AGEING AND HUMAN SKILL

BY

A. T. WELFORD

FELLOW OF ST. JOHN'S COLLEGE
CAMBRIDGE

A Report centred on work by

the Nuffield Unit for Research

into Problems of Ageing

GREENWOOD PRESS, PUBLISHERS
WESTPORT, CONNECTICUT

Library of Congress Cataloging in Publication Data

Welford, Alan Traviss.
    Ageing and human skill.

    Includes bibliographies.
    1. Age (Psychology) 2. Motor ability--Testing.
3. Age and intelligence. I. Cambridge. University.
Psychological Laboratory. Nuffield Research Unit into
Problems of Ageing. II. Title.
[BF701.W395 1973]   155.6   73-1409
ISBN 0-8371-6799-X

Originally published in 1958 by Oxford University Press,
London

Reprinted with the permission of Oxford University Press

Reprinted by Greenwood Press, Inc.

First Greenwood reprinting   1973
Second Greenwood reprinting   1975
Third Greenwood reprinting   1977

Library of Congress catalog card number   73-1409

ISBN 0-8371-6799-X

Printed in the United States of America

MEMBERS OF THE
NUFFIELD UNIT FOR RESEARCH
INTO PROBLEMS OF AGEING

Director:

A. T. Welford	1946–56

Research Staff:

C. G. A. Allan	1946–49
Betty M. Bernardelli	1946–47
Ruth A. Brown	1946–56
A. B. Cherns	1947–48
Hilary M. Clay	1949–56
A. E. Earle	1950–51
M. A. Jeeves	1954–55
H. Kay	1948–52
A. Kendon	1956
H. F. King	1949–55
J. A. Leonard	1950–52
W. T. Singleton	1950–53
D. Speakman	1949–56
J. Szafran	1947–55
(Assistant Director 1953–55)	
Jean G. Wallace	1949–55
Gillian C. Webb	1946–47
N. L. Webb	1950–53
N. T. Welford	1949–55

Research Staff attached under a scheme sponsored by the Panel on Human Factors of the Committee on Industrial Productivity

R. M. Belbin	1948–53
A. E. D. Schonfield	1949–50
Antonia M. N. Shooter	1948–49
and	1950–51

Fulbright Research Fellows

W. K. Kirchner	1954–55
J. R. Simon	1955–56

Workshop Mechanic

G. Baker	1946–56

PREFACE

THIS book is the final report of the Nuffield Unit for Research into Problems of Ageing, which was attached to the Psychological Laboratory at Cambridge from 1946 to 1956. The work was conceived as an extension of the research on skilled performance initiated in the Laboratory during the Second World War under Sir Frederic Bartlett and the late Dr. K. J. W. Craik. It has attempted to study changes of performance from young adulthood through the middle years to the sixties and seventies and has thus been concerned with *ageing* rather than solely with old age. The results have shown that it is in these middle years that some of the most important age changes become noticeable, and that it is often at these earlier ages that practical measures to deal with problems of old age may best be taken.

The present book replaces an earlier interim statement under the title *Skill and Age: An Experimental Approach*, published for the Nuffield Foundation by the Oxford University Press in 1951. It is, however, more than just a new edition. Some four to five times as much work by members of the Unit has been covered, so that instead of describing and discussing experiments individually, studies have been grouped under several broad topics. At the same time, opportunity has been taken to outline work by others whose research has seemed especially relevant to the problems under review, although no attempt has been made to cover the literature completely. The topics have been dictated by the areas in which it has been possible to make studies: we are not yet in the fortunate position of being able to turn the evidence around, so to speak, and group it in terms of questions of practical importance to older people. It looks, however, as if the day when this can be done may not be far off. Developments in the study of ageing and of human performance in general during the last few years have profoundly changed our understanding of both.

The fact that most of the work described here has already appeared in scientific journals or symposia has made it possible to omit many technical details such as the results of statistical significance tests. An attempt has, nevertheless, been made to give the main quantitative results in the form of figures and tables together with references to the papers where fuller information can be obtained. The material in the former book has been similarly incorporated in a condensed form. Statistical significance tests have been applied in all appropriate cases to results outlined here but not previously published, and no age trend or other difference has been mentioned without qualification unless it has been found to be significant at the 5 per cent. level or better.

The work of the Unit has included both laboratory and field studies which, as explained in Chapter III, have been regarded as complementary. Although they have been so treated throughout this book, most of the field studies are in fact described in the latter part of Chapter V and the first part of Chapter X, while the laboratory experiments occupy most of the rest of Chapters IV to X. A reader interested mainly in one side of the work can thus easily omit the other.

The Unit has been greatly indebted to Dr. E. R. F. W. Crossman and to Mr. R. L. Gregory, who have given freely of their help and advice in several of the experimental studies and to Dr. Eunice Belbin and Dr. B. O'Doherty for permission to use unpublished material. It is impossible to give individual acknowledgement to the many others who have assisted the work in various ways, either by advice, by active help or by taking part in experiments. Special mention should, however, be made of Mr. L. V. Green of the Dunlop Rubber Company, of Mr. R. E. Stonebridge, and of the Glisson Road Cambridge British Red Cross Over-Sixties Club for their repeated efforts on the Unit's behalf in the very difficult task of finding subjects. I am very grateful to Miss R. A. Brown, Miss H. M. Clay and Dr. R. H. Thouless who have read the proofs of this book. My gratitude is also due to Mr. L. Cattermole and Mrs. J. Wordie who prepared the typescript drafts.

Finally, my sincere thanks are due to former colleagues in the Unit whose work has provided the material for this book, to Sir Frederic Bartlett who gave the work its start and guided its early stages, to the Nuffield Foundation whose generous and continued support made the research possible, and to those at Nuffield Lodge whose gracious dealing has made the task of administration a pleasant one. Thanks are due also to the Panel on Human Factors of the Committee on Industrial Productivity for a grant which provided for most of the industrial studies.

The Unit was disbanded in 1956, but it is hoped that a foundation has been laid on which others will be able to build.

6 *June* 1957   A. T. WELFORD

ACKNOWLEDGEMENTS

ACKNOWLEDGEMENT is gratefully made for permission to reproduce the following diagrams and other material:

S. Barkin, R. M. Belbin, and the *British Journal of Industrial Medicine*. A quotation on pp. 122–3.

The *British Journal of Psychology*. Figs. 4.2, 4.7, 4.8, 7.9, 7.10, 7.11, 7.12, 7.13, 8.4, 9.1.

Ruth A. Brown and *Occupational Psychology*. Fig. 5.1.

Messrs. Butterworth & Co., Ltd. Figs. 4.13(a), 8.3.

Hilary M. Clay. Figs. 8.4, 8.5, 8.6, 8.8, and a quotation on p. 219.

E. R. F. W. Crossman, J. Szafran, and *Experientia*. Figs. 4.15, 7.5, 7.6, and quotations on pp. 102 and 166–8.

The Ergonomics Research Society. Fig. 4.5.

Gerontologia. Figs. 8.5, 8.6.

The *Journal of Gerontology*. Figs. 8.8, 9.2, 9.3, and quotations on pp. 199–201 and 219.

H. Kay and the *Quarterly Journal of Experimental Psychology*. Figs. 6.7, 6.8.

H. F. King. Figs. 9.2, 9.3.

Messrs. E. and S. Livingstone, Ltd. Figs. 4.6, 4.9, 4.10.

W. R. Miles and the National Academy of Sciences, Washington. Fig. 4.1 and a quotation on p. 65.

J. C. Raven. Fig. 9.1.

W. T. Singleton. Figs. 4.5, 4.6, 4.7, 4.8, 4.9, 4.10.

D. Speakman. Quotations on pp. 199–201.

J. Szafran. Figs. 6.5, 6.6.

E. Verville, N. Cameron, and the *Journal of Genetic Psychology*. Fig. 7.8.

Jean G. Wallace. Figs. 7.9, 7.10, 7.11, 7.12, 7.13.

H. C. Weston and the Illuminating Engineering Society. Fig. 7.1.

The *Journal of Educational Psychology*. Fig. 6.1.

Acknowledgement is also due to Messrs. J. and A. Churchill, Ltd., and the Ciba Foundation for permission to use the substance of an article by the author (Welford 1957) in Chapter III, and to *Occupational Psychology* for permission to reproduce the substance of an article by Shooter *et al.* (1956) in Chapter X.

CONTENTS

I

ON THE NATURE OF AGE
CHANGES IN PERFORMANCE

As its title implies, this is a book about skill as well as about age. Middle and old age hold, as it were, a magnifying glass to human performance so that many facets present but scarcely noticeable in the twenties have become important by the time we reach the sixties. It is almost certain that had the work on which current psychological thought is based been done with older people, many points of emphasis would have been different and some of the concepts richer. As it is, those researching on problems of human performance in relation to age often find themselves having to rethink ideas current in the general field of their subject, and would seem able, if they paused a little from time to time in their work, to make significant contributions to the study of performance in general.

Many, probably most, of those who approach the study of human skill and age will have the very practical aim of helping men and women in later life to maintain their efficiency and thereby their self-respect. They will thus wish to know the nature of the work for which older people are best suited and the best methods of retraining those who for one reason or another have to change their jobs before they retire. Others will be interested in the nature of ageing from an academic and theoretical point of view and will wish to study age changes in human performance as the expression of a biological and social process.

These two approaches and their requirements, although different, should not be regarded as opposed. It has often been said, with considerable truth, that theoretical studies in psychology divorced from any applied aim quickly lose perspective and become confused with minutiae. On the other hand, it is certain that the applied aim is better served by an understanding of the fundamental changes occurring in human beings as they get older, rather than by a series of *ad hoc* studies of whether old people can or cannot do this, that or the other job. It would seem that, so far as studies of skill are concerned, by far the greatest, and in the long run quickest, contribution to the welfare of older people is to be made by studying the changes with age of normal human capacity. These are basic to the work people can do and enter into almost every aspect of daily living.

Many of the studies of human performance and age made between the two world wars have measured changes of ability at particular tasks without offering any explanation of why these changes should have come about, or have tried in a qualitative way to demonstrate the effects of the influences which obviously vary with age, namely changes of the physical organism and length of experience. They seem often to have been made with the unexpressed hope that some of these influences, especially the organic changes, would prove unimportant and the others amenable to medical, psychiatric or social treatment enabling the effects of age to be halted or reversed. These studies have contributed valuable factual knowledge and suggestions for more fundamental work but must in the long run prove of subsidiary significance to researches upon what, for want of a better term, we may call the 'mechanism' of human performance. There are two aspects of this mechanism both of which it is important to keep in mind: firstly, the physical and chemical working of the various structures of the body; secondly, the way in which these interact with one another and with the environment to produce behaviour. The first is essentially a matter of physiology, the second a matter of processes or 'systems' involving relationships in time between physiological and environmental events, often expressed in the form of conceptual 'working models' specifiable in mathematical terms.

Research has usually attempted to isolate and study separately a number of supposedly basic components of capacity such as intelligence or learning ability or visual acuity, and on the basis of changes with age in these to build predictions about complex performance in terms of their interaction. Just what constitutes a 'basic component' of performance is not easy to identify and it is desirable to approach our problem also from the other end by taking complex, continuous performances and making analyses to reveal their essential 'key' features. We shall in the chapters which follow be dealing mainly with this second type of approach because although initially slower at yielding tangible results it appears likely to produce quicker insight into the problems as a whole.

Almost all the research on ageing which has been done so far has the depressing characteristic that the changes are downward with the years, and indicate only by implication, if at all, ways in which improvement occurs. Obviously there are ways in which a man or woman matures and ripens into old age: the difficulty seems to be, however, that these concern subtle aspects of human functioning which have not yet proved amenable to scientific investigation. It may be hoped that future studies will make them so. Meanwhile, the results of research on ageing tend often, as Wechsler (1935) has pointed out in a vigorous passage, to be unpopular. Yet we cannot escape them and we must agree that it is not by glossing over or neglecting older people's difficulties but by seeking to understand them that we can best open the way to their removal. The most positive contribution research has made in this direction up to the present is that it has been able to *delimit* areas of change and to specify not only conditions which act to the disadvantage of older people *but also those which do not.* If we cannot point to ways of reversing age trends, we can at least show how their effects may be minimized.

Broadly speaking, popular current theories to account for the changes that come about with increasing age fall into two main types which follow what we have already noted as two obvious influences. The first is that these changes are the result of the physical maturation of the organism from birth to early adulthood, and its subsequent degeneration—the physical organism in this instance being taken to include not only the body in general, but also the brain and nervous system and thus the 'mental' organism as well. The second type maintains that these changes are essentially due to environmental factors, the effect of which increases with the extent to which the organism is in contact with them, and therefore increases with age.

It is clear that neither of these theories in its crude form is adequate. Any activity by an individual is the result of the interaction between the capacities he brings to a situation and the characteristics of the environment, and it is with these interactions that we must deal if we wish to study human activity and experience. Each interaction between the organism and its environment modifies the organism so that when it confronts later situations it is different from what it was before. What the organism is at any moment of time is therefore the result of a long chain of interactions stretching from birth or before up to the present, and in this chain hereditary maturation-degeneration factors and environmental influences are intimately and inextricably mixed.[7]

We may, however, for practical purposes, and providing we remember what we are doing, dissect out of this chain various relatively constant and pervasive features which can, up to a point, be dealt with separately. In particular for our present study we may separate:

1. Certain results of bodily changes which characterize individuals of different ages.
2. Features of the social environment both present and past which seem to exercise a general steering influence over individuals or groups of individuals for relatively long periods.
3. Specific experience affecting methods of dealing with particular situations or problems.

We shall proceed to consider in turn these three factors, and their probable effects with increasing age. In doing so it must be clearly recognized that we are merely outlining some tentative working hypotheses based on current doctrine in experimental psychology, on the findings of previous workers in the field of ageing, and on remarks and suggestions made in the course of numerous conversations that the author and his colleagues have sought from time to time with people of different ages, and with employers, managers, doctors and others. Although these tentative hypotheses have been shaped by the results of previous work, they must be regarded more as a guide to future research than as an interpretation of what has already been done.

1. *Bodily changes*

The successive changes of bodily, including neural, structure which take place between birth and old age are clearly such that, if the human organism is viewed as a piece of anatomical and physiological machinery, it rises to a peak of efficiency in the early twenties and thereafter slowly declines. It therefore seems inevitable to say that as regards bodily mechanism the progress from young adulthood onwards is essentially one of gradual deterioration.

Although these physical deteriorations are in many cases easy to detect and measure, their effects on performance are far from easy to determine. They undoubtedly limit the range of the organism's *potential* action and are likely to lead to some restriction of actual action. This is readily observable in cases of extreme old age, although it is questionable how far it applies to the 'I can't do all I used' of middle age.

The nature and extent of the limits on actual action resulting from any disability depend on the demands of the task the subject is trying to do and upon the extent of his other capacities. Often the capacity impaired will not normally be used to the full, as, for example, muscular strength when writing with a pen or dealing a pack

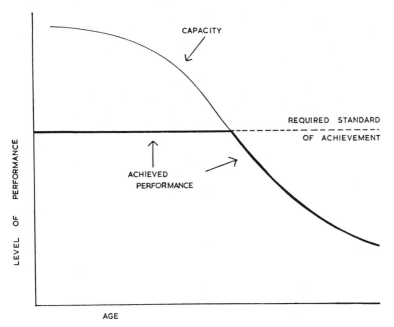

Fig. 1.1. Relation between capacity and achievement when a limiting factor is present

Level of performance may be in terms of speed, accuracy or probability of adequate performance.

of cards. The limitations upon performance in these cases lie in the control of action or in some 'expected' standard of achievement rather than in strength, and muscular strength can fall a long way before it becomes the limiting factor. The relationships between failing capacity and achieved performance in a case like this are shown diagrammatically in Fig. 1.1. Achievement is independent of potential capacity until this falls to a point at which it becomes the limiting factor. Beyond this point achievement shows a functional dependence upon the capacity concerned.

A further complication arises from the fact that it seems as if the organism, when confronted by a difficult situation, makes what use it can of the capacities it has so that any deficiency is at least partly overcome by a change of method. If, to take a very simple example, a parcel is too heavy to be carried in one hand it may be carried in two or rested on the hip.

It is obvious that compensatory changes in performance can occur only to the extent that the task or portion of the task concerned permits of attack by a variety of slightly different methods, allows variations in the timing of constituent reactions, and so on. It is also clear that the extent to which these conditions occur is largely dependent upon the extent to which the method and timing of the task are under the subject's own control. Where such control can be fully exercised, compensation is likely to occur, but where the performance is narrowly constrained in either the form or timing of the constituent reactions, compensation will be virtually impossible.

Examination of what an organism suffering from a physical disability achieves in a complex task may therefore reveal four results. Firstly, a few things which formerly could be done cannot now be done at all because the disability limits performance and no compensatory change of method is possible. Secondly, some things cannot be done as easily as they could before, because changes of method, although possible, do not compensate fully: former levels of achievement may be maintained but only with increased effort. Thirdly, performance at many tasks will not be affected because the demands of the task are still well within the capacity that remains or because compensation can be made effectively. Fourthly, in some cases over-compensation may occur so that achievement is actually improved.

Measuring physical deficiencies as such will thus not enable us to make any very accurate prediction of achievement at a complex task, and the degree of degeneration will be a poor indicator of inefficiency. It seems necessary therefore, if we wish to study the effects of these deficiencies, to turn our attention from total achievements to the details of the methods whereby these are attained, and to make an analysis of the complex performance and examine the different parts thus abstracted from the whole. Such parts in a total performance can, if the analysis has been well done, be much more closely linked to anatomical and physiological features of the organism than is the total performance to which they contribute. In so far as these features change with age we may therefore expect to be able to detect certain uniformities of method within any one age group.

On the other hand, any deficiency in the anatomical and physiological mechanisms will cause compensation in order to maintain performance. The ways in which people do this are likely to differ from one individual to another. We may therefore expect that the physical deficiencies associated with age will be accompanied by a decrease in the range of activities of any one individual but an increase in the variation between individuals. In any actual case we are likely to find both uniformities and increased variations associated with advancing age, and it is possible that the degree of uniformity or variability found in any one portion of a total performance within an age group can give us some indication of its origin and consequent modifiability.

It is important to recognize that many different bodily changes of this kind can occur because many organs—sensory, central and motor—are involved in the production of behaviour. These all age at different rates so that it is in principle impossible to assess a single 'biological age' for an individual as a whole. We have to do this for each organ separately unless groups of organs are found to be correlated in their rate of ageing.

2. *Features of the social environment*

Just as an individual has inevitably to live within the framework of his physical constitution, so he has to live within the framework of his physical and social environment, which we may therefore expect to find exerting certain restricting and channelling effects upon his activities. Three factors which may be considered as essentially environmental seem especially likely to affect differently the performances of different age groups.

Social demands

It seems likely that such social demands as the need to support a family may exert a very considerable effect upon what a man is willing to do and how hard he is willing to work. The incentive will be to some extent 'forward acting', in the sense that it will tend to operate before the family becomes expensive and may die away before the children have actually become self-supporting, so that on the average we should expect to find its main effects powerful during the thirties and perhaps early forties, and tending to die away thereafter. It is probable that such incentives as this can operate without the individuals being aware of them, and that, in so far as they become socially conventionalized, their influence extends to those who do not actually possess family responsibilities themselves.

The desire to maintain his social position in the community will also probably exert a considerable effect upon what man is willing to do. Its effect is likely to reinforce and prolong the effects of family responsibilities, and in addition, since social prestige is something which a man builds up in the course of many years, to produce resistance to anything tending so to change the social pattern as to constitute a threat to his position.

The exact effects of these influences upon performance are, of course, difficult to demonstrate quantitatively. We may expect, however, that though they will have little effect if any on what a man *can* do, they will tend to narrow the range of what he is *likely* to do, by concentrating his activities in the service of certain ends directly or indirectly connected with these pervading aims.

Although in general they are likely to increase carefulness, accuracy, efficiency of performance, and the other qualities normally demanded in employment and associated with 'responsibility', they may not always do so. Especially in cases where family or social demands are greater than the individual's ability enables him to meet, there is likely to be frustration and conflict which may lead to the disruption of efficient performance. If so we should expect to find similarities between such disruption occurring among old men whose failing physical powers make them unable to meet the demands of their position in society, and that occurring among men in middle life whose responsibilities are in excess of their abilities.

Popular beliefs about the abilities of different age groups

⸱ Research in other fields makes it appear possible that popular beliefs of the type that 'older workpeople cannot make the pace' or that 'you cannot teach an old dog new tricks' exert a considerable effect upon the performance of men belonging to the age groups to which they refer, even though the men concerned may be quite unaware of this influence and, indeed, may stoutly deny it.

Again, the influence on performance will probably be a restrictive one, and again it will restrict not so much what can be done as what is likely to be done or what a man is willing to do. The beliefs will act on the individual by setting up *expectations* regarding his performance. These in turn will lead to a lowering and narrowing of levels of aspiration which will often be in conflict, and sometimes serious conflict, with his desires to live up to his responsibilities and position in society. At the same time he may compensate for disabilities which he does not actually possess or over-compensate for those he does possess, and thus produce or accentuate the effects on performance that follow from real disabilities—including the improvement of achievement that may result from over-compensation. A further possible adverse effect is that questioning of the beliefs may lead an individual to 'examine himself' and bring into consciousness many habitual activities and skills which, if left undisturbed, would have done their work quietly and efficiently, but which break up on being subjected to scrutiny.

Features of the past environment

The hypothesis that what an individual is at any particular moment of time depends upon a continuous chain of interactions between organism and environment, stretching back to birth or before, implies that we can never in any practical case equate the environmental backgrounds of different age groups, because the changes in social, educational and material conditions during the past century inevitably mean that the childhoods of different age groups have been spent under different environmental conditions. The importance of this point is enhanced by the probability that not all portions of the chain of interactions are equally significant, but that it is these very childhood and adolescent periods that are in many ways of predominant importance.

As the influences of such early environmental conditions can only affect the present state of the individual via a long chain of intermediate experiences and activities, their effects on present actions will be complex and difficult to predict. We should expect, however, that in spite of considerable variation between individuals, they would tend to produce certain inter-individual uniformities which would be associated with particular generations of the present population. These uniformities are not, strictly speaking, effects of age as such, but since they attach to present-day age groups they must be taken into account if we are studying the differences between these groups.

3. *Specific experience*

In dealing with each environmental situation as it arrives an individual seems to use what may be thought of as a repertoire of methods and abilities which have been built up in his dealings with similar problems in the past. If this repertoire provides some ready-made means of dealing with the situation which appear suitable, these are used more or less without change. If, however, no ready-made means of dealing with the situation prove adequate, it seems as if some new means are built up and are thereafter available for dealing with future situations. The individual's ability is thus widened, or in other words the number of things he can do is increased.

We should therefore expect that as age increases, ability to deal with new situations should rise, not only in the sense that an individual has greater knowledge and more techniques at his command, but that he has a broader basis on which to construct new ways of acting. This would be true when dealing with a situation which is actually confronting a subject, but it would apply especially when anticipating future events. In any real-life situation a great deal, perhaps most, of what an individual does is in the nature of making responses which are in preparation for or in anticipation of things which will happen in either the near or remote future. It seems as if the pattern of action for dealing with a future event is laid down in advance so that either, when the event occurs, it triggers off a pre-formed response, or the response is begun before the event actually arrives. These anticipatory adjustments must inevitably be dependent upon past experience and, other things being equal, may therefore be expected to become more complete and better formed as age increases. It is probably by means of such anticipation that much of the compensation made for physical defect is carried out by older persons. If this is so, we ought to be able to detect larger differences between age groups in situations to which anticipatory adjustments cannot be made than in situations where they can, and we should expect to find older people voluntarily seeking a predictable environment.

Certain tendencies are likely to operate, however, to modify this increasing ability and rising efficiency. One obvious possibility is that the increases due to experience are overtaken and cancelled by failures of fundamentally organic origin, not only in the sense of failing sensory or motor functions but of disabilities of central origin in the recall and control of material carried in memory—the subject may be thought of as having an increasing store of experience but a diminishing ability to use it when it is required. Apart from this possibility three others may be mentioned which derive essentially from the accumulation of experience as such.

(a) Although the possession of an increased number of ready-made responses should lead to an increased chance of having one which is appropriate for dealing with any new situation which arises, it is likely also to lead to difficulty in choosing the most appropriate one so that in a new situation there will tend to be a conflict of tendencies to response which will produce hesitation, disorganization and confusion.

(b) It seems that in many cases certain methods or features of methods which have been found successful in dealing with a particular type of situation 'work loose' from their original setting and become general tendencies or methods which are applied in dealing with a wide range of situations, and may come to colour almost the whole of an individual's activity. There are thus built up in an individual certain dominant responses or modes of response which tend to be applied to all types of situation and problem whether they are appropriate or not. They obviously make for increased uniformity of activity within any one individual, but are likely to lead to increased variability between individuals in a group. Their relationships to age are difficult to predict. Inasmuch as they are built up in the course of experience, we should expect their effects to increase and harden with age. Further, we should expect these generalized tendencies to increase in importance as physical disability called compensatory mechanisms into operation. They are, however, in opposition to the tendencies noted in the previous paragraph. It would seem that investigation of the conflict between these two kinds of tendency is of major importance to any study of human efficiency, especially as between persons of different ages.

(c) Although in the course of experience an individual will learn how to do an increasing number of things and what to do in an increasing number of situations, this process consists not only in learning what to do, but also what *not* to do in any particular situation. In other words, value judgements are made about actions: some things are recognized as *worth* doing, others as not. In one sense, of course, knowing what not to do, or what is not worth doing, is just as much a positive ability as knowing what to do. From the point of view of one studying overt behaviour, however, the two are different, and while learning what to do may increase the number of things which *can* be done, learning what not to do will greatly reduce the number of things *likely* to be done. Two points follow from this third tendency. Firstly, we may expect that with increasing age should go, other things being equal, a rise of skill in dealing with recurrent situations, but that this should be accompanied by a stereotyping of the method employed. The second point relates to the lack of confidence which is sometimes reported in middle and old age. There are doubtless often deep-seated psycho-pathological reasons for this, but it is worth considering whether the accidents and hard experiences of life tend to shake a man's confidence in his own powers. All people experience some successes and some failures in the course of life, and make some achievements and some mistakes, but of these it seems to be the unpleasant events and the discrepancies between goal and achievement which tend to be noticed. There is, of course, sound biological reason for this in that an animal which did not give priority in its behaviour to dealing with dangers and difficulties would be at a grave disadvantage. The question is whether this tendency has a cumulative effect and whether some trends associated with age are the result of undue stress upon past failure leading to bitterness and crabbing of effort. The answer is important because, in so far as this is true, age trends might be reversible if people could reconcile themselves to letting their past die and realize that over-caution born of past mistakes can cripple their present activities.

The combined effects of organic changes and experience

The sum of the various organic and environmental influences upon performance in relation to age has sometimes been represented as in Fig. 1.2. Curve (A) for the organic factors rises to a peak in early adulthood and then declines. Curve (B) for experience rises throughout life. The curves in Fig. 1.2 are arbitrary since we do not know precisely what shape they should be—even if they are valid at all. Curve (A) is based roughly on intelligence-test data representing the ability to perform a kind of 'mental gymnastic' which depends mainly on organic factors. The curve (B) is the integral of (A) on the assumption that it should depend upon cumulative exposure to environmental stimulation, and upon the level of (A) in the sense that this will determine the extent to which environmental stimulation is converted into experience. It will also, however, depend upon the extent to which forgetting takes place, and will be limited by the fact that as experience accumulates the chances of anything new happening will diminish. The former, if its rate does not vary with age, will lower the whole curve proportionately. The latter will tend to flatten it towards the upper end.

Although Fig. 1.2 is a gross over-simplification, it brings out a point which is often neglected, namely that the results of ageing will differ widely as between one task and another depending upon the

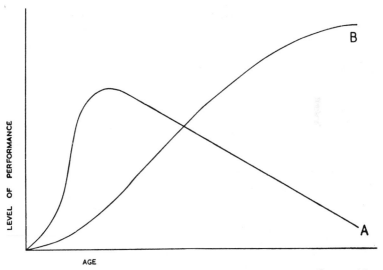

FIG. 1.2. Hypothetical curves relating performance based on organic capacities (A) and experience (B) with age

extent to which various capacities are required for their performance. Tasks which make their chief demands upon organic capacities will tend to follow curve (A), those demanding knowledge and experience curve (B). In most cases both types of demand would be made and the result would be intermediate between (A) and (B) according to the balance of demands and the extent to which compensation for deficiencies of organic origin could be made by knowledge gained in the course of experience.

Since both the organic factors and experience vary from one individual to another, it follows that just as we cannot assign to an individual a unitary biological age but have to consider the various structures of his body separately, so we cannot think of a person as old or young in relation to all tasks equally, but must consider each, or each type, separately in terms of the demands it makes.

Fig. 1.2 is, however, misleading in that it neglects the implications of Fig. 1.1. As it stands it would imply that if, say, a task was dependent upon experience at all, the more (relevant) experience possessed by the subject the better the task would be carried out. Normally, however, all that is required is certain special knowledge or understanding or 'knack' and if a subject possesses this, he will be able to do the task unless his performance is limited by some organic or external factor: improvement of performance with very long experience would only result from the subject getting to know how to deal with certain rare contingencies. The same argument applies to organic capacities: provided these are sufficient, variation in their level will not affect performance. It follows that for 'easy' tasks making little demand on either organically based capacities or experience people of all ages should perform about equally well. With a task making somewhat more demand on the organic side we should expect a curve similar in shape to (A), the level becoming lower and the slopes steeper with progressively more severe demands as shown in Fig. 1.3(A). Strictly, a family of curves should be drawn for every function involved in the performance, and these would all have different slopes and probably different ages at which the maximum was attained, but since probably only one would be limiting, all except this one could reasonably be neglected. In the same way, increasing demands for knowledge and experience in a task easy as regards the organic side should lead to a family of curves of type (B) as shown in Fig. 1.3(B). Tasks making some demands of each type should lead to results intermediate between the two with peak performance coming at somewhat later ages than in (A).

The fact that many performances show a rise with age from childhood to the early twenties and thereafter a decline until by the time old age is reached achievement has fallen again to childhood levels has led some people to think of ageing during the adult decades as a process of 'involution'. The view is given currency in that we sometimes speak of people suffering from senile mental disorders as being in 'second childhood'. Clearly, however, any resemblance between old age and childhood must be essentially fortuitous and superficial. Performance may return to childhood levels of achievement but the past is not genuinely uncovered a second time. The changes that come with age must be underlain by uni-directional changes and

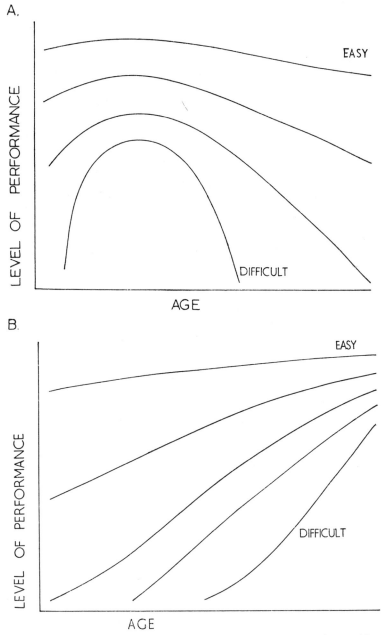

FIG. 1.3. Hypothetical curves relating to performance based on organic capacities (A) and experience (B) with age, taking account of limiting factors

ongoing processes. Because of this the comparison which is often recommended of old-age decline with child development is at best trivial and at worst likely to be seriously misleading. The two may be in some ways similar, but in others, especially regarding the interaction of organically determined capacity with experience, they must be profoundly different.

We have spoken of age changes as if they were continuous from early adulthood onwards but the rates at which they occur at different periods of life may not be the same. Apart from the limiting factors discussed in connexion with Fig. 1.1, disease or accident may take a rapid toll of organic powers, while experience may lead to insights which suddenly increase understanding and the ability that this implies. These changes will come at ages which differ from one individual to another. For this reason they may be concealed in a smooth age trend if the performance of a group of subjects is averaged. They may nevertheless have to be taken into consideration when assessing the meaning of these trends.

II

ON THE NATURE OF SKILL

THE foregoing discussion has been concerned with the changes that come with age in terms of people and their relationships with their environments. We turn now to a more detailed consideration of the mechanism of skilled activity within an individual. The term 'skill' is used somewhat differently in industry and in psychology. In the former a man is regarded as skilled when he is qualified to carry out trade or craft work involving knowledge, judgement, accuracy and manual deftness usually acquired as the result of a long training, whereas an unskilled man is not expected to do anything which cannot be learnt in a relatively short time. Semi-skilled jobs are regarded as intermediate: involving the characteristics of skilled work but to an extent which demands a training extending over weeks or months rather than years. The fundamental questions of interest to those concerned with industry are: 'What characteristics in a job will make it easy or difficult for any given man to learn it?' and 'Which jobs will require a man who has been through an apprenticeship and which will require a shorter training?' In other words, one asks what is it that differentiates between work which makes greater and lesser demands for training. The picture is not, of course, in practice quite as simple as this. Industrial organizations show, as do all social institutions, a degree of inertia so that in the course of time jobs may change in character but not in grading as regards skill. In these cases, the skill-demands of a job may be largely a matter of its history. Again, classification in terms of training is clearly too narrow, as some recent attempts to give a skill-rating to *responsibility* have recognized.

A psychologist's approach is to ask the question: 'When we look at a man working, by what criteria in his performance can we tell whether he is skilled and competent or clumsy and ignorant?' In other words, he asks: 'How is complex performance organized and what is it that differentiates between more and less trained or expert levels?' The psychological concept of skill is thus wider than the industrial in two ways. Firstly, skill in the psychological sense can exist in the performance of many jobs which in industry would be graded as semi-skilled or unskilled. Secondly, and more important, the psychological use of the term covers so-called 'mental' operations as well as manual. Indeed, from the psychological standpoint, the distinction between manual and mental skill is difficult to maintain in any absolute sense. All skilled performance is mental in the sense that knowledge and judgement are required, and all skills involve some kind of co-ordinated overt activity by hands, organs of speech or other effectors. In manual skills the overt actions clearly form an essential part of the activity and without them the purpose of the skill as a whole would disappear. In mental skills the overt actions play a more incidental part, serving rather to give expression to a skill than forming an essential part of it. They thus may be varied within fairly wide limits without destroying the nature of the underlying skill.

In spite of these differences all skills, industrial and psychological, motor and mental, appear to possess three characteristics which provide us with a convenient framework for discussion:

A. They consist essentially of the building of an organized and co-ordinated activity in relation to an object or a situation and thus involve the whole chain of sensory, central and motor mechanisms which underlie performance.

B. They are learnt in that the understanding of the object or situation and the form of the action are built up gradually in the course of repeated experience.

C. They are serial in the sense that within the overall pattern of the skill many different processes or actions are ordered and co-ordinated in a temporal sequence.

Within any skilled performance these characteristics are closely bound together, and in order to gain an adequate view of the nature of skill all must be considered.

A. THE RECEPTOR-EFFECTOR ASPECT OF SKILL

We may think of the chain of processes which leads from stimulation falling on the sense organs to the resulting behaviour as being in three parts. First, there are what may be called *receptor* processes which have to do with the reception of the incoming signals by the sense organs and their interpretation. At the opposite end of the chain are what may be called *effector* processes which shape and carry out the resulting action. Between these there occur what may be termed *translation* processes which relate perception to action. It is not always easy to decide in a particular case where the line should be drawn between receptor and translation processes or between translation and effector, but many cases seem clear enough to show that the distinction ought to be made.

We shall consider these three types of processes in turn.

1. The receptor side

Skilled performance would seem in the first instance to depend upon two important principles of what may be broadly termed perception: first, that perception is essentially an *organizing process*, and second that in this process *past actions and experience* play a leading role.

Organization in perception

Between the receipt of stimuli by the sense-organs and the attainment of meaningful perception it seems that a chain of processes occur which are of considerable complexity, although often they take place so quickly that they are quite unconscious and perception appears to be 'immediate'. The broad fact that these are organizing processes is obvious enough. For instance, in visual perception the incoming data from the eyes are integrated, grouped and ordered so that normally we see not just a mosaic of more and less stimulated points, but coherent objects which have form and structure. It is also obvious that normally we do not perceive with only one sense at a time, but that data from different senses are organized together, and that the resulting perception, although it is predominately, say, visual or auditory, has been partly shaped by stimuli coming through other sensory channels. A well-known example is the fact that it seems easier to hear what a man is saying if we can also see him speaking.

The process of grouping and organizing may be thought of as consisting essentially of the *abstraction of constants* from the total mass of data presented in space and over time, together with the selection of some data as dominant and important while the rest are relegated to the background and more or less neglected. This process makes perception substantially independent of the precise details of stimulation—words are, in an important sense, the same whether written, printed or spoken. Data thus organized are no longer treated as complexes compounded out of a multitude of separate elements, but as *single units*. The perceived wholes are thus in a very real sense 'simpler' than the stimuli giving rise to them. Psychological simplicity is, in fact, not the same thing as objective simplicity, but is essentially dependent upon the degree to which the data can be organized into larger units of this kind.

It appears that such a treatment of the data is by no means the end of the perceptual process but that it is often—probably typically—followed by one or more of three further types of organizing activity. Firstly, a unitary whole which has been built up may be analysed into parts, as when we examine an object in detail. This analysis, although it involves breaking up a whole into smaller units, is not simply the reverse of the unifying process: each of the parts is itself a unified whole, and each is still recognized as belonging within the framework of the larger whole out of which it has been analysed. Secondly, certain features of the whole may be further abstracted and become perceptual units on their own: for instance, when reading a passage of prose we may become aware of features such as style. Thirdly, a number of unitary wholes may themselves be subjected to further processes of selection and integration which result in the formation of still larger units, as when reading we integrate words into sentences, sentences into paragraphs, and so on.

Although perceptual units built up in these ways may appear in consciousness as being present 'all at once', they often result from the integration of data which are not all present at the same instant, but which extend over a considerable period of time. When reading, for instance, the material organized into a paragraph has taken an appreciable time to observe. In perceiving an object which is too large to observe at a single glance, we are putting together data from many individual glances which may have taken place over several seconds or even minutes. Some perceptual units, such as musical themes or visually seen movement, have indeed an essentially temporal character, the perceived wholes being by their very nature configurations in which time is a necessary dimension.

The number of stages passed through on the way to full meaningful perception probably tends to vary somewhat between individuals and within the same individual according to circumstances. The same is true of the time taken: often they occur, as we have already said, very rapidly; often, however, they take a considerable time, so that it is impossible to draw a hard and fast line between perception and thinking.

Whether rapid or slow, perception seems to involve mental activity and effort by the observer, so that the attainment of meaningful perception is not a mere process of 'registration', but is essentially a kind of *response* to the material presented. We may conveniently call this a *perceptual response* to distinguish it from the overt action which may be taken in dealing with the presented material once it has been perceived.

The role of past experience

Some of this organization is doubtless the result of the hereditary constitution of the organism. Certainly hereditary constitution sets some *limits* to the organization which takes place in the sense that we cannot do what we have no inherited potentiality for doing. But it is clear that for almost all important purposes organization at each stage of the perceptual process represents the application to the incoming sense data of material brought by the observer to the present situation from the past. In precisely what form this 'past' is available for use in the present is not known, but a number of important principles of the *manner in which it is used* are known with fair certainty. This fitting of terms from past experience to incoming data is part of the process of giving them 'meaning'. The word is confusing, however, because it is used to cover three rather different types of process, namely *identification, setting in a context* and *significance for ensuing action*. It is the first two that concern us here, the last belonging more properly to a discussion of the translation process.

As regards identification, perception is, as we have seen, essentially an integrative process if it is considered in terms of incoming data, but in terms of the results achieved it is a matter of discriminating or differentiating one object from another, of recognizing similarities and differences. The process of identification involves placing the object presented to our senses in one of a number of categories provided by our past experience. The categories may be broad and general or narrow and precise and it would seem that the amount of data required and of 'perceptual work' increases as the categories become more specific. Thus when crossing a road, the identification of an oncoming vehicle as a car rather than a lorry, omnibus, &c., is easier and quicker than if we have to specify the make, colour, style and other details of the car.

The progressive, hierarchical nature of the classification by which objects are identified in perception is shown by the fact that often an object is specified as belonging to a particular major class with some extra detail which enables it to be placed in a sub-class. For example, we may say a vehicle is an *omnibus* painted *red*. The classes and sub-classes appear to behave as unitary 'codes' applied to incoming material in such a way that it is invested with all the characteristics normally associated with the class or sub-class concerned. In this way a great deal of 'perceived' detail is not really perceived but inferred, in the sense not only that some detail not actually present is believed to be so, but also that some detail in fact present is not observed. Usually, although not always, the inference is either correct or not in serious error, and this fact results in a substantial economy of effort in perception. The concept of 'economy of effort' or 'economy of specification' appears to be of widespread application to perception and to hold out important possibilities of quantitative treatment (Attneave 1954; Hochberg and McAlister 1953).

While identification may be thought of as the aligning of present data with past experience similar to them, placing presently perceived objects into a context or 'framework' involves setting them in relation to other things very unlike themselves. This framework or setting is both spatial and temporal, so that an object is perceived as located in space, for example in a room or in relation to other objects such as the controls of a machine; and events are perceived as localized in time, and series of events can be perceived as forming sequences and rhythms. Some kind of simultaneous spatial and temporal reference enables movement and causal relationships to be perceived.

The relating of data to past material does not always take place after the data have been received: some of the perceptual 'work' involved is often, indeed usually, done beforehand and this enables identification to be made more easily and quickly when the data actually arrive. It seems that this can be done in one of three ways. Firstly, we may know definitely that certain major categories of possible identifications are excluded. Thus, we find it easier to identify a series of pictures if we know in advance that they will all be of, say, animals than if they may also include buildings, scenery and various other types of object. We shall even find it easier if we know that *most* of the pictures will belong to a particular category so that there is a bias in favour of one category as opposed to others. Secondly, terms from past experience having an essentially sequential character will imply future events as soon as the initial member of the sequence is identified. Thus, for instance, having identified a tune by the first few bars, we are expecting the remainder. Thirdly, we seem able to use the various present data and material from past experience to, as it were, 'compute' predictions of future events and by doing so we are able to expect sequences we have never experienced before.

It would seem that in everyday perception we unconsciously use these various methods to build up a kind of running hypothesis constantly predicting a little ahead of events. The accuracy attained is usually sufficient to effect a very considerable saving of time in dealing with moment-to-moment events, and indeed renders us unaware of most of them, leaving only the rare, unexpected events to engage our conscious attention. This constant prediction enables action to be taken which has reference not to the state of affairs immediately present, but to a state that is expected to exist in the future, as for instance when, in driving a car, adjustments of the controls are made not to the present positions of vehicles on the road, but to the positions they will occupy a few seconds hence.

The result of this continual short-term prediction is that when incoming data are familiar they are identified and fitted into context *immediately* and without any intervention of consciousness. When, however, data are novel or unexpected, there seems to be an active search for terms of past experience which are 'fitting' or 'appropriate', and there may be use of images, searching for analogies, and a considerable amount of trial and rejection before satisfaction is reached.

Each new perceptual response leaves the observer different from what he was before, so that the 'past' which he brings to deal with any new data is in some way changed. The amount of change may, of course, be either small or large and will depend to some extent on the time-scale involved—a series of small changes from second to second may add up to a large change over a longer period. Whether small or great, however, it appears not to be due to the mere addition of another experience to a 'stock' already existing. The past experience brought to deal with any incoming signal seems not to consist of an aggregate of past impressions, but appears to be in an organized or *schematized* form which is affected by each new impression in a manner which can be compared to the *modification* of a 'plastic' model.

2. *The translation process*

The relating of perception to action is a process which is often thought of as an aspect of perception, constituting the forward-looking part of 'meaning' in the sense that it confers upon perception significance for subsequent action. Alternatively, it might be regarded as a preliminary stage of the effector process. It would seem, however, to be sufficiently distinct from both to be considered separately as a link between the two.

A good example, as the term implies, is translation from one language to another: material perceived in the one language must be converted into the other to make a verbal or written response. Other examples are contained in the use of codes of various kinds. Most important for skilled performance are relationships between display and control studied under that title by many authors (e.g. Garvey *et al.* 1954, 1955), under the heading of 'stimulus-response compatibility' by Fitts *et al.* (1953, 1954) and under the title of 'transformations' by Crossman (1956).

When lifting an object by hand from one position and putting it down in another the relationship between what is seen and what is done is straightforward. The actions of the hand are closely related to the perceived positions and movements of the object. Similarly direct relationships between what is seen and done obtain when using hand tools. With machine tools and other mechanical and electronic devices, however, the relationship between perception and action may be complicated in several ways. For instance, a side-to-side motion of a pointer on a scale may result from a rotary motion of a control knob. Or again, the force required on a control lever may bear no directly linear relationship to the force it controls.

Many translations seem to be, as it were, ready to hand or 'built into' the repertoire that a man can bring to bear upon a task. This is obviously so in the case of direct hand movements, and, for most people, of such basic educational attainments as reading. It also applies to machine controls with which certain 'expected' relationships between actions and their effects have been demonstrated. Thus, for instance, clockwise rotation of a knob is expected to make the pointer of a horizontal scale above it move from left to right. Or to take a more homely illustration, most people would be confused by a tap that had to be rotated anti-clockwise to turn it off. These display-control relationships are learnt in the course of experience and their precise form is thus more a matter of individual experience channelled by social convention than of any fundamental characteristic of the organism. Doubtless almost any set of relationships could be learnt in time. They seem to be much easier to master, however, if those in any one set are all consistent according to a single rule than if different rules apply to different displays and controls. It thus appears that, like perception, the translation process works on an economy principle in the sense that if a single translation can be applied to all display-control relationships, or at least all in a given task, less data have to be carried by the subject's memory and less uncertainty arises when any control has to be used.

In a task for which no translation has already been built up the subject has to construct one *ad hoc*. An elaborate case of this would arise in the breaking of an unknown code. A very simple case is that of making movements when all we can see of what we are doing is in a mirror. Left-right movements are normally not affected and cause little difficulty. Back and forth movements are, however, reversed and make it surprisingly (to most people) difficult to trace a design seen in a mirror. Other examples are discussed in Chapters IV and VI. It frequently seems possible to analyse these translations into one or more specifiable stages of spatial, symbolic, or other transformation. Thus, in the mirror case we have to make a single spatial transformation of the far-near dimension.

Once a rule of translation has been built up, putting it into use can often precede the signal which would normally initiate it. When a particular signal or type of signal is expected we can often carry out the translation process and prepare responding action before it arrives so that when it does, it, as it were, triggers off a pre-formed response.

3. *The effector side*

The translation process may be thought of as a response to perception and in turn as a stimulus to effector action, initiating a chain of events containing a series of stages which are, in an important sense, the reverse of those leading from an external stimulus to perception. That is to say, there is a transition from a unitary integrated process to a series of detailed muscular movements. The nature of the events on the effector side is not at all well known—no doubt because they are usually unconscious—but it seems clear that they involve a progressive differentiation and particularization.

The first of them is probably some kind of general *orientation* or *attitude* which determines in broad outline what is to be done. Next, perhaps, come what may be called *general methods* of dealing with the object or situation concerned, and these are followed by particular *knacks* and *dexterities* which in turn bring into play detailed muscular movements.

It should be noted that throughout the functioning of the effector side there seems again to be an organizational quality which is similar in several important ways to that of the receptor side. In particular:

(*a*) At each stage there is the use of pre-existing patterns of response. As with the receptor side, some of these may be innate; but it again seems clear that, though their limits are set by innate capability, this limitation is in most cases small compared with the influence of past learning and experience.

(*b*) The organization of muscular movements produced by the effector side has a reference which is not only spatial but also temporal, so that movements do not occur as isolated units but are bound into sequences. This is especially noticeable when actions are performed in a rhythmical manner, but is an essential characteristic of all manipulative operations and, indeed, of all bodily movements except the very simplest reflexes. In this connexion it is to be noted that, just as a series of signals may lead to a single perceptual response, so a single translation may lead to a series of actions.

(*c*) The attitudes, methods, knacks and so forth which are brought into play in the building of effector action show a generalized quality in that they do not lead to exact stereotyped muscular movements. The actual movements made on any occasion are adapted to the requirements of that occasion, and, as these requirements are never quite the same twice, the precise way in which the actual movements occur varies from one occasion to the next, even when a performance is nominally repeated exactly.

Human performance appears to be almost infinitely variable. It is often assumed that we achieve this variation because we acquire in the course of time a very large number of pre-formed responses which can be put to use as occasion requires. The variability of the performance seems, however, too great to be reasonably accounted for in this way except in a few very special cases. It would appear better to think of the central mechanisms as capable of producing a response which is formed *ad hoc* by a kind of 'calculation' based on many influences derived from the present aims and past experience of the subject and the sensory data of various kinds available at the time. We should, in other words, think, as Craik (1943) urged, of the whole receptor, translatory and effector system as a kind of calculating machine capable of receiving several different inputs and producing an output which is derived from the various input parameters acting in concert. Such a system results in a response which is unique on each occasion, although it is determinate and based on constants which are, at least in principle, discoverable.

B. THE LEARNT ASPECT OF SKILL

From what has been said of the receptor-effector aspect of skill it will be clear that when a man meets a situation or carries out an action he necessarily and inevitably does so in terms of what he brings to it from previous experience. When he is meeting the situation or carrying out the action for the first time, he will have to build up his manner of doing so from a past experience which has been shaped by other situations and actions, some of which will be relevant and some not, so that success will depend to a great extent upon the way in which he selects from various alternatives. When he has to do the same thing again, however, the case is very different, because the past experience he brings will have been modified by his experience of the first occasion. In other words, learning has taken place.

The effects of meeting the same situation repeatedly are complex, and a number of variables, such as the time elapsing between one occasion and another, have been shown to influence them. For our present purpose, however, the points to be noted are, first, that the organization carried over from one occasion to another tends to become firmer and more complete the more it is used, and second, that although the organization undergoes considerable modification with repeated use, the way in which the task is performed the first time it is met may largely determine the manner of its performance subsequently (Welford, Brown and Gabb 1950). In relation to studies of ageing this underlines the point made in the previous chapter that if we are fully to understand present performance by older people it may be necessary to go a long way back into the past, to a time when industrial, social and other demands were considerably different from what they are today.

It appears that the carrying over of organization takes place in all three types of process, perceptual, translation and effector, and also occurs at various perceptual and effector levels so that the skill that is built up has typically some relatively specific and some more generalized features. On the receptor side, a subject learning a skill gradually acquires an increased comprehension of the data presented in the task, and, by recognizing the ways they hang together, may often be able to carry on with less sense data than he did at the beginning. He may, for instance, as Szafran has shown (p. 184), be able to carry out by touch and kinaesthesis alone a task in which he formerly needed to supplement these with vision. The translation process changes in the course of practice by becoming readier in the sense that 'rules' are built up, and quicker so that in a well-practised skill the relationship between perception and action appears 'immediate' and it is difficult to recognize the presence of the translation process except in a logical sense. Effector action in the course of learning becomes more accurate and better timed with the result that it is smoother, requires less checking for correctness of outcome and takes less time although the actual speed of movement may not increase.

The main results of these changes with learning, apart from the saving of time and increased precision, appear to be two. Firstly, the subject acquires a greater ability to anticipate future data and to plan actions ahead, and at the same time the size of the 'unit' of his performance increases. The classical data on this point are those of Bryan and Harter (1899) who explained their results on learning morse code in terms of the fact that as men become more skilled they seem to pass from dealing with letters as units to words and even to whole phrases. More recent evidence indicating the manner of this achievement has been given by Vince (1948b, 1949) who has shown that in tasks such as responding to signals in very rapid sequences or making rapid series of actions the number of discrete perceptual-motor 'units' which can be dealt with is only about two or three per second, but that performance can be greatly speeded up by grouping signals so that several are dealt with together as a single unit. Skilled typists, morse-operators and pianists execute individual movements of printing letters, making dots and dashes or pressing notes very much more rapidly than this, and it seems clear that they can only do so by dealing with whole words or phrases as single perceptual-motor units.

The second result of change in skill during the course of learning seems to be that when learning becomes very thorough, conscious control seems to drop out. What exactly happens when this stage is reached is not known. It seems frequently to be associated with the acquisition of rhythm and thus, presumably, with the attainment of larger 'units'. Often it is said that the performance has been passed over to the 'lower centres' of the brain. This statement is, however, unsatisfactory. If it means that the cortex is no longer functioning, it is clearly untrue. If it means that so-called higher mental processes of decision or thought no longer occur, it merely restates the observed facts in a physiological language for which there is no justification. Work by Leonard (1953) suggests that some dropping out of consciousness occurs when the subject is working under such conditions that he gives his whole attention to signals on the display and has no time or need to give attention to his responding actions. It seems fairly clear (Welford 1952a) that this can only occur when the actions are of an accuracy such that their outcome is not in doubt. We might thus expect that well-practised actions could be carried out with relatively little conscious attention. More generally the view seems to be tenable that what we recognize as consciousness in the full sense—as opposed to merely not being asleep—arises essentially when some uncertainty requires to be resolved and that the apparent loss of conscious control in highly practised skills is a result of the virtual elimination of uncertainty in performance.

The discussion of conscious attention in this kind of connexion will seem to some readers to smack of an archaic type of psychology. The extent to which a subject is or is not aware of what he is doing appears, however, to be such an important and widespread variable in skilled performance that some serious account must be taken of it in any comprehensive treatment of skill.

C. THE SERIAL NATURE OF SKILL

The foregoing treatment of skill has several times required the mention of temporal factors, integration of data in time and the performance of sequences of actions. Let us now, as it were, turn our problem round and consider specifically performance in its temporal aspects. Except in the very simplest reflexes, and perhaps not even then, human activity never consists of discrete stimulus-response chains. Rather it is to be conceived as involving a constant stream of incoming data and outgoing actions all to some extent interconnected. We shall here consider four points about this serial aspect of performance and its changes in the course of the acquisition of skill.

1. *Feedback from effector to receptor*

The subject obtains data about his own actions and their results in three ways. Firstly, actions of a manipulatory kind, by affecting external objects, modify the data fed into the receptor side. Actions of a non-manipulatory nature, such as the subject changing his position without doing anything to an external object, nevertheless change his relationship to external objects and thus similarly modify the data fed into the receptor side. Secondly, the muscular contractions and relaxations and the changes of posture involved in taking action modify the proprioceptive stimuli inevitably accompanying any external stimulus, and thus further modify the data fed into the receptor side. Thirdly, connexions in the brain between motor cortex, sensory cortex and cerebellum almost certainly enable some kind of data derived from central effector functioning to be fed into the receptor side without any necessary involvement of the peripheral musculature or overt action.

As a result of information fed back in these ways there *appears* to be a mixing of receptor and effector processes, so that not only is effector function dependent upon receptor, but receptor function is in a considerable measure determined by effector. For example, embarking on a course of action may produce a selective orientation towards subsequent sense data so that the field of attention is narrowed and the observer is set to organize incoming data in a particular way. Whether this occurs or not, the point reached by one action will inevitably be the starting-point of the next. We can thus say that as regards both action and perception each response does in a very real sense grow out of the responses which have gone before.

The whole system of receptor and effector interaction appears to be analogous in many important ways to the *feedback* systems met in certain kinds of electronic and mechanical apparatus, such as regeneration and degeneration in radio sets, governors on steam-engines and mechanically assisted steering-gear on ships. By analogy with such systems the effect of feedback from effector to receptor might be either *positive* as when the taking of action encourages its own continuation and reduction of action tends towards cessation; or *negative* as when the taking of action tends to cessation and reduction mobilizes efforts for continuation. A type of negative feed-

back system is widely recognized in biology under the term 'homeo-
stasis'.

Human behaviour in which there was a predominance of positive
feedback would tend to be erratic and clumsy—the reverse of what
is normally regarded as skilled. For performance to be skilled in the
sense of being smoothly efficient and accurate, negative feedback must
predominate, although both positive and negative may be operating.

Negative feedback makes a system self-regulatory and would
seem to give to skilled performance two important characteristics
where information about the results of action is available to the
subject. Firstly, action in relation to any external object will tend to
be 'pulled into line' in the sense that it will be more closely related
to the requirements of the object and situation than to momentary
variations in the subject. Secondly, performance tends to remain
constant in the face of disturbing influences, so that variation of the
conditions under which the task is done has, within limits, little
effect on achievement. The compensatory adjustment of method in
the face of difficulty noted in the previous chapter would seem to be
dependent upon such feedback, although other conditions are also
necessary for its occurrence.

It must be emphasized that a negative feedback system implies
a potential over-sensitivity and over-activity balanced by an active
inhibitory force. Macpherson et al. (1949) have provided evidence
confirming that this is so in the case of a simple task done with
knowledge of results. It means, however, that negative feedback will
only operate to produce constancy of achievement when the task is
such that the subject's capabilities are not fully stretched under the
easiest conditions, and when the conditions are not so adverse that
even the simplest task can be performed only with great difficulty.
For constancy, or approximate constancy to be attained, the subject
must be working within his capabilities, and the external conditions
must be within the limits of tolerance.

2. Limits of speed

The various mechanisms in the chain from sense organ to effector
all take time to function. The sense organs themselves normally take
very little, while effector action usually takes a great deal—so much
so that industrial work study has often attempted to obtain analyses
of performance essentially in terms of the times taken by overt
movements. The limits to speed of performance as a whole are usually

set by the time required for the central mechanisms to act in discriminating one signal from another, in carrying out the translation process and in selecting responding action. These are the processes which largely occupy *reaction time* (i.e. the time from the onset of a signal to the beginning of the responding action) in a reaction-time experiment. What must surely rank as one of the most important advances in psychological knowledge in recent years has been the demonstration by Hick (1952*a*) that choice reaction times can be regarded as a linear function of the amount of 'information' (in the information theory sense) transferred from display to control in making a response. Thus, for example, reaction time in a choice-reaction experiment is linearly related to the logarithm of the effective number of equi-probable choices. This formulation provides an approach to a rational basis for the explanation of variations in the speed of performance, and also enables speed and accuracy to be treated in the same terms: inaccuracy can be regarded as failure to transfer enough information and thus is expressible in terms of time saved. The inverse relationship between speed and accuracy expected by this formulation is not always shown in a practical case since it assumes subjects do not take time correcting errors and are not disturbed by noticing they have made them: it does, however, hold in principle.

Hyman (1953) has shown that the rate of gain of information remains, on average, constant even though choices are not equi-probable and Crossman (1953) has opened up wide possibilities by showing that it also remains constant for the continuous performance of sorting packs of cards into different numbers of categories. Hick (1952*b*) has discussed the fact that although the rate is constant for different degrees of choice within the same type of material, it varies considerably between different classes of material. Work by Crossman (1956) has shown that one at least of the important variables affecting rate is the nature of the relation between display and control, the rate being much higher when this is direct and straightforward; it is, for example, very much higher when in a choice reaction-task stimulus lights appear directly over the reaction keys than when the key is indicated by a light whose position is not directly related to the corresponding key. It seems clear, therefore, that rate of information transfer is greatly dependent upon the nature of the translation process involved.

The work has been further extended by Fitts (1954) who has proposed a formulation following Hick's law which holds for simple hand and arm movements over distances of 2 to 16 inches. The time taken by the back and forth movements of 'dotting' with a stylus alternately on two targets was found to be proportional to the logarithm of the ratio between twice the length of the movements and the width of the targets.

The time taken by discrimination is normally small compared with that taken by the translation process, but when objects to be discriminated are closely similar it becomes substantial. The mathematical treatment of discrimination time has been discussed and a formulation proposed by Crossman (1955). According to this, the time taken for discrimination is a linear function of the reciprocal of the difference between the logarithms of the quantities which are being compared.

Turning now to serial performance, it is clear that often these various times all enter into the determination of the speed of performance. Thus, when each action must depend upon the results of the last, the total time will depend both on the times taken by central processes of perception and translation and also upon the time required to make the responding actions. Experiments have shown, however, that some overlapping of processes can often occur with consequent saving of time. Thus, discrimination can very often overlap with choice (Crossman 1955) as is understandable in the sense that if discrimination involves the progressive elimination of various classes of possible identification, the exclusion of classes of possible response might proceed step by step with this. Evidence for this view has been provided by Leonard (1954). It is likely, however, that such overlapping can only occur when the translation between display and control has been so thoroughly learnt that successive stages of elimination on the receptor side can be related in detail to those on the effector. Where this cannot be done discrimination seems likely to have to reach an advanced stage before choice can begin so that the times taken by the two processes become more or less additive.

Other cases of overlapping are that a signal can be received while the central processes are dealing with a previous signal; the central processes can deal with one signal while the effectors are making a response to a previous signal; and it seems that the monitoring of an action or sequence of actions can often be carried out by mechanisms substantially independent of the control of movement by the translation process.

We have noted that the human perceptual-motor 'mechanism' receives input data continuously and simultaneously over several channels, and is able to take action continuously and simultaneously with various effector organs. Somewhere between input and output, however, there seems to be a single channel which we may term a *decision mechanism* receiving data, initiating action and, where necessary, checking the occurrence and results of action. The time taken by this single channel to function fills almost all the *reaction time*, so that a signal arriving during the reaction time to a previous signal has to wait to be dealt with until the single channel is clear. The channel *may* also be filled and cause delay in dealing with incoming signals during and shortly after a responding action if sensory data fed back from the effectors capture the subject's attention. Delays from this cause tend, however, to drop out as the subject's performance becomes more precise and requires less monitoring. When this happens performance becomes substantially faster because central processes leading to the next action can overlap with the preceding movement (Craik 1948; Vince 1948a; Welford 1952a and references there given; Davis 1956).

We must regard the decision mechanism as a single channel of *information* and the channels feeding it are channels of information rather than of stimuli. Evidence for this view is that although in certain circumstances the two ears can act as separate channels, two sounds from different sources can also be separated in spite of the fact that both are being received by both ears. Each such channel presents data to the decision mechanism with some of the work of perception already done and each seems to be equipped with the capacity for some short-term storage of data so that signals can be held if the decision mechanism is 'busy' (Broadbent 1954).

The decision mechanism appears not to act continuously but intermittently taking in perceptual data from the receptor side and issuing, as it were, 'orders' to the effector side which seem then to be carried out without further control by the decision mechanism even though a fairly substantial sequence of actions is involved. It thus seems essentially to involve certain types of translation process, where some fresh connexion between receptor and effector has to be made. It does, however, appear to embrace discrimination, translation and choice all together so that it cannot be equated with translation in any simple sense.

The decision mechanism appears to be concerned fundamentally with the *resolution of uncertainty*, which we have previously suggested is intimately associated with conscious attention. On this view, when a performance is so thoroughly learnt that it becomes 'automatic', it can be carried on while leaving the decision mechanism virtually free: for example, an 'automatic' performance such as repetition work in a factory or simple knitting can be carried out while a person's attention is given to talking or reading. Consistent with this view is the fact that if a mistake is noticed or a relatively difficult portion of the task occurs such as turning a row in knitting, the conversation or reading is usually interrupted. Just what happens when an activity becomes 'automatic' in this sense is not known but it would seem that a programme of action and expected events is laid down and that so long as input data are consistent with those required by the programme, the decision mechanism is left free. Any discrepancy, however, whether due to an error or to an unexpected event will cause the decision mechanism to be 'captured' and a new or revised programme set up.

3. *'Higher' units of performance*

Bryan and Harter suggested that the succession of units of performance from letters to syllables to words and even to phrases mastered by a morse operator as he becomes more skilled constitute a 'hierarchy of habits' the levels of which can be conceived in terms of the size of the unit. How the higher units are related to the lower and how they are formed out of them was not pursued in detail, and the application the authors made of the hierarchy of habits concept was limited to the task they were studying. Work on skill suggests that this concept can be applied more widely and does indeed denote an important principle of performance in general.

Let us consider by way of example looking up a telephone number and dialling it. Looking up the number will require a series of actions, turning over pages, running the finger down the columns, and so on. It will involve a constant inter-play between receptor and effector functions, each turn of a page being made in response to information on the page open at the time in relation to the information sought. The various actions are all in one sense discrete receptor-effector units but are bound together by the aim of finding the number required. In another sense, however, they are all receptor activity aimed at obtaining information. When this has been done it is translated into a series of turns of the telephone dial which are then made.

These are again in one sense discrete receptor-effector units each requiring the observation of a number and turning the dial. Again, however, they are in another sense all effector activity using the information previously obtained. We can think of the whole operation as a single unit of performance incorporating many smaller units, and that both the larger and the smaller units are similar in the sense that information is gathered and used to direct action to a specific end.

The hierarchical ordering of units of performance is perhaps better illustrated in some industrial skills. If, for example, we went into a workshop where a man was using a lathe and interrupted his activity at a particular instant of time, we should find a detailed muscular action in progress—say a twisting of the wrist to turn a handwheel on the tool carriage. The action would, however, be only one of a series required to move the tool over the surface of the work. This again would be only one part of the cycle of operations required to machine the article concerned, and the article might be only one of several needed for the job of construction on which the man was engaged. The action, the series of actions, the cycle of operations, and the job of construction are all in a sense units of performance of a task. The larger units at each level embrace the smaller, organizing, co-ordinating, 'steering' and indeed 'driving' or motivating those which lie below. They do this not only in a formal analytical sense, but also by setting constants for the smaller units: for instance, the speed at which a smaller unit of performance is carried out will depend in part upon the tempo of the larger unit to which it belongs (de Montpellier 1935; Wehrkamp and Smith 1952; Denton 1953).

Were we to ask the man on the lathe what he was doing we should be asking an ambiguous question because an answer in terms of any of the units would be correct. The actual unit he chose to give as his answer might be expected to depend on the level at which the outcome of his actions was least certain. Units higher in the hierarchy would be 'taken for granted', those lower would have become more or less 'automatic'. If this view is correct, we should expect the level at which awareness is centred to rise as the operator becomes more expert and masters larger and larger units, but that it might fall again if conditions of work, fatigue or other factors made the performance of smaller units sufficiently difficult for their outcome to be in appreciable doubt.

Where conditions require or permit virtually exact repetition of a unit many times, performance tends to become highly stereotyped in the course of practice, and the whole cycle can be run off very much as a chain response with each member acting as the cue for the one that follows. Even in this case, however, the unit seems to behave as a whole rather than as a simple chain because it is often impossible, and almost always difficult, if a cycle is interrupted to begin it again in the middle without some rehearsal of the parts already completed.

Where conditions are more fluid and in early stages of practice performance appears to be more variable. The precise sequence of sub-units may differ from one performance to another in much the same way as the precise form of an action varies with detailed circumstances. Often the results of each sub-unit will indicate what should be done subsequently, as when in looking up a telephone number the names appearing on each page of the directory opened indicate which way the pages should next be turned. Sometimes, however, the subject will have no alternative but to *remember* at each stage what he has done and what still remains to be done to complete the task. Thus in dialling a telephone number it is necessary to remember as each figure is dialled what remains to be done because the dial itself gives no indication of what has been completed.

4. *Short-term retention*

The last point focuses attention upon an important factor implicit in the whole idea of higher units of performance and the integration of data over time, namely *short-term memory* retaining data early in a series until they can be combined with later, holding data while the decision mechanism is 'busy' and keeping a tally of what has been done in a complex task. Short-term memory has come into prominence in recent thought, partly because of analogies with electronic digital computers and the possibility that the self-regenerating circuits sometimes used for storing information have their counterpart in self-re-exciting neuronal circuits in the brain. The importance of short-term retention does not, however, depend upon this analogy but must be reckoned as an essential factor in many types of human performance.

Studies of short-term memory have shown it to be of surprisingly limited capacity, especially under conditions where information has to be stored over intervening activity (Kay 1953; Brown 1955; Mackworth and Mackworth 1956; see also Chapter IX). There can be little doubt that it is one of the factors limiting the size of higher units of performance that can be built, and that it sets a rather sharp limit upon the amount of advance information a subject can use in a serial task. The span of short-term memory can, however, be extended if instead of individual pieces of data whole 'schemata' or 'sub-routines' or 'codings' can be retained as the units of data (see Bartlett 1951; Pollack 1953; Miller 1956). This means that one of the most effective ways in which short-term memory can be used is to retain information about what material stored in longer-term memory should be brought into play and in which order.

One of the aspects of short-term retention as yet insufficiently explored is the maintenance of *orientation* in space and time—the running retention of data which give a spatial and temporal framework in which our present position can be fixed and in terms of which events can be placed. Essentially similar to this would seem to be the framework built up in conceptual thought and in terms of which it appears to be carried out. When we think about a relatively complex problem it would seem that we have to gather a certain amount of data and hold it all together in a conceptual framework as a prerequisite for performing 'mental manipulations' upon it. It would appear that the maximum levels of conceptual thought that some so-called 'power' tests attempt to measure, are largely determined by the capacity of short-term retention which limits the size of such a framework in any particular individual and under any particular circumstances. Further consideration to this problem is given in Chapter VIII. Meanwhile, we have to recognize that considerations of short-term storage of information are inevitably bound up with the serial aspects of any performance which goes beyond the simple 'chain-reaction' pattern.

LOCATING CHANGES IN SKILL

It is clear from the foregoing that changes in skill for better or worse may be located in many different mechanisms. Of these, however, the peripheral receptor and effector organs are probably of comparatively minor importance. Well-formed efficient sense-organs and muscles will favour the establishment and maintenance of skill, and impairment of either will tend to cause its breakdown, but a great many experiments and clinical observations on both animals and human beings have shown that there can be impairments of both sense-organs and peripheral effector organs with relatively little loss of skill.

Much more important would seem to be the central receptor, translatory and effector mechanisms concerned with the organization of data and the shaping of action. For example, any failure to organize the incoming data or to co-ordinate the data coming from different sensory modes such as visual, tactile and proprioceptive, will result in these not providing an adequate basis for full meaningful perception and subsequent action. As regards the central mechanisms concerned with bringing past material to bear upon the present situation, two types of failure appear to be possible. Firstly, there may be failure to carry over from the past to the present, either because the appropriate learning has not taken place in the past or because there has been forgetting or because for some reason the past material required is temporarily 'unavailable', as, for instance, when we fail to recall something which at other times we can recall perfectly well. In such cases there may be a total breakdown of performance or some alternative means of dealing with the material may be adopted which is less than fully effective.

Secondly, there may be failure to exercise adequate *control* over the process of bringing past experience to bear on the present situation. The effect of this may sometimes be that incoming data 'touch off' more than one organization of past experience with the result that perception or action is confused. More commonly it means that insufficient identification of incoming signals is achieved or that too crude a rule is applied in the translation process or that a wrong action is initiated. In all cases we can say that insufficient information is transmitted from display to control because somewhere along the line the signal has been placed in the wrong class or into one which is insufficiently precise. In other words, the 'encoding' has been incorrect or not detailed enough. As has already been mentioned, coding involves the application of an organization of past experience which carries a wealth of detail not immediately perceived so that much of what is thought to have been perceived is in fact inferred. Any error of encoding will result in this inferred detail being to some extent incorrect, and the ensuing action being in consequence inappropriate. Lack of control of this type will often appear as a touching-off of an identification by some detail of the presented material which may attract attention but be of little relevance to the material as a whole.

A similar type of failure may arise with well-learnt serial performances. It would seem that in the course of repetition the organizations concerned with the performance of a task become more complete and act with less reference to external stimuli, and that this may sometimes lead to a breakdown of skill. What seems to happen is that a sequence of actions 'runs itself off' with insufficient reference by the later members of the series to the effects of the earlier members. Essentially this is, of course, a failure of the feedback via the object manipulated which would normally keep the skilled performance and the object in close relation to one another. But it seems clear that it is often not so much a failure of the feedback to take place at all, as of a failure to use the data provided by it to control the pre-existing organization.

Lack of control of a rather different type may be shown in tasks where it is necessary not only that certain actions should be performed, but also that they should be carried out in the correct sequence. A type of breakdown of skill sometimes occurs in which the subject produces the correct actions but fails to order them in the correct sequence. This essentially represents a breakdown of higher units of performance with a consequent failure to control the smaller units.

The location of any change of skill within the scheme outlined is unfortunately seldom easy. Any change of moderate degree which affects only one part of the chain of events from 'stimulus' to 'response' is likely to make little difference to overall achievement provided that the dynamic character of the skill remains unaffected, as this will enable compensation for any deficiency to be made. At the same time any gross failure in one part of the system is likely to affect all the others to some degree, so that when a substantial change of achievement does occur it may be difficult to ascertain whether it is due to some severe failure of one part of the mechanism, or to a more general impairment. Because of this, it seems clear that any attempt to study changes of skill must make as thoroughgoing an analysis as possible of the performance, in order to assess separately the functioning of the different mechanisms involved.

In making such an assessment when skill deteriorates, it has to be recognized that we are usually looking for signs of a *partial impairment* because a total disability of any part of the mechanism would usually lead to such gross effects that it could be located without much difficulty. Partial impairment of the efficiency of any stage may show itself in one or more of six ways:

(i) Very often the first signs of breakdown will be that the component actions of a complex performance change while the overall achievement remains constant.

(ii) Temporary breakdowns of function may occur to such an extent that obvious errors are made. These breakdowns may be of several different kinds, due, for example, to some event in the chain failing to occur at all, or to some inappropriate event occurring, or to an otherwise appropriate event occurring at the wrong time.

(iii) More subtly, any reduction of data from external objects will, owing to the dynamic nature of skill, tend to increase the part played in shaping the performance by the schematized past experience brought by the subject to the situation. Any impairment of the early stages of the receptor side will, therefore, tend to produce relatively little change in a skill which has already been firmly established, but will make for a marked deterioration of performance at unfamiliar tasks. In the wider field of everyday behaviour, the same impairment would seem to be a reasonable explanation of the tendency of some older people, especially those showing clinical senility, to display poor comprehension of the present situation combined with detailed remembering of past events.

(iv) It would appear probable that a very common impairment is the result of a mechanism becoming insensitive and requiring a greater input than usual to operate it, but operating more or less normally if this greater input is provided. This kind of sensitivity would seem to be shown not only in sensory functions but also in cases when the subject requires more than the normal amount of information for the solution of a problem or the forming of a judgement, although the solution or judgement may be sound enough once the information required has been supplied.

(v) It appears that impairment may frequently lead to a condition in which the various receptor mechanisms work satisfactorily in the sense that they do not cause errors, but work more slowly.

It is not clear how far this last type of impairment should be distinguished from that leading to insensitivity, as there exists a wide class of mechanisms, among which are almost certainly some of those in the brain, in which speed of operation rises with level of input, so that if input is kept constant impairment will show as a loss of speed, or if speed is kept constant impairment will show as the requirement of higher input. An important example of such a mechanism has been indicated by work on sensory sensitivity following the implications of the fact that incoming signals take the form of nerve impulses superimposed upon an appreciable amount of random nervous activity or 'neural noise'. What the subject's central mechanisms must do in order to perceive a signal is to distinguish the increase of impulses produced by the signal from temporary bursts of random noise. Since random bursts of high intensity are very improbable, signals producing a larger increase of impulses will be recognized easily, but weak signals may be indistinguishable from background noise. Duration of signal as well as absolute instantaneous intensity is, however, also important. Random bursts of noise tend to be of short duration, so that the recognition of weak signals will become easier as the period for which the incoming signal lasts becomes longer. Reduction of signal intensity or increase in the level of randomness of the background noise can thus be compensated by the cumulation of input data over a longer time. Work on this subject will be considered and the theoretical treatment set out in more detail in Chapter VII.

Though the implications of 'signal to noise ratio' have so far been worked out almost entirely with regard to the sensory field, it seems reasonable to suppose that it could in principle be applied to all stages of the chain from sensory input to overt action. Insensitivity of the various central mechanisms, weak signals by one to the next, or high levels of noise in the brain could lead to slowness of performance or to the need for more input data to achieve control of, say, translation by perception or of effector processes by translation.

(vi) When performance is *paced* in the sense that signals for action occur at times which are not of the subject's choosing and action has to be carried out within time limits, other types of breakdown arise owing to the limited capacity of the organism as regards speed of information transfer and short-term retention. At high speeds there may be chronic overloading of these mechanisms. The kind of breakdown that occurs is illustrated in an experiment by Vince (1949): responses lag farther and farther behind signals until a 'blocking' occurs, then signals are missed until the subject can once more get his responses into step. Even where speeds are slower, so that on average they are well within the subject's capacity, irregularities in the spacing of signals may result in several coming together and causing temporary overloading. The decision mechanism will for a period after each signal be fully loaded so that other signals following within this period will have to be stored in short-term memory. If so many arrive that the subject's short-term memory is overloaded, some signals will be missed. If adverse circumstances or any other cause reduce the capacity of short-term memory the tolerance to such bunching of signals will be reduced. Similarly, any slowing of the decision process will not only interfere with the accurate timing of responses, but will also throw an undue load upon short-term memory and lead to the same result.

Once such overloading leads to breakdown, a vicious-circle situation may easily arise: the missing of some signals disturbs the flow of performance and interferes with the subject's expectations by disrupting the 'coded' sequences. As a result, incoming signals have to be dealt with piecemeal and in consequence take more decision time so that performance is slowed. This slowing aggravates the very factors which have brought it about, and the whole performance tends to get worse and worse until some limit is reached and performance is stabilized at a lower level.

This is the kind of breakdown which seems to occur in fatigue at some kinds of complex tasks (e.g. Davis 1948). In these, an initially adequate performance becomes disrupted owing either to endogenous changes in the organism which slow decision or lower the capacity of short-term memory or to irrelevant stimuli which capture the subject's attention and thus interfere with the decision processes and take time which is needed for the task the subject is endeavouring to carry out (Welford 1953a).

Impairments of all these kinds we have outlined in the last few pages appear fairly obvious in some people of extreme old age. Whether, however, the changes occurring in people during middle and early old age are to be regarded as essentially of the same kind but of lesser extent, is a matter for investigation.

III

METHODS OF STUDYING AGE CHANGES

It is relatively easy in principle to obtain factual information about changes of performance with age, but to gain an understanding of the nature and causes of these changes is a matter of unusual difficulty. This is due partly to problems inherent in all psychological research and partly to certain of these being intensified when age changes are studied. We shall not here be concerned with large-scale fact-finding investigations such as surveys of the numbers of men in different industries or on various grades of work. These have been used in the attempt to study human capacity in relation to age and, when carried out by personal inquiry rather than by circulated questionnaires, are of value as indicators of issues for more intensive study and as checks on theories formulated by such study. They are, however, ill-adapted to provide a thorough understanding of changes of performance with age leading to theoretical explanations or detailed solutions of practical problems—their use for these purposes is not impossible but tends to be extremely laborious and expensive. The reason is that surveys which are easy to make are so only because they deal with whole industries or factories or with classes of work such as skilled, semi-skilled and unskilled, whereas the differences of demand upon human capacity are between individual operations, of which many making a variety of different demands are usually included in the larger groupings. We shall instead concentrate on the methods of more intensive studies consisting firstly of experiments, usually conducted in a laboratory, and secondly of studies of actual work in industry either by means of factory records or by direct observation and measurement of industrial performance.

Four topics will be considered:

1. The relative merits of these different sources of data.

2. Problems arising from the complexity of the human 'mechanism'.

3. Questions of motivation—are younger and older subjects equally willing to try their best?

4. Certain other problems arising from the need to compare subjects of different ages or to test the same individuals more than once.

1. Experiments and industrial studies

Experiments are well recognized as probably the most powerful tool we possess for the study of human performance. They essentially use tasks specially constructed to bring out some particular aspect of performance, such as speed or accuracy of movement or ability to perform one or other type of intellectual operation. The task may take any of an almost infinite variety of forms from drawing lines on paper or sorting a pack of cards to simulations of high-grade skills such as flying an aircraft or driving a car which involve substantial and elaborate apparatus. Whether simple or complex they aim at obtaining a sample of the subject's performance under controlled conditions where a precise record can be taken for subsequent analysis.

One important limitation of experiments is that it is seldom possible to continue them for a long time—usually a few hours is the maximum and in most cases about half an hour is all that can reasonably be demanded of a subject. This gives rise to two opposing objections. The first is that if older people are less resistant to fatigue than younger, they might be able to maintain a performance for a short period at a level which would be impossible over a longer working spell, and the experiment would thus unduly favour older people. Smith (1938), for instance, found in an experiment in which subjects were required to assemble nuts and bolts, that the lowering of performance between men in their thirties and fifties was somewhat greater for a eight-hour spell than it was over a period of half an hour. The second objection is that if older people are slower at learning an unfamiliar task, difficulty shown by them in performing an experiment might disappear with long-continued practice, and the experiment would thus give a falsely *un*favourable impression of their capacities.

Both these objections tend to be exaggerated. Exercise tolerance has been shown in several studies to diminish with age but normal performance is seldom limited by physiological capacity in this sense. What little we know about mental fatigue in older people suggests that fatigue effects may sometimes become *smaller* with age at least until the sixties (Botwinick and Shock 1952). The reason presumably is that a lower level of performance by older people produces a lower rate of fatigue decrement. As regards improvements with practice, the results of laboratory experiments such as those of Brown in Chapter IV (p. 70) and Szafran in Chapter VI (p. 136) suggest that, in some cases at least, these are in about the same *proportion* in all age groups, so that although *absolute* differences of performance might be reduced by long-continued practice, *relative* differences would remain about the same. However, our present knowledge bearing upon these problems is scanty and both would repay further study. Meanwhile the point would seem to be in principle valid that the observations made in brief experiments need to be checked against long-practised skills to sort out continuing age-differences of performance from age-changes of capacity to deal with short-duration and unfamiliar tasks.

These objections do not apply to studies of industrial work. Observation and measurement of work in industry cannot be as closely controlled as an experiment, but are usually more so than studies of other everyday activities and thus provide tasks practised to an extent far beyond what is possible in the most protracted experments, yet capable of quantitative study in terms of output and a number of other measures.

For the clearest results experimental and industrial studies need to be closely integrated. Experiments need verification from industrial investigations: these need guidance from experimental results and can in turn give rise to further experimental inquiry.

2. *Problems arising from the complexity of the human 'mechanism'*

When we study the behaviour of a whole human being we are attempting, even more than in other biological studies, to understand the working of mechanisms of extreme complexity which for almost all practical purposes we cannot *directly* observe. One important result of this complexity is that investigations, whether experimental or industrial, have to sort out the effects of the many different mechanisms, sensory, central and motor, contributing to a single final result. This means that in neither kind of study is it sufficient to take a simple measure of performance such as amount achieved in a given time at a single task.

We need to expand our study in three ways: firstly, by measuring performance under conditions whieh are systematically varied to limit one of the constituent mechanisms only, varying, for example, either the display of information or the responding action required while keeping the remaining conditions the same.

Secondly, we need to take several different measures of a subject's performance: a single score of overall achievement leaves out of account variations in the manner whereby this achievement was attained. Thus, one subject may have been deliberate and accurate, whereas another may have been quicker but have wasted so much time making errors that he has achieved no more than the one who was slower. We need to measure various component actions of the performance separately, ending up, ideally, with a double analysis both of what the subject has done in terms of accuracy, types of error and form of his actions and also of the time he has spent over each. When making such a study it is important to bear in mind that total achievement is often by no means the same thing as the generally accepted criterion of success. In many cases this criterion has the status of a score dealing with only one part or aspect of the performance. For instance, in dart-throwing and many similar aiming tasks, the score obtained on the target is a matter only of accuracy and takes no account of the time taken in aiming or the way in which the aiming was carried out. A full study of performance at such a task requires, as a measure of total achievement, some integration of accuracy with time taken. For analysis, accuracy needs to be broken down into, perhaps, vertical and horizontal components, and it may be necessary to study the relationship of each throw to the next, so as to obtain scores which indicate the nature of corrections made for errors. The total time similarly may need to be split up to indicate how it was spent: for example, how much was spent taking aim and how much was spent observing the results of each throw.

Thirdly, all these scores need to be examined for variation during the course of the performance: thus one subject may start slowly and speed up while another maintains an even tempo throughout, and yet another proceed by a series of bursts of activity with intervening pauses.

Many important studies have been done without entering into this amount of detail, and indeed few have dealt with all three types together, but significant differences have been shown between age trends in closely similar tasks, in different constituent actions of the same task and in the serial course of performance, so that each type of detailed treatment should be considered and only rejected from a particular study after making sure that important data are not likely to be thrown away. Such a procedure is apt to be laborious both in reading records and handling the large quantities of data obtained, but alleviation is possible in some cases if records are taken in a digital form suitable for direct feeding to an electronic or electro-mechanical computer (N. Welford 1952, 1955).

The same considerations apply to industrial studies based on production records. Figures for overall output can often with advantage be supplemented by records of wasted material and faults, and by figures for changes in all these with variations in the precise nature of the job and over periods of time. This is not to say that significant use of production records cannot be made without this extra information, but there are indications that it is in such features as continuity of activity rather than overall production that early signs of change with age at industrial work are to be found.

3. Motivation

Two questions are often raised about whether older and younger people are equally willing to co-operate in ageing studies, and whether unwillingness by older people distorts the results. The first is that the subjects of almost any intensive study must for obvious human and practical reasons be volunteers, and it may well be that these are on average bolder and somewhat abler than their contemporaries. If so, and if the older subjects are in fact more highly selected in this respect, age trends in their performance might be unduly favourable. The second objection is that experimental tasks are almost always artificial and may be regarded by older people as trivial and not worth serious effort, with the result that age trends in performance might tend to be less favourable than they ought.

With regard to the first question, most investigators have found difficulty in obtaining middle-aged and old subjects. It is fairly easy to obtain men in their twenties, but in the thirties and over they become increasingly unwilling. Many plead lack of time, or raise other difficulties, or agree to come and then forget. These pleas are, of course, sometimes well justified, but it is quite clear that in most cases they are excuses and that the real reason for unwillingness is fear of being tested and in particular of doing badly and appearing foolish. They seem to know well the popular opinion that as one advances through middle age one's ability falls, and do not wish to have this demonstrated upon themselves.

The fear manifests itself in several ways. For example, typical remarks made by older subjects before being tested are: 'You don't really want me, do you? I shan't be very good.' 'You can't expect too much of me; after all I'm nearly sixty.' 'So this is where you make a fool of me, is it?' After being tested older subjects almost always ask how they have done and demand to know how their results compare with the average or with those of younger subjects or of any friends known to have been tested previously. Even when told that scores are strictly confidential they sometimes persist in attempts to obtain information about friends. This strong interest in the relationship of one's performance to that of others is seldom shown by subjects in their twenties although one may suspect it is sometimes present but unexpressed. Visible relief and pleasure are frequently shown by older subjects upon being told they have 'done well'. Yet even when told this many criticize their performances and produce reasons such as eyestrain, tiredness or preoccupation with other problems, for not having done better. Frequently their actual performances in no way merit this self-criticism.

It has certainly been our experience that although many older subjects are unwilling to be tested, once they consent they approach their task with every intention of putting forth their best efforts and are fully as well motivated as those younger. Objective confirmation of this was obtained in the case of one experiment (p. 65) in which subjects were asked after completing the task to estimate the time they had spent. Almost without exception both younger and older substantially underestimated the time, usually assessing it at about half its actual length. Indeed if there is any difference of motivation it is on the side of the older subjects, and if their performances are in any way adversely affected by motivational factors it is not by undermotivation but by over-motivation leading to anxiety with the consequent danger of disorganization.

Older subjects are, however, sometimes unwilling to sustain their initial effort. The first instance noted among the experiments by the unit of which the writer was a member was in an extremely irritating, noisy task (p. 163) which required the subjects to make several long series of judgements with no knowledge of whether they were doing so correctly or not. It seems reasonable in this case to suppose that the older subjects found the task disappointingly trivial and unrewarding. Subsequent instances, however, seemed to be due to a different cause. They were all in very difficult experiments, and what appeared to happen was that the older subjects would try the task but then realize it was beyond them and give up. The clearest example is contained in a series of experiments by Clay (1957), described in Chapter VIII. She found in these that time taken rose with age up to a point but thereafter dropped sharply. The drop in the time was, however, associated with an increase in the number of errors. It seemed as if the subjects up to the age at which the 'break' occurred could complete the task by taking extra time and were willing to do so, but that for the oldest subjects the task was virtually impossible. They came to realize this fairly quickly and gave up after a short time. They did in fact take the most sensible course open to them in the circumstances, but it is clear that their unwillingness to continue was essentially the *result* and not the *cause* of their poorer performance.

Between the two extremes of irritatingly trivial and impossibly difficult, older people seem to enjoy experiments once they can be persuaded to try and, especially where they can see some results for their efforts, become thoroughly absorbed in the tasks.

Motivation in industry should, on the face of it, differ little with age since all the men or women studied are doing their daily work. There are, however, two suggestions frequently raised which would make this view too naïve. We have already noted in Chapter I the possible influence of family responsibilities. The decline of these, for most men in the fifties, might lead a man to be content with lower piece-work earnings or to transfer from piece-work to day work. A considerable number of men do in fact move from very arduous jobs in their early fifties (Richardson 1953) and piece-rate earnings show some tendency to decline at about the same age, but in view of striking changes of performance in experiments which also occur at these ages it seems doubtful whether such attitudinal factors are mainly responsible for the industrial trends.

The second suggestion regarding motivation in industry is that tacit agreements sometimes exist in a shop or factory that younger employees will work at less than maximum rate in order to 'give the old ones a chance' or to ensure that they will themselves be able to maintain the pace when they are older. Very little is known definitely about the effects of either of these factors.

4. *Problems arising from the need to compare subjects of different ages or to test the same individuals more than once*

What is probably the most recalcitrant and all-pervading methodological problem for ageing studies derives from the fact that a human being carries his history with him. Each new situation is dealt with in terms brought from past experience and in its turn modifies the experience brought to bear on future situations. The organism is thus constantly changing; its present state cannot be fully understood without some reference to past events, and we can never assume that it is the same on two different occasions—indeed we can be sure it is not. For many purposes these variations may be unimportant, but they do, at least for certain tasks, carry three important implications. Firstly, part of the variation between people of different ages living at any one time will be due to the fact that they were brought up under different conditions. Secondly, any study or testing of an individual will itself affect his approach to subsequent situations so that a prolonged study cannot be wholly independent of the effects of its own earlier stages. Thirdly, differing experience and development serve to magnify the variations between individuals, and may profoundly affect their capacities.

All this means that at the very least we must study *groups* of people and compare substantial numbers in order to assess age changes. We cannot base any valid inference about the average capacity of older people from the exceptionally good or bad performances of a few individuals or from the occasional striking old men and women held up as examples of what older people can do in industry, politics and other walks of life. We have to think in terms of average trends, yet even these may upon occasion be of doubtful significance. A common finding is that the performances of older and younger people, say of a group in the twenties and another in the sixties, show a clear change of *average* achievement but with a much wider scatter in the older age group than in the younger—many of the older group are well within the range of the younger, others well outside. The problem in a case like this is to decide whether the older group is comprised of some individuals who have changed greatly and some who have not changed at all, or whether all have changed to some extent with amount of change following a non-linear function. Only in the latter case can we justifiably regard the arithmetic mean as a representative measure of the performance of the older group. In the former case we should have to substitute for the mean a statement in terms of the proportion of subjects attaining or exceeding a given level of performance. Fortunately for ease of statement the use of the mean does seem to be justified in most instances.

Other implications of the role played in human performance by past experience concern problems of sampling and differ according to whether the studies are (a) *experimental* or *industrial*; (b) *cross-sectional*, examining groups of different ages in the population at one time, or *longitudinal* following a single group over a substantial period of time; and (c) aimed at obtaining *theoretical* insight, or at the solution of an immediate *practical* problem. Each of these classifications is independent of the others giving a somewhat unwieldy array of eight types if all possible combinations are considered. The independence of (a) and (c) may at first sight be surprising since experiments tend to be used in theoretical research and industrial studies in practical. We have already pointed out, however, that industrial studies can contribute significantly to theoretical issues and there is a growing tendency to use experiments as a means of furthering practical research.

The obvious difference in the present context between theoretical and practical studies is that the former are directed to an attempt to understand the nature of ageing, whereas the latter are concerned with problems such as employment or social welfare to which the ageing process may be an important but nevertheless ancillary consideration. The main methodological difference between the two is concerned with *sampling for cross-sectional studies*.

Cross-sectional researches with a *practical* aim need to be done with a strictly *representative* sample of the population to whom the practical issues relate. They might thus require a representative sample of the population of the country as a whole, or of a particular town or factory or occupational group. The sample should be of the present living population in each case with no consideration of whether death, disease, emigration, education or any other cause has had a selective effect on the older age groups. Refinements to this basic requirement may be needed if, instead of dealing with a present problem, we are trying to anticipate one in the future. We might, for instance, need to control education to allow for changes in schooling over the years, or health to allow for changes in the treatment of disease, but the principle is still the same—we are attempting to obtain a representative sample of a population, in this case a future one.

The essential requirement for a theoretical study is a sample in which older and younger people are *comparable*. This is a much more difficult type of sample to obtain with human subjects because differential effects of death, disease, education, occupation and so on must be taken into account, and because in a rapidly changing world parts of the economic, social, material and educational backgrounds of subjects will inevitably differ with age even among people of the same status in every other respect. The problems of obtaining comparable samples differ between experimental and industrial researches, and we will therefore deal with the two types separately.

Experimental studies

The obvious procedure is to attempt to equate the backgrounds of the subjects in the different age groups. Unfortunately, just what background factors are important appear to differ from one task to another in a manner which, with present knowledge, is not entirely predictable. There is, however, some evidence upon three types of factor: (*a*) educational and occupational level, (*b*) occupational 'skill', and (*c*) family relationship.

(*a*) *Level of education and occupation*. Several researches have shown that declines of performance with age are less among people of high educational or occupational level. Effects have been shown for problems involving 'ingenuity', translating an artificial language, giving synonyms and antonyms, symbol-digit substitution, completing number series, giving meanings of words, giving analogies and solving arithmetic problems (Sward 1945); recall of a passage of prose and a 'test of concentrated attention' (Pacaud 1955*a*, *b*). The tasks have in common that they involve fairly high-grade intellectual activity, judgement or the use of verbal or other symbols. With more straightforward sensori-motor tasks, differences of performance with educational and occupational level are usually small (Pacaud, op. cit.).

These findings may be linked with the result, often obtained in experiments and mental tests, that the difference with age between the best performers shows less decline than between those whose performance is poorer. This result occurs with a wide variety of tasks such as the Matrices test and word meanings (Foulds and Raven 1948); memory, both short and long term (Gilbert 1941); and sensori-motor tests (Pacaud, op. cit.). It is clearly another facet of the tendency noted earlier for variation between individuals to increase with age. It could in some cases be an artefact in the sense that the task may not stretch the ablest individuals and may thus fail to show differences at the highest levels of ability. This cannot be the complete explanation however, and there seems no doubt that age declines are less among the best performers at least in a relative if not always in an absolute sense.

(b) *Effects of occupational skills* can sometimes completely reverse a group age trend for a particular individual. An example in an experiment by Szafran (1951) is described in Chapter VII (p. 186). In a task in which hand actions had to be carried out blind, a subject aged 49 who had considerable experience in dark rooms performed far better than any other subject tested either younger or older. The connexion between occupational skill and experimental result in a case like this is clear and reasonably easy to guard against when making up groups of subjects. Aspects of skill and tendencies to action of occupational origin do, however, appear sometimes to 'work loose' from their original settings and become generalized to performances seemingly remote from their originals. For instance, in an experiment where subjects were required to throw at a target (Szafran and Welford 1949) an apparent slowing with age turned out to be due to the inclusion of a large proportion of servicemen in the youngest age range. Subsequent tests confirmed that men with recent army experience carried out the task significantly faster than those who had been in civilian life throughout the Second World War. It seems impossible to control such influences in advance without building up a systematic body of knowledge on the nature and extent of occupational 'transfer' effects. Until this is done they must be reckoned as an unknown hazard for the experimenter.

(c) Control of *family relationship* by comparing different generations of the same family would seem to be an obviously desirable procedure in studies of ageing, yet it is one which is seldom used. Doubtless this is in part due to the difficulty that would be caused by the additional constraint in the selection of subjects, but it may in part also be due to the curious unwillingness of psychologists in the past to admit the role of hereditary factors in determining human capacity. Resemblances between parents and children have been demonstrated in a number of performances such as intelligence tests (Jones 1928). Family resemblances in behaviour have been shown to be in part the result of heredity and in part the result of similarity of environment, but work by Kallman (1957) on twins living apart suggests that heredity plays a larger part than has been supposed hitherto.

For a large-scale study we should take care to see that the numbers in each age range are balanced for these and any other background factors suspected as being of importance. For a small-scale experiment aimed at establishing a qualitative rather than an exact quantitative result it is probably sufficient to concentrate on subjects from one particular background—say from a single factory or a university population. The inferences we can make will be restricted owing to the restricted range of subjects, but usually not seriously so. An alternative procedure which overcomes this limitation is to take two or more groups of widely different background in each age range— in effect to do the experiment twice on different types of subject. By this method we not only achieve a high degree of control but also throw light upon whether differences of background are in fact important for our experimental task.

Four other methods of very different kinds are sometimes useful for ensuring or checking the comparability of subjects in different age ranges.

(i) When we know, or have reason to believe, that the observed age trends should progress smoothly over several age groups we can assume, provided our experimental method has been rigorous, that any marked deviation from a smooth progression is due to an accident of sampling. What appears clearly to be a result of this kind is contained in an experiment by Weston (1949) on changes of visual acuity in middle age (see p. 153).

(ii) Some investigators, notably Thorndike *et al.* (1928), have given their subjects a preliminary task such as an intelligence test, and selected groups in different age ranges with equal means and scatters of test score. This is undoubtedly a powerful method of control provided we know what the preliminary task measures. The inference from the experimental results is, of course, affected in the sense that any trend is relative to that which would be observed in results of the pre-test for an unselected population, but this, far from being a disadvantage, opens the way to a rather precise method of assessing the relative magnitude of age trends for different types of capacity.

(iii) Somewhat similar to this last method is one used by Szafran, Kay, Clay and others (see Chapters VI and VIII) which consists of presenting the experimental task in two or more different forms and noting the difference of age trend between them. In all the cases cited one form has been found to give much less age trend than another and we can thus use it as a base line for a relative statement about the effect with age of the factor by which the one form of the task differs from the other. This method appears to be of wide and rather simple application. Its value will depend, however, to some extent upon the easiest form of the task not being so easy that every subject can do it equally well. The task and the method of scoring must be such that some individual variation can be shown if the similarity between the older and younger subject's performance at the easiest form of the task is to be more than a trivial result.

(iv) The most radical method of overcoming the problem of comparability is to abandon the use of human subjects in favour of animals whose background and experience can be rigidly controlled. There is, of course, some hazard in using the results of animal experiments as an aid to the interpretation of human performance, but in so far as ageing is due to biological processes common to different species, animal studies would seem capable of supplying invaluable checks upon human research. Experiments on animal behaviour in relation to age seem in fact to show very much the same trends as human studies, and thus tend to confirm that background factors cannot by any means wholly account for changes of human performance with age.

The difficulties inherent in cross-sectional studies can be avoided by following a group of individuals over a substantial period of time. The longitudinal method does, however, have two difficulties of its own which severely limit its usefulness.

(a) The method essentially involves testing a subject's performance and retesting it once or more later in life. This requirement means that any age effects are inextricably mixed with any learning effects. These latter can be very marked. For example, Heim and Wallace (1949, 1950) have shown that substantial gains in score on an intelligence test are made when it is taken more than once even when the subjects have no knowledge of their success or failure on earlier occasions, and that these gains transfer to another intelligence test not taken before. Their results were, however, for tests given only one week apart and thus may not be an entirely valid objection to longitudinal studies such as that of Owens (1953) using intelligence tests at intervals of many years. The effects of a single experience can, however, without doubt be long-lasting, and we need to know more about them before we can be confident as to the meaning of the results of longitudinal studies using material of the level of an intelligence test on more than one occasion.

With repetitive tasks such as sensori-motor skills this difficulty can be, at least largely, overcome by training the subject before each test until he has ceased to improve with practice. Unfortunately, however, this may take a long time and make the test unduly time-consuming.

With problem-solving and other tasks where 'insight' can be gained the task cannot be used more than once, and subsequent tests have to be done with similar but different problems. The problems must either be equated for difficulty or must be presented to different subjects in different orders in a balanced design. Even with different problems, however, substantial learning effects in the way of tackling particular types of problem are likely to enter, so that the longitudinal method would seem seldom appropriate for the study of performance at this kind of task.

(b) The obvious objection to longitudinal studies that a very long wait is required if the study is to span a substantial part of a man's life, can be overcome in some cases by using animals. Where animals are unsuitable, it may be possible to resort to a mixture of the longitudinal and cross-sectional methods. A group of subjects covering a substantial age range is tested and the same group is tested again after a period of years. For some functions this period can be as short as five years, as with Weston's (1949) experiment already mentioned. For most tasks, retesting at intervals over a period of ten to twenty years would be better. This method has been little used because although it avoids the necessity of extremely long waits it still requires, with preparation before the first test and analysis of results after the second, a term of years longer than the duration of most research projects.

Industrial studies

Problems of equating subjects for education, occupation and other background features do not usually arise in industrial studies because these normally relate age and work done and so control them automatically. They have, however, their own problems of control which depend upon the type of industrial data used.

(a) *Production records* or *studies of actual work done* provide what are at first sight the most valuable and informative data on performance, but are subject to serious limitations. The most important of these is that a marked fall in productivity would be unlikely to be tolerated for long by either the employer or the man concerned, so that if productivity falls much as a man becomes older he is likely to move or be moved to another job. Older people left on the job will thus be unrepresentative of their age group, and inferences based on their performance will be unduly favourable to older people. Selection in the opposite direction by promotion will also occur, although probably less often, and may result in age trends appearing unduly *un*favourable to older people. We cannot without further evidence be sure in any particular case that these two selective trends balance. Progressive selection of this kind is not overcome by a longitudinal study of men who have been on the same job for a long period of years, because the fact that they have been so may imply that they are a selected group whose performance has declined or risen less than that of others.

Studies of work done in industry, whether cross-sectional or longitudinal, are thus valid only if labour turnover and transfers to other jobs are negligibly small. Ideally they require also a substantial group of people well spread over the age scale and all doing *exactly* the same work, since what are minor variations of work from the industrial point of view may imply major differences in the psychological demands the work makes. This requirement is very seldom satisfied in industry but can be at least partly overcome by relating each man's performance to the average of men in a particular age range—say the thirties—or in the whole group who are doing the same work. Wackwitz (1946) has used such standard measures to compare one operation with another in his extensive and important study of industrial workers in Holland.

(b) It can be argued that if productivity figures are invalidated by progressive selection in favour of the most able, the *age distribution* of the men remaining on the job should give an indication of whether capacity to do the operation remains high with advancing age or declines. The age distribution for a job may, of course, be affected by factors such as age policies in the factory concerned or the age structure of the local population, but comparing the age distribution of one job, or group of jobs, with another in the same factory would seem to be a possible method of obtaining data on capacity in relation to operation. The data is crude, lacking all the subtleties of detailed studies of actual work done, but is a better method to use than production figures when labour turnover is high.

Age distributions may, however, be misleading if, as often happens, there is a policy of recruiting young people in preference to older, because they will then be dependent upon the history of the job. If the job has expanded the age distribution will have too many at the young end; if it has contracted, too many at the old. It will for the same reason also be affected by such factors as the availability of labour in the district and competition with other jobs. Even where such recruitment policy is absent, it may be difficult to decide whether a shortage of older people on a job is due to their failing to maintain performance or to their finding difficulty in learning the job with consequent restriction of placement. Age distributions are, however, by far the easiest industrial data to obtain and would seem capable of giving valuable preliminary information for comparing one class of job with another provided due precautions are taken to ensure that the recruitment policy and history are similar for both. Work by Murrell, Griew and Tucker (1957) has provided a striking example of stability in differences of age distributions between jobs over a period of eight years in a situation where there was no ascertainable selective placement.

(c) The most reliable criterion of difficulty for older people at a job is that substantial numbers leave at a relatively early age. The reliability is clearly greater for men's work than for women's, and comparison between jobs in terms of age at which people leave must be made separately for women and men. People transferred within the factory to other jobs must be included as well as those who leave altogether. The reasons given for leaving or transferring should be regarded with caution. Clearly when people leave because of gross disease, or move from the district for family reasons, we can hardly regard their decisions as being influenced by a growing difficulty with age at maintaining performance at their jobs. Reasons such as this are, however, likely to apply equally to all jobs and therefore not to affect comparisons between them. Other reasons such as disagreements with management, dissatisfaction, and even, as Richardson (1953) has pointed out, many cases of sickness, do seem to be associated with jobs which we should expect on other grounds to become a strain as people grow older. Indeed, it would seem that in the absence of strong indications to the contrary *all* moves from jobs compared should be counted regardless of reason. A possible exception to this is where people leave for promotion or a better-paid job; and a more rigorous criterion would be therefore to count all moves to *lower-paid* work for any reason other than serious incapacity due to disease or accident and genuine redundancy. Anyone looking at changes with age can, however, scarcely fail to wonder whether many moves to better-paid work are away from jobs which would soon have become a strain if the move had not been made.

One practical research procedure is to make a preliminary comparison of jobs in terms of age distribution after excluding those where there is evidence of younger people restricting output or where a difference of history from other jobs is likely to vitiate a comparison. After this preliminary sorting, selected jobs can be compared in terms of proportions leaving or transferred to other work, and jobs with low labour turnover can be examined for changes of performance with age.

Two important research possibilities for the future in this field may be mentioned. The first is the detailed study of performance at jobs where substantial numbers leave relatively young to see whether early signs of strain can be detected in changing methods or manners of work. The second is to use the cohort technique of taking a group, or set of groups of different ages and following them over a number of years not only at one place of work but also if they leave to go elsewhere.

CONCLUSION ON METHODOLOGICAL PROBLEMS

It seems clear that many of the methodological problems commonly supposed to attach to the study of human performance in relation to age are less serious than they are usually believed to be. Difficulties arising from the brevity of laboratory experiments can be met by studies of work in industry. Motivation among older subjects does not seem to be a serious problem. The bewildering complexity of human capacity can, at least to a considerable extent, be sorted out. Various background factors affecting the comparability of subjects of different ages can be controlled. Many difficulties in the way of precise quantitative studies do not apply to work aimed only at qualitative results.

On the other hand, it seems equally clear that no one way of studying ageing is wholly free from methodological objections and that we can thus seldom, if ever, draw certain conclusions from a single experiment or industrial study. In view of this it seems wiser to carry out several small-scale studies using different methods rather than concentrate the whole research effort on a few large-scale investigations. Even a study using thousands of subjects recruited haphazardly would be at the mercy of possible sampling errors. The use of a number of small-scale studies each controlling different variables enables us to gather on our way a great deal of valuable information upon the effects of various background factors influencing age trends, and although giving a mass of data which it may often be difficult to integrate, holds the promise of the attainment of results having a greater degree of generality.

IV

SPEED AND ACCURACY OF MOVEMENT

'You say the saw slipped. It wouldn't have slipped unless you let it!'

AN OLD CRAFTSMAN-TEACHER

I T is so obvious that people's actions tend to become slower as they grow older that we seldom stop to consider whether all aspects of performance are equally affected and what the causes of slowing may be. Research bearing on these questions will be surveyed in this chapter and may be said at the outset to answer the first question with an emphatic negative. The second is a more difficult question and cannot be answered with the same assurance, but some general indications seem clear enough.

The classical work in this field is that of Miles (1931) who took several measures of performance from 863 men, women and children with ages ranging from 6 to 95 and with as nearly equal numbers in the adult decades as he could obtain. He divided his readings into two classes which he termed 'reaction tests' and 'motility measures'. The former included two simple reaction-time procedures, namely, the times taken by the subject to lift, in the one case, the forefinger of his dominant hand, and, in the other, his foot, from a key, on hearing a buzz. The motility tasks included a 'digital extension-flexion test' involving raising and lowering the forefinger of the dominant hand from a key as quickly as possible; turning the crank of a hand-drill mechanism as fast as possible, first with the dominant hand and then with the other hand; and a somewhat complex movement entitled 'manual reach and grasp' consisting of raising the finger from a key, transferring a pencil from one hole to another, and moving the hand back to the key.

The reaction tests also included a task entitled 'pursuit reaction'. The measure was the error, in terms of time, in stopping a pointer rotating at 2 r.p.sec. at the zero position on a dial by pressing a key. Because of his reaction time the subject had to initiate the process before the pointer reached the zero position, but it did not matter how long before it was initiated so long as the action became effective at the right time. Errors were attributable not so much to slowness as to 'randomness' of timing due either to irregularity in choosing the instant to initiate reaction or to uncontrolled variation in the reaction time. In either case, pursuit reaction yields a measure of one type of *uncertainty of outcome* of the subject's intended action. When speaking of Miles's reaction times we shall not include this 'pursuit reaction' because it would seem to be a task making demands fundamentally different from those made by the others.

Miles's results, given in Fig. 4.1, show that in all cases some slowing with age occurred. Norris *et al.* (1953) have pointed out that this slowing cannot reasonably be ascribed to falling speed of nerve conduction because this could account for only about 4 per cent. of the change of reaction time from the thirties to the eighties. Confirmatory evidence comes from an experiment by Birren and Botwinick (1955a) who showed that age differences of reaction time are closely similar whether the responses are given by the finger, jaw or foot—that is, by members involving very different lengths of efferent nerve path.

It thus seems clear that the slowing must have been in the sensory or central processes or in the time actually taken to make movements. Miles observed that changes with age were greater and began sooner with the motility measures than with the reaction tests, and concluded that the main locus of slowing in older people lay in the making of movements rather than in the central activities of comprehending data and selecting a response. His results do in fact agree fairly well in this respect with the still earlier data obtained by Galton (1885, 1889; see Koga and Morant 1923; Ruger and Stoessiger 1927). It is true that some other measures of reaction time (e.g. Bellis 1933) have shown greater changes with age than were found by either Miles or Galton before him, but this does not affect the *relationship* between the two types of measure taken by them. It rather suggests that their volunteer subjects were perhaps not entirely representative of the upper age ranges nor comparable with the younger subjects. Miles recruited the relations and friends of Girl Scouts with the reward of payment to the troop funds, while Galton's subjects were visitors to an International Health Exhibition. In both cases it seems likely that only those both active and unusually willing to risk having their performance tried would have submitted to testing, and that slightly different conditions of recruitment might have yielded more severe age changes.

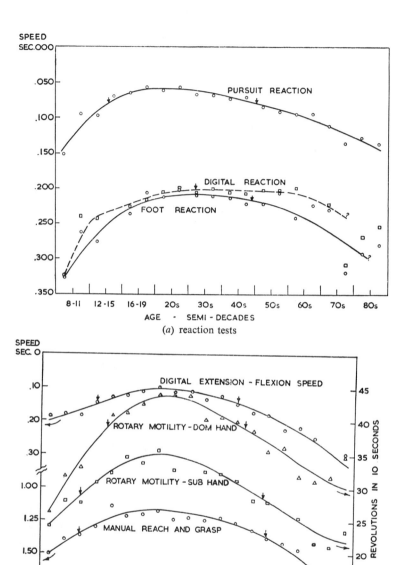

(a) reaction tests

(b) Motility Measures

FIG. 4.1. Results of tests by Miles of reaction time and manual motility. Means per subject

Miles's results have set a trap for the unwary and have often been taken to indicate that the cause of age declines lies more in the peripheral motor mechanism than in central brain processes —a view seemingly in accord with the fact that maximum strength of grip and other measures of muscular power decline with age (Fisher and Birren 1947). Miles himself avoided this pitfall and proposed instead an explanation in terms of 'conservation of effort'. He says:

It is well known that cortical function is economical of energy and that motor function is spendthrift. A possible theory then for the slower and more difficult action in the old is that neural conservation mechanisms are built up or become more potent with increasing lifetime. A particular decrement according to this theory would not be chiefly chargeable to a defect in the mechanism but to a positive check on it—a neural governor device protective of the mechanism. The weight of years may be in large part neural inhibition-interference to action. This is perhaps the core, or the basic behaviour element, in the caution and proverbial good judgment of the old.

Miles recognized that this explanation went far beyond the facts of his study, but more recent work has shown that a kind of conservation may well be one factor making for slowness among older people. The same work has also shown that Miles's reaction tests were a rather special case and that the locus of slowing with age lies more in the capacity of central processes for rapid action than in the execution of movement.

Fuller insight into the causes of slowing with age, and several leads to subsequent work, have come from two exploratory experiments by Brown. In the first of these the subject was confronted by an apparatus on which was a plate carrying two pieces of graph paper approximately 6×4 inches. His task was to move, by means of a handle, a pointer with a spot on it so as to make the position of the spot on the right-hand piece of graph paper similar to that of a small steel ball about $\frac{1}{16}$ inch in diameter on the left-hand piece, relative to vertical and horizontal co-ordinates on the two pieces. The layout of the grids and pointer is shown diagrammatically in Fig. 4.2. When the subject thought the pointer was in the correct position, he pushed a small button mounted on the handle. If his judgement was correct, the ball started to move about the left-hand grid. If it was incorrect, nothing happened. He went on making attempts until he was successful in starting the ball, and was instructed that as soon as this happened he was to press a key at the side of the apparatus which stopped the ball in a new position on the left-hand grid, and was then to start the cycle of operations over again.

It will be seen that the experiment set a fairly complex task, the nature of which was such that the subject had to make the same achievement each cycle of operations, causing the ball to move and

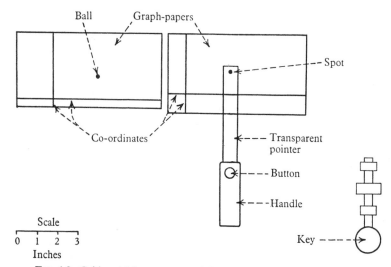

FIG. 4.2. Grid-matching apparatus. Diagram of display and controls

stopping it again. The pattern of hand-movements required was, however, different for each cycle so that the task did not involve the building up of any strictly stereotyped succession of movements. At the same time the task was sequential in the sense that the completion of each part of the cycle set the stage for performance of the next.

Table 4.1 shows an analysis of the attempts made by the subjects in two age ranges during half an hour's work. The unsuccessful attempts were divided into two classes: (a) 'small errors' due to minor errors of plotting, and (b) 'large errors' resulting from attempts to plot by reference to the edges of the grids instead of to the co-ordinates—which were placed in different relations to the edges on the two sides. The striking feature of Table 4.1 is that although the younger subjects were quicker in the sense that they made more attempts in the half hour, they also made many more small errors. Compared with this, the differences between the age ranges in the number of successes was not great and was in fact not statistically significant.

TABLE 4.1. *Grid-matching experiment. Analysis of recorded attempts*

Means per subject

		Age range	
		18–29	45–82
Successful attempts			
Without previous error		80	67
After errors		51	30
Total successes		— 131	— 97
Errors			
Small errors		210	74
Large errors		15	16
Total errors		— 225	— 90
Total attempts		356	187

In Table 4.2 is given an analysis of the average times per cycle. The older subjects took longer over each part of the cycle except the making of small errors.

Taking Tables 4.1 and 4.2 together, the older subjects clearly appear as slower but more accurate, with their greater accuracy at least partly compensating for slowness. It would indeed seem relevant to ask whether it was the younger or the older subjects who, from the

TABLE 4.2. *Grid-matching experiment. Analysis of mean times per cycle in seconds*

	Age range	
	18–29	45–82
Between stopping the ball and making the first attempt to restart it	8·73	14·51
Making small errors	6·36	4·98
Making large errors	0·39	1·43
Between starting the ball and stopping it again .	0·86	1·11
Total cycle times	16·34	22·03

practical standpoint, showed the better average performance. Such a question is by no means easy to answer, and depends very much on what we regard as the criterion of 'goodness'. If we are interested in the number of times the ball is made to move in a given period of time, that is to say in the total amount achieved regardless of any other considerations, then the younger subjects must be regarded as, on average, better. However, the older subjects achieved their results with less effort wasted on errors, so that their performance can at least be said to have been more *efficient*. Finally, if we were interested in accuracy, as we should be if every error represented waste of valuable industrial material, we should regard the older subjects as, on the average, clearly superior.

The scores in the tables give by themselves very little indication of why the older people were slower, but questioning and observing them at work suggested that different reasons operated to delay the older subjects in different parts of the cycle.

The longer time between stopping the ball at the end of one cycle and making the *first attempt*, whether successful or unsuccessful, to start it again, appeared not to be due to slowness of moving the pointer because this occupied only a small fraction of the time. Nor did it seem to result from the older subjects finding any gross difficulty in seeing the grid lines: had they done so, we might have expected them to make more instead of fewer small errors than the younger subjects. Minor degrees of difficulty with the fairly fine visual task imposed by the grids may, however, have played some part, if indirectly. The main direct cause of slowing was clearly an *increased carefulness* on the part of the older subjects when positioning the pointer. In this respect, the younger and older subjects displayed a profound difference of method. The younger tended to swing the pointer into position with a kind of sweeping motion, stop it and press the button, all more or less in a single movement, seeming to look at the graph papers as a kind of 'general setting' within which they located the ball and the pointer immediately. The older subjects tended to look carefully and in detail at the graph paper, move the pointer into position and check the accuracy of this position by looking rapidly back and forth from one grid to the other, often several times, and sometimes counting the squares on the paper, before they pressed the button. It is understandable that the younger subjects' method should lead them to make a great many small errors.

Whether the older subjects' greater carefulness was due to caution as such, born of hard experience in the past, or whether it was an indirect effect of some failing ability, it is not possible to say. Some evidence in favour of the latter view comes, however, from the time taken over large errors. This cannot reasonably be regarded as having been due to any defects of vision or of the effector mechanism, but appears to have resulted from some lessening of the older subjects' power to comprehend the essential static features of the display. If so, it raises the interesting possibility that, just as older subjects took longer to comprehend the features of the display which remained the same throughout the experiment, so they also took longer to comprehend each change introduced into the display by shifts in the position of the ball between runs; and that the carefulness shown in their performance was a compensatory reaction to this increased difficulty. The evidence from the present experiment is, of course, quite insufficient to support such a view alone, but it may be noted in anticipation of what is to be said later that this view accords well with the evidence from some other experiments.

The reason for the longer time taken by the older subjects to stop the ball once it had been started, appears to have been, at least in part, of a quite different kind. Although the instructions were that the ball should be stopped *as soon as* it was started, many of the older subjects often waited until the ball was in an 'easy' position near the co-ordinate lines before stopping it. This action appeared to be an interesting case of *planning* the work as a whole: the subjects were willing to take longer over one part of the task in order to save time and trouble over a subsequent part. The fact that this contravention of instructions appeared frequently among the older subjects and hardly ever among the younger, suggests that the tendency towards planning may increase with age.

It must be emphasized that although the results in Tables 4.1 and 4.2 represent the trends of the groups tested, there were some individuals who departed markedly from the general run. The most striking of these was a man in his late fifties who attained 342 successes during the half-hour. This was about 40 per cent. higher than the highest performers in the younger group; well over twice that of his nearest contemporary; nearly four times the mean of the rest of the older group; and over $2\frac{1}{2}$ times the mean of the younger. His method of work was quite different from that of his contemporaries. Instead of a careful positioning of the pointer before making an attempt to start the ball, he swung it rapidly into position and pressed the button immediately. If the ball did not start, he proceeded to make several rapid attempts within a small circle round the point at which he had made his first attempt. Had it been possible to test very large groups of subjects, he would probably have been found to be in the 'tail' of a continuous distribution. Whether or not this is so, his result serves to raise the interesting problem of how far the changes associated with increasing age are likely, while lowering the average standard of performance, to produce a few exceptionally able individuals. With regard to this problem, two points may be mentioned. First, that exceptional performers in the higher age ranges have been found in many experiments, and second, that the exceptional performance by this subject seemed to be fairly specific to a particular type of task. He took part in several other experiments afterwards and in only one (the tracing task, to be described next) did he show a similar striking achievement.

The last point is in line with what would be expected if the changes accompanying age are to be thought of as due to a restriction of the range of things which can be done. Performance at any task is the result of the interaction of what the subject brings to the task and the demands of the task itself. It will attain a high standard when, and only when, the 'fit' between these two is good. If the range of what the subject brings diminishes with age, the *likelihood* of an older subject attaining a high standard at any task will be reduced, but the ability to do so at *some* will remain and may indeed increase.

The grid-matching experiment set a task into which both accuracy and speed entered, but the main stress almost inevitably tended to be laid on accuracy, at least by the older subjects. In Brown's second exploratory experiment an attempt was made to render the requirements for accuracy less stringent so that the stress was more upon speed.

The main task consisted of tracing with a stylus 'as quickly and accurately as possible' over brass figures 1–0 inlaid in an aluminium plate. Each subject traced five times over the figures as shown in Fig. 4.3(*a*), then five times over the reversed figures as in Fig. 4.3(*b*) and then again five times over the normal figures. The apparatus was arranged so that as soon as each figure had been completely traced a bell rang indicating that the subject could proceed to the next. If at any point he made an 'error' by running the stylus over the edge of a figure on to the surrounding aluminium plate a buzzer sounded. Before the main task began, he wrote the figures 1–0 once on paper; he also wrote them reversed once before and once after tracing the reversed figures.

Times taken over the tracing task, shown in Fig. 4.4, indicate a marked slowing with age after the thirties. Again, however, some of the older subjects traced very rapidly—the third quickest of the whole group was a man of 74, beaten only by two undergraduates in their twenties. The increasing variability, both absolute and relative, of performance with increased age is shown in Table 4.3. Again subjects appeared to differ with age not only in speed but also—perhaps

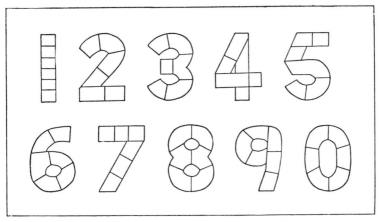

FIG. 4.3(*a*). Diagram of plate with normal figures used in tracing task

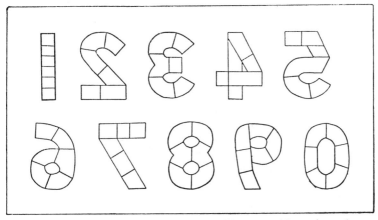

FIG. 4.3(*b*). Diagram of plate with reversed figures used in tracing task
The figures were 2⅜ inches high and ½ inch wide

mainly—in the balance they struck between speed and accuracy. Comparing Table 4.4 with Fig. 4.4, it will be seen that the thirties maintained speed at the expense of accuracy while from the forties onwards accuracy was restored at the expense of speed. This inverse relationship between speed and accuracy was found also to hold within each age group except the oldest.

TABLE 4.3. *Individual variations in times taken to trace ten figures fifteen times*

Age range	Standard deviation in seconds	Standard deviation divided by mean
20–29	42	0·21
30–39	51	0·25
40–49	92	0·34
50–59	89	0·32
60–69	100	0·31
70–79	174	0·43

TABLE 4.4. *Errors made in tracing ten figures fifteen times*

Age range	Mean errors per subject
Twenties	20·5
Thirties	54·3
Forties	29·7
Fifties	8·8
Sixties	17·4
Seventies	7·3

At first sight the main lines of the results from Brown's two experiments appear to accord well with Miles's work. In both there is, on average, a marked fall of activity or 'motility' with age and the increased care and accuracy could be regarded as a means of conserving action. There are, however, indications in the results of both these experiments which suggest not, as Miles implies, that slowing with age is due to a desire or need to conserve action as such, but that *limitation of speed with age lies in slowing of the perceptual and translatory mechanisms controlling movement.* The grid-matching task was obviously one involving perception and translation to a much greater extent than motor action. In the tracing task the subject was required not only to make movements but to make them in a controlled manner by limited amounts first in one direction then in another, according to the shape of the pattern he was tracing—in other words, according to the dictates of the display. From split second to split second he had to make changes of direction and speed which depended upon the direction and speed of his movement in the immediate past and the point to which these had led him. His effector action at any time was thus dependent upon *knowledge of the*

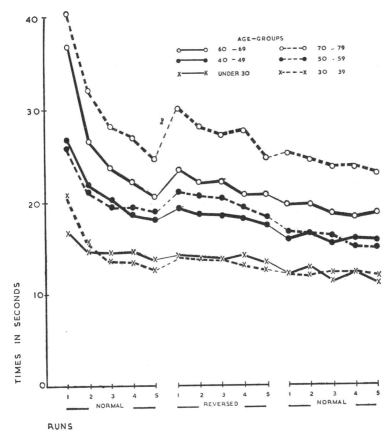

FIG. 4.4. Times taken per subject to trace ten figures (1-0)

results of what had already been done—in other words, upon the *perception* of the relationship of his present direction, speed and position to the display.

General theoretical considerations regarding continuous movement make it virtually certain that in normal young subjects central processes concerned with the control and monitoring of movement do normally limit the speed together with the accuracy of action. The general problem has been discussed by Vince (1948*b*) and by the present author (1952*a*). We have already mentioned in Chapter II the quantitative treatment of the relationship between speed and accuracy in terms of information theory given by Fitts (1954). The importance of such central control in producing age differences of motor performance is suggested by the work of Birren and Botwinick (1951) who found a correlation which rose with age between writing speed and the obviously central task of adding. Some more indications may be obtained by comparing the results for tracing normal and reversed figures shown in Fig. 4.4. The reversal of the figures clearly tended to slow performance to an extent which increased with age in spite of the fact that the actual movements required were of the same extent and of closely similar form—indeed identical in some cases. Further evidence for central control as a cause of slower movements by older people is contained in the times for *writing* reversed figures shown in Table 4.5, where the effect of reversal in relation to age was greater than in the tracing task. These results will be discussed again in Chapter VI.

A conclusive answer to the question of just how far perceptual and translatory processes and how far motor factors account for slowing with age cannot, however, be obtained from a tracing experiment of this kind, because the central processes are almost certainly taking place while the movements are in progress. It is, therefore, not possible to say which is limiting, or whether each becomes limiting at different points in the performance. The question has, however, been pursued in a number of subsequent experiments where the times taken by action and by the central processes guiding it could be measured separately. To these we shall now turn.

TABLE 4.5. *Times taken in seconds per subject to write ten figures* (*1–0*) *once*

Age range	Normal way round	Reversed, first time	Reversed, second time
20–29	7·3	21·3	12·4
30–39	7·7	20·3	14·5
40–49	9·3	33·8	20·9
50–59	7·7	31·9	22·8
60–69	11·7	34·9	25·1
70–79	12·5	55·5	37·2

Locating slowness: reaction time and movement time

The first clear suggestion that when reaction time and movement time are recorded separately it is the former that shows more change with age, came from an experiment by Szafran (1951). The subject sat in a kind of cockpit facing a panel of nineteen small light bulbs. Around him at nearly arm's length were targets, one corresponding to each bulb. The cockpit was modelled on an apparatus used by Fitts (1947). When one of the bulbs on the display went out, the subject had to move a stylus he was holding from a small metal plate directly in front of him to the target corresponding to the extinguished light. Twenty targets had to be located in this way with full opportunity to see them and their surroundings, then twenty more while wearing goggles which left the lights visible but which completely obscured everything else.

The main results of this experiment as a whole will be described in Chapter VII and do not concern us here. Those of interest in the present context are firstly, that the times taken between a light going off and the subject initiating a response to it by lifting the stylus from the plate, showed a substantial and significant rise with age in both conditions, whereas the time spent moving between the plate and the target showed a small increase in one condition and a small *de*crease in the other. The results are shown in Table 4.6 and show clearly that in this experiment it was reaction time and not movement time that became slower with age. We cannot be certain whether the

TABLE 4.6. *Times to initiate responses and times to execute movements in Szafran's 'cockpit' experiment*

Means per response in seconds

	Age range			
	Twenties	*Thirties*	*Forties*	*Fifties*
Time from appearance of signal to beginning of responding movement				
Without goggles. . .	0·75	0·85	1·03	1·06
With goggles . . .	0·96	1·13	1·55	1·67
Duration of responding movement				
Without goggles . .	0·99	1·11	1·07	1·27
With goggles . . .	1·36	1·29	1·21	1·17

older subjects were *unable* to initiate their movements more quickly than they did, or whether they were making sure where they were going to move before they started whereas the younger subjects were starting a movement quickly and then modifying it as it proceeded.

The evidence from this experiment might be questioned because the instructions did not specifically mention speed and the subjects may, therefore, not have been working as fast as possible. Such an objection is almost certainly unimportant because there seems to be a natural tendency for subjects in sensori-motor experiments to feel they should work as fast as possible consistent with the degree of accuracy required. In any case, the indications were confirmed in serial reaction experiments by Leonard (1952) and by Singleton (1954, 1955) where the objection did not apply.

In Leonard's experiment, two groups with average ages of 27·6 and 26·9 years were compared with two further groups having average ages of 69·5 and 66·6. The subject sat facing a display of five neon bulbs at the corners of a regular pentagon. On the table in front of him was a board with a brass disk 1¼ inches in diameter corresponding to each light bulb, and an additional similar disk in the centre, with its edge 1¾ inches from the inner edges of the other disks. The task as presented to one of the older and one of the younger groups was to slide a stylus from the centre disk to one of the other disks indicated by the corresponding neon light being on, and then return to the centre disk as quickly as possible. On reaching the centre disk again, the light would change, indicating that the stylus should be moved to a different disk, and so on for 100 signals in a continuous random-order series. The subject was thus set a continuous serial reaction task in which time spent on the centre disk could be regarded as a four-choice reaction time (four-choice and not five, because the same disk was never indicated twice running), and the time moving to the outer disk could be considered as a movement time.

The other two groups of subjects, one younger and one older, were given a similar task, except that the light changed as soon as the indicated outer disk was touched with the stylus. The effect of this arrangement was to give the subject advance information of the direction in which he would have to move after touching the centre disk so that the time required to make a choice of direction, which in the first condition almost inevitably had to be spent at the centre disk, could now be spread over the times at the outer and centre disks and the time moving between them.

The results given in Table 4.7 are for the last twenty-five responses of the hundred when the subjects had had some opportunity to get over initial difficulties with the task. The pattern of results under both conditions was clear: the older subjects took substantially longer than the younger, but practically the whole of the extra time was spent on the disks; the times spent actually moving were closely similar for both younger and older. Of course, some of the time spent on the disks was taken in moving across them, but broadly speaking

TABLE 4.7. *Analysis of cycle times in Leonard's serial reaction experiments*

Means per cycle in seconds

	Light changing when centre disk touched		Light changing when indicated disk touched	
	Twenties	*Sixties*	*Twenties*	*Sixties*
On centre disk . .	0·39	0·58	0·19	0·36
Moving from centre to indicated disk . .	0·15	0·18	0·17	0·15
On indicated disk . .	0·20	0·34	0·19	0·43
Moving from indicated to centre disk . . .	0·11	0·14	0·14	0·16
Total time on disks .	0·59	0·92	0·38	0·79
Total time moving between disks	0·26	0·32	0·31	0·31
Total time per cycle .	0·85	1·24	0·69	1·10

it seems that slowness by the older subjects was not in actual movement but in changing direction and making choices where to move next.

Table 4.7 shows that the younger subjects were able under the second condition to make good use of the advance information and, compared with the first condition, shorten the time spent at the centre without substantially lengthening the other time components. Presumably they were able to overlap their choice reaction time to some extent with changing direction on the indicated disk and moving back to the centre. The older subjects also made use of the advance information in the sense of reducing the time spent at the centre, but achieved this at the expense of longer time spent on the indicated disk. Leonard reports that the main difference to an observer between the performances of the older and younger subjects was that the former tended to treat the outward and return movements as separate, whereas the latter appeared to treat them more as a single response. Why this difference occurred is difficult to say and the problem will be considered further in conjunction with rather similar results obtained by Singleton, whose experiments were undertaken to follow the leads given by Szafran and Leonard. In doing so opportunity was taken to obtain an even more rigorous separation of reaction times and movement times and also to achieve greater control of the accuracy of movement.

The apparatus used in the first of these experiments is shown in Fig. 4.5. The subject sat on the chair with the lever between his

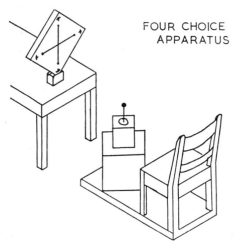

FIG. 4.5. Apparatus used in Singleton's first experiment

knees. The lever was made to move over a distance of about 4 inches in slots, forward, back, left and right, each direction corresponding to a neon light at the end of one of the arms of the cross on the display. When one of the lights came on, the subject had to move the lever as fast as possible to the end of the appropriate slot and back again to the centre. If he moved in the correct direction the light went out as soon as he reached the end of the slot, and the next light came on as soon as he returned to the centre. The task was thus, like Leonard's, a serial one, each response bringing on the next signal. To make it more difficult, the apparatus was arranged so that in order to put out a light the subject had to move the lever in the direction opposite to that in which the light appeared: thus to make the left-hand light go out he had to move to the right, and to make the top light go out he had to move the lever towards him. The task was again a four-choice one (since the same light could occur twice running) but with a complication in the translation process between display and control.

The fact that the lever worked in slots meant that it did not have to be accurately guided beyond the gross orientation into one of the four possible directions. It was fitted with a system of locks which prevented the subject accidentally overrunning when he got back to the centre but did not prevent his leaving again in response to the next light. The whole arrangement made it possible to regard the

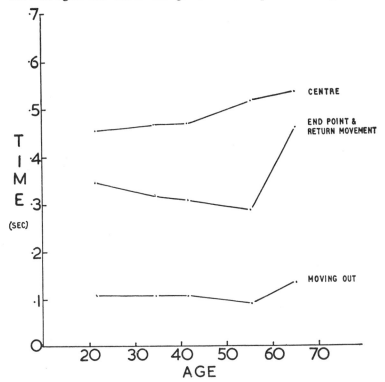

FIG. 4.6. Component times in Singleton's four-choice serial reaction task. Mean times in seconds per response

time spent at the centre as a measure of serial reaction time, and the time spent while the lever was moving in the slots as a near approximation to a 'pure' movement time, uncomplicated by the need for current sensory control and guidance.

Fig. 4.6 shows the times taken by groups of subjects in decades from the twenties to the sixties over three portions of the whole cycle of reaction and movement: time at the centre, time moving out from the centre to the end of the slot, and time spent at the end and moving back again to the centre. The times taken were those for the last of six trials each of sixty-four signals, so that the subjects had had time to settle to the task. In arriving at the average times only correct responses were considered. Errors, such as moving in the wrong slot, did not seem to be related to age, so that excluding them from consideration would not appear to vitiate age comparisons.

The centre time shows a small—perhaps rather surprisingly small—rise with age which was nevertheless very consistent and statistically significant. The times for the two movement components show a *fall* as far as the fifties followed by a rather sharp rise to the sixties. It

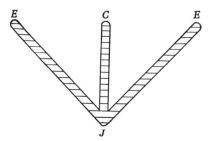

FIG. 4.7. The shaded area represents the possible paths of movement in Singleton's two-choice task

was unfortunately not possible to score time spent at the end point separately from the return movement, but comparison of the 'end point plus return movement' time with the 'outward movement' time and observation of the subjects made it clear that nearly all the extra time taken by the sixties was being spent at the end point.

Singleton observed much the same pattern of results with different subjects in a similar task using a simpler display but a more complex movement. There were on the display only two neon lights placed horizontally. The paths for the lever are shown in Fig. 4.7. The lever rested at C, and when one of the lights came on the subject extinguished it by moving the lever via J to the end-point E on the same side as the light. He then returned via J to C and on his reaching there the next light in the series came on. Each subject was given three trials of forty-eight signals of which the second and third trials were scored, the first being used for practice. The times taken at the points C, J and E and the times moving from one point to another are shown in Fig. 4.8. Quantitatively the results differ somewhat from those of the four-choice experiment, but the trends are similar. The times spent at C, J and E all rose sharply from the fifties to the sixties and that at C, which corresponded most closely to the centre time in the former experiment, rose appreciably from the thirties to the forties. The rise to the sixties of time spent at C was greater than

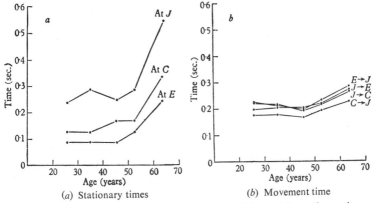

FIG. 4.8. Component times in Singleton's two-choice serial reaction task. Mean times in seconds per response

in the four-choice experiment, due probably to the oldest subjects deciding in which direction to move before leaving C instead of overlapping their decision with the action of moving from C to J. In this respect they behaved like Leonard's subjects.

The times spent moving fell slightly until the forties and then rose, but the increase was small compared to that at the points C, J and E, where the lever was stationary.

These two experiments by Singleton, together with those by Szafran and Leonard, all point to the same conclusions, namely that the main locus of slowing with age in sensori-motor performance lies not in the speed of movement but in the time taken by central processes initiating, shaping and monitoring movement.

Having said this, however, a number of questions immediately arise. We shall deal here in turn with three about which it seems possible to say something constructive. Firstly, how generally does this conclusion apply? In particular, the experiments of Leonard and

Singleton all set sensori-motor tasks involving very light movements of small extent. Would perhaps larger movements have revealed greater slowing with age in the actual movement time? Secondly, when slowing does occur, what is its cause and how is the extra time spent? Thirdly, how can the conclusion we have suggested be reconciled with Miles's results?

Slowing of longer movements with age

The attempt was made in Singleton's experiments to ensure that each movement was prepared before it began and that once it started it could be run off 'ballistically' with no monitoring beyond that of the kinaesthetic control in the effector mechanism. The results obtained from these experiments and those of Leonard and Szafran are surprising in that from watching older people it is obvious that many of their movements do become slower. The reason would appear to be that many—perhaps most—movements in real life are not made ballistically but are subject to current sensory control. For instance, when we reach to pick up an object we usually guide our movement up to the last half-second or so by sight. Two further experiments by Singleton show the difference of time taken between such visually monitored movements and those where detailed control is unnecessary.

In the first, the subject moved his hand from side to side tapping with a stylus on two targets 1 inch in diameter and 18 inches apart. He was told to touch the targets alternately as quickly as possible without making 'errors' by touching the surrounds. Few errors were in fact made and there was no obvious trend in these with age. Each subject had three trials: the first of twenty-five 'taps', the second and third of fifty 'taps' each. The experimenter signalled when each trial had been completed, so that the subject did not have to count the number of taps made.

The second experiment involved moving a lever from side to side fifty times as fast as possible in an 18-inch slot, while making sure to hit the stops at the end of the slot. This task was given after a number of other somewhat similar tasks with the same lever which served to allow the subjects to become acquainted with the apparatus. The completion of the required number of movements was again signalled to the subject so that he did not have to count.

Results for the two experiments are shown in Fig. 4.9. The times taken for the visually guided movements were about twice those for the movements of the same extent in the slot and rose more steeply with age. Their rise was very much in the manner of the stationary times in the two-choice experiment. It seems clear that the limits

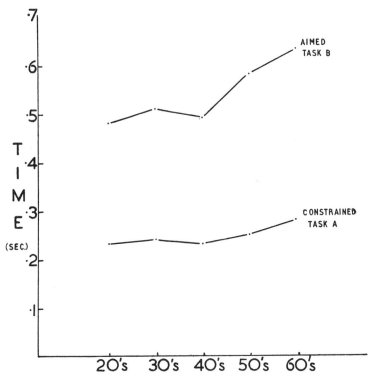

FIG. 4.9. Times for two types of repetitive movement. Means per movement
A. Moving lever in slot
B. Tapping with stylus

of time for the visually guided movements were set largely if not entirely by the perceptual and translatory processes involved in the guidance and that it was these which accounted for the slowing with age.

The times taken to move the lever in the slot were analysed further to determine the precise locus of such slowing as did occur among the older subjects under this condition. The results set out in Fig. 4.10 show that, rather surprisingly, the times for the first and last quarters of the movements showed no rise with age, indicating that the acceleration and deceleration phases were carried out as fast by the older subjects as by the younger. As in Singleton's four- and two-choice experiments, there was a sharp rise in the time spent by the sixties at the end stop where the direction of movement was changed: this is

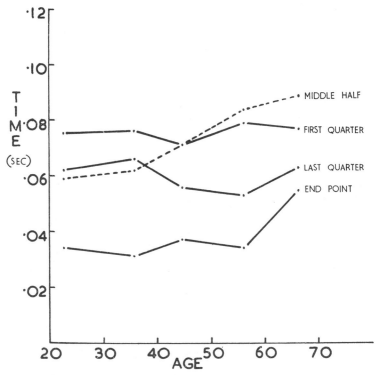

FIG. 4.10. Component times of simple lever movement. Means per movement

a matter to which we shall return later. The main slowing, however, occurred during the middle half of the movement, and it seems reasonable to suppose that this represented a genuine slowing of movement as such with age.

Taking all Singleton's experiments together two points about movement speed with age appear to emerge. Firstly, older people do seem to be genuinely capable of making short movements of a few inches as fast as can younger. Secondly, with longer movements, speed of movement *as such* may in some cases slow the performance of older people. In any situation, however, when the movement must be accurately aimed, the limits of speed and their change with age

will be set by the perceptual and translatory processes guiding movement: the speeds of the actual movements observed will have been
'tailored' to fit the times required by such central control.

These points emphasize the fallacy in the argument that slowing
of movement with age is due to failing muscular strength. This is
often advanced on the assumption that the maximum force a subject
can exert upon, say, a hand dynamometer, will indicate the power
that he can put into causing hand movements to be made rapidly.
We see that during the acceleration phase of movement, when
muscular strength might, if anywhere, be expected to have its
maximum effect, there is no trend with age. More important, we see
that if failing muscular strength did limit the maximum speed of
movement that could be attained in some circumstances, it would
have a substantial effect only in cases where movement did not
require to be accurately aimed.

The nature of the change with age in the central control of movement

Upon this matter it is possible to ask a number of questions regarding the precise points at which time is spent in a serial task and
how these times vary with the nature of the task. Five questions will
be considered here upon which some evidence is available.

(a) How far is slowing with age due to caution and how far to a lowering
   of capacity?

This is an extremely difficult question to answer conclusively, but
it would seem reasonable to suppose that if slowing was entirely due
to caution it should be possible by forcing the pace of work to per-
suade older people to drop their excessive carefulness and raise their
speed to the same level as that of younger people, without any fall
of accuracy. One of the most frequently used paced tasks in experimental studies is that of *tracking* in which the subject is required
to make movements to match or compensate for movements of a
mark on a display. This type of task aroused interest in relation to
gun-laying problems during the Second World War and has some
clear affinities to steering a car. It suffers from the disadvantage that
severe technical and theoretical problems are involved in scoring
performance, and of the many methods proposed, from very simple
measurements to elaborate mathematical treatments, none is wholly
satisfactory. Tracking is a convenient task, however, in that it can
very simply, by changes of speed and other conditions, be made to

cover the range from extremely easy to impossibly difficult. At the same time the intellectual demands it makes are relatively slight so that the task is readily understood.

We shall in the present connexion consider a group of three tracking experiments. In the first of these the subject had to keep a pointer, which he could move from side to side by raising or lowering a lever held in his right hand, in line with a second pointer moved by an irregularly shaped cam. The pattern of the cam was such that the swings of the target did not repeat until forty had been completed. In the apparatus for the second and third experiments the target-pointer was replaced by a track on a paper strip which was drawn down past a window, and the subject had to 'drive' a ball point pen along the track. He did this by moving the pen from side to side by means of a steering wheel as the track came past. The window was fitted with a shutter which could vary the amount of track seen ahead of the pen. The pattern on the paper was such that it did not repeat until ninety-four swings of the track had occurred. Samples of the track and of the course steered by subjects are shown in Fig. 4.11.

For the first experiment four scores for the movements of the subject's pointer were taken at each of five speeds: integrated time and distance off target; number of reversals; extent of movement; and time-lag relative to the target. Of these the third and fourth were the most interesting. The first proved misleading for reasons which will appear shortly, while the second showed that approximately the correct number of swings was made by all subjects at all speeds. This last point makes it clear that all the subjects were making a real effort to track although doing so at the two higher speeds was obviously a considerable strain and many subjects appeared tense. There was, however, no evidence at any age of fatigue in the sense of a break-down of performance towards the end of the experiment.

The average distances moved per minute by the subject's pointer and hand are set out in Fig. 4.12. The most noticeable feature of the scores plotted in this figure is that the extent of movement, unlike the number of reversals of direction, did not rise steadily with speed. At the two lower speeds both age ranges moved to an extent related to the rate of movement by the target-pointer. Beyond this speed, however, the amount of movement by the older subjects hardly rose at all. The younger subjects increased their movement a little from the second lowest to the middle speed, but made no further rise thereafter. The general form of the results closely resembles those obtained by Vince (1949) for responding with a morse key to different rates of discrete signals.

Broadly speaking, the older subjects as they passed from the lowest to the next higher speed maintained the correct *amplitude* of movement by increasing average *velocity*. As they passed to the middle speed and beyond they maintained the same velocity, but the swing-

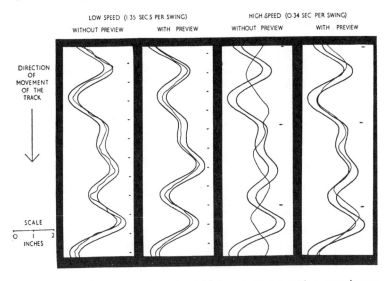

LOW SPEED (1.35 SECS PER SWING)   HIGH SPEED (0.34 SEC. PER SWING)

WITHOUT PREVIEW   WITH PREVIEW   WITHOUT PREVIEW   WITH PREVIEW

DIRECTION OF MOVEMENT OF THE TRACK

SCALE

0   1   2
INCHES

FIG. 4.11. Samples of record in the second and third tracking experiments performed by a subject aged 40

The track is indicated by the double lines, the course of the subject's pointer by the single line. The small marks on the right-hand margins of the record are at 1-second intervals.

ing of their pointer in response to the swings of the target-pointer became progressively less as the speed increased. The younger subjects showed essentially the same change, but for them it came at the middle speed.

Failure to maintain amplitude of swing must be regarded as a breakdown of tracking. On this criterion, therefore, performance by the younger subjects broke down at the two higher speeds, and performance by the older subjects at the two higher and also at the middle speed.

The time-lags, set out in Table 4.8, show that the older subjects lagged considerably more than the younger at the lower speeds, but

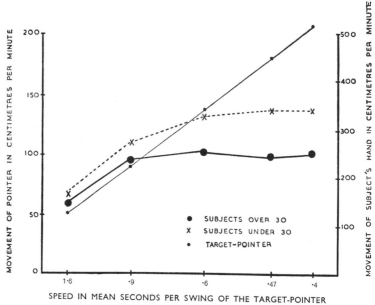

Fig. 4.12. First tracking experiment. Average distances moved by subject's pointer. Means per subject per minute.

TABLE 4.8. *First tracking experiment. Mean time and phase-lags*

Speed in mean seconds per swing of target-pointer	1·6	0·9	0·6	0·47	0·4
Subjects under 30					
Time-lag (secs.)	0·10	0·15	0·24	0·30	0·30
Phase-lag (degrees)	11	31	73	118	134
Subjects over 30					
Time-lag (secs.)	0·24	0·28	0·31	0·30	0·29
Phase-lag (degrees)	27	55	94	120	129

at the highest two speeds both the age groups seem to have reached a common ceiling of about 0·3 second. These time-lags can be thought of as shifting the subject's movements through a phase angle relative to the movements of the target-pointer. Comparing the phase angles in Table 4.8 with the time-lags and with the distances moved in Fig. 4.12 it can be seen that, at the speeds at which the subjects reached the ceiling of 0·3 second, the phase-lags were more than 90 degrees and the amount of movement had fallen short of that required. Now when the phase-lag exceeds 90 degrees the courses of the two pointers are so far out of step that the score for integrated time and distance off target would actually be *lower* if the subject were merely to hold his pointer stationary in a central position and make no attempt to track. It appears that what the subjects did when lagging to this extent was to maintain a semblance of tracking by making the correct number of swings but to cut down the amplitude of swing thus keeping misalignment to a minimum. This is really the best the subject can do in the circumstances: he will match the shorter swings of the target and 'catch the longer ones on the way back'. In addition, by doing this his swings will tend to be less differentiated so that, in accordance with Hick's law, they would require a shorter reaction time to prepare and would thus tend to keep the time-lag from rising further (Crossman 1957). The effectiveness of this course of action was shown in the fact that although the older subjects made a substantially greater 'time and distance off target' score at the lowest speed they were equal to the younger at the next two speeds and actually made a smaller score than the younger at the highest two speeds.

It is unlikely, however, that the advantages of swinging short were consciously realized by the subjects. After the experiment they were all asked whether, if they had to teach someone else to do the task, they would be able to offer any advice, but their replies never gave the slightest hint that they recognized the advantages of tracking at low amplitude. Certainly to the author when he tried the task himself the method was quite compelling—it seemed to be *impossible* to make long swings of the lever at high speeds.

The task did not impose any severe visual demands, and the movements required were very unlikely to be setting limits to performance. There seemed, in fact, no doubt that explanation of the breakdown of performance at the high speeds and the lower speed of breakdown among the older subjects was due to the times taken by central processes, in other words, to reaction time.

The question of just what effects lengthening of reaction time would have on paced performance and what possibility there might be of mitigating any difficulty encountered by older people is bound up with the theory discussed in Chapter II (pp. 31–35) regarding the limitation of the capacity of the central processes. Two alternative views have been discussed by Craik (1948). The first is that a longer

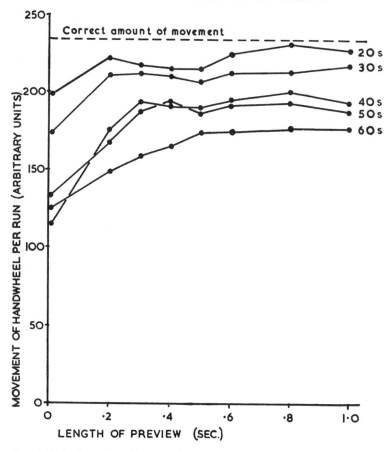

FIG. 4.13(*a*). Second tracking experiment. Movement as a function of preview. Means per subject per run of ninety-four swings of the track at a speed of 0·39 second per swing

reaction time merely implies that a longer time must elapse between the giving of a signal and the emergence of responding action, but that successive signals can follow each other without limit to rate of input. Craik rejected this view on an interpretation of experimental evidence although not specifically in relation to age. Indeed, such a theory is essentially unlikely to be correct because it would imply that as reaction time lengthens the capacity of the central processes increases. The lengthening would be analagous to an escalator running at the same speed down a longer shaft: the time elapsing be-

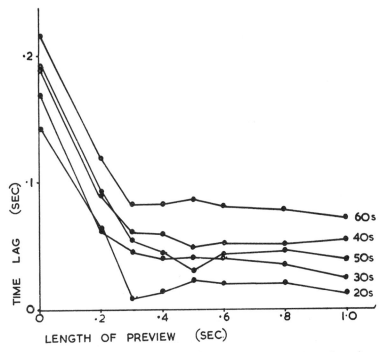

FIG. 4.13(b). Second tracking experiment. Time-lag as a function of preview. Means per subject per run of ninety-four swings of the track at a speed of 0·39 second per swing

tween a person getting on at the top and off at the bottom would be longer and the number of people on the escalator at any one time would increase, but the number carried per hour would remain the same.

The alternative view is that with the slowing goes a genuine limitation of *capacity* in the sense that less can be dealt with in a given period of time. The analogy would be with an escalator of the same length running more slowly, or better with a lift taking longer to complete its journey. The time elapsing between a person getting on and off would be lengthened and the number carried per hour would decrease.

The two subsequent pursuit-meter experiments provide evidence that the second rather than the first of these views is correct as a description of the effects of slowing with age. If the first were correct it should be possible to overcome the difficulties of older people at tracking tasks and make their performance equal to that of younger people very simply by giving them a view of the track sufficiently far in advance for them to be able to overcome their longer reaction time by looking a little farther ahead. If the second view is correct such preview should have only a limited effect and the only way to equate the performances of older and younger subjects would be to reduce the speed to a point at which the amount of information was within the older people's capacity to deal with in the time. Accordingly, in the two further tracking experiments speed and preview were systematically and independently varied.

Subjects in one of these experiments were given practice at several speeds and then two runs, one with preview of 3 seconds and one with none, at a low speed followed by several runs at a higher speed with varying amounts of preview. The age differences at the low speed were relatively small. The results for the higher speed are set out in Fig. 4.13 (a) and (b) and show striking improvements in either time-lag, amplitude of movement or both in all age groups up to a preview of 0·3 second but relatively little thereafter. The oldest subjects improve slightly beyond this point, which is understandable in that we should expect longer preview to improve performance up to the point at which it covered the range of a subject's reaction times. There is, however, no indication that lengthening preview beyond about 0·5 second brings the performance of the different age groups any closer together.

In the third experiment subjects performed runs at several different speeds both without preview and with the maximum possible preview obtained by opening the shutter to its fullest extent. The length of preview thus provided varied with speed but was never less than one second. The actual speeds given to the different age groups were varied in order to cover what seemed likely to be the most important range without making the experimental session unduly long. Amplitudes of movement attained are plotted in Fig. 4.14(a) in a manner similar to Fig. 4.12. Time-lags are set out in Fig. 4.14(b). Quantitatively the results varied somewhat from those of the first experiment due doubtless to changes in the task resulting from differences in the apparatus used; the pattern of results was, however, the same. Without preview there was, as in the first experiment, a tendency for amount of movement per minute to remain constant as speed rose above a critical level. With preview the amount of movement rose with speed to a much higher level in all age groups but the separation

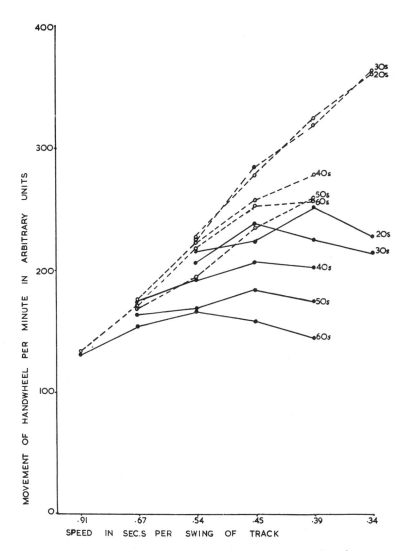

FIG. 4.14(a). Third tracking experiment. Movement of subject's pointer as a function of speed of track. Means per minute

Dotted lines: with preview
Solid lines: without preview

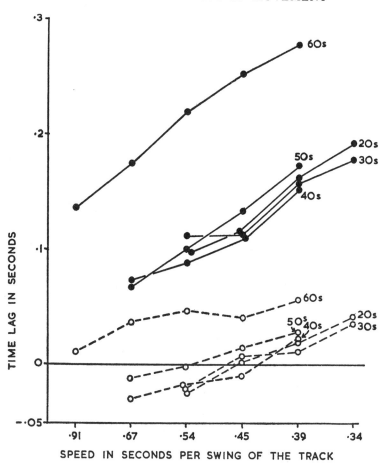

FIG. 4.14(*b*). Third tracking experiment. Time-lag as a function of speed of track

Dotted lines: with preview
Solid lines: without preview

between the age groups, which was shown without preview, still remained, except that the sixties attained greater amplitude than did the fifties. This should be taken together with the fact that they also showed a greater time-lag. We may note as a general point in passing that the time-lags rose fairly steadily with speed and at about the same rate in all age ranges.

The increase in the amount of movement which came with preview is an indication that actual movement as such was not the limiting factor in these experiments under the 'no preview' condition. Two further direct checks on this point were, however, made in the third experiment. One was to require all subjects at the end of the experiment to swing the steering wheel first one way and then the other several times as fast as possible: all subjects of all ages did this at a speed far in excess of the highest required in the experimental runs. The other check consisted of giving all subjects additional runs at the speed of 0·39 second per swing with the steering wheel geared up so that smaller movements were required to match the swings of the track. The results, set out in Table 4.9, show that in the 'no preview'

TABLE 4.9. *Third tracking experiment. Movement and time-lags as a function of display to steering wheel ratio*

Means per subject at speed of 0·39 second per swing of the track

	Age range				
	Twenties	Thirties	Forties	Fifties	Sixties
Movement in arbitrary units					
With preview Steering wheel:					
(*a*) Normal .	205	205	162	152	154
(*b*) Geared-up .	214	212	184	174	182
Difference *b−a* .	9	7	22	22	28
Without preview					
(*a*) Normal .	101	95	75	74	56
(*b*) Geared-up .	128	123	95	99	80
Difference *b−a* .	27	28	20	25	24
Time-lags in seconds *With preview*					
(*a*) Normal .	−0·013	0·008	−0·001	0·034	0·064
(*b*) Geared-up .	−0·013	0·007	−0·005	0·031	0·055
Difference *a−b* .	0	0·001	0·004	0·003	0·009
Without preview					
(*a*) Normal .	0·162	0·204	0·180	0·215	0·291
(*b*) Geared-up .	0·156	0·155	0·169	0·186	0·337
Difference *a−b* .	0·006	0·049	0·011	0·029	−0·046

condition the amount of movement increased to about the same absolute extent in all age groups and thus brought about some relative improvement among the older subjects. With preview the older did improve somewhat more than the younger with the higher gear, but the amount of movement attained by the younger subjects was in any case so near to that required that they had less scope for improvement than the older.

Taken together these tracking experiments give support to the second view discussed by Craik, as opposed to the first, and indicate that lengthening of reaction time with age is accompanied by a genuine lowering of capacity in the sense that less data can be handled in a given length of time. The experiments show also that under paced conditions older subjects do not, when forced to work fast, do so without sacrificing accuracy. Thus they provide evidence for the view that slowing of performance among older people cannot wholly be accounted for in terms of an excessive caution which they could be forced to abandon under suitable conditions. It would, therefore, appear that if caution is the cause of slowness it has been so deeply ingrained into the attitudes of older people that it cannot be set aside at will and must, if it hampers performance, rank as a genuine disability of middle and old age.

The difficulties of the older subjects were mitigated a little and their performances brought relatively nearer to those of the younger by adequate preview and facilitation of the motor task, but improvements wrought in these ways were clearly small compared with the effects of reducing speed. At lower speeds the performances of the older subjects were indistinguishable, at least on the criteria used, from those of younger.

(b) *How far is slowing due to some factor in the reaction time preceding movement and how far does it result from processes following movement?*

In Szafran's experiment already described (p. 75) slowing was clearly due to some factor in the reaction time, but in Leonard's and Singleton's part at least might have been due to some secondary or checking process following the execution of a movement.

Evidence upon this point comes from an experiment by Jeeves using Singleton's four-choice apparatus. The arrangement was the same as in Singleton's experiment except for two features; firstly, that the relation between display and control was 'direct'—that is to say when the left light came on the subject had to move left, and so on, and secondly, that in some runs the light did not come on immediately the subject returned to the centre, but was delayed by either

0·1 or 0·2 second. Two groups of subjects, ten with ages ranging from 18 to 34 and eight with ages ranging from 58 to 71 were compared after several practice runs under each of the three conditions.

If the time spent at the centre was entirely taken up with processes in the reaction time preceding movement, such delays should add progressively to the centre time so that the time with a delay of, for example, 0·1 second would be that amount greater than the observed centre time with no delay. To put it another way, we should expect that if we deducted the amount of delay from the observed centre time the difference (which is essentially the *reaction* time) would be equal to the centre time when there was no delay. If, on the other hand, the centre time were taken up with processes resulting from the preceding movement, these should be able to take place during the delay and the observed centre time under delay conditions should be the same as that under conditions without delay, up to the point at which the lengths of the processes resulting from the preceding movement and of the delay are equal.

Jeeves's results, set out in Table 4.10, showed that *reaction time*

TABLE 4.10. *Serial reaction times and movement times as functions of delay in the appearance of signals*

Means per reaction. All times in seconds

	Amount of delay		
	0·0	0·1	0·2
Reaction time: i.e. centre time minus delay			
Younger (18–33)	0·335	0·298	0·307
Older (58–71)	0·412	0·362	0·356
Outward movement time			
Younger	0·085	0·075	0·068
Older	0·136	0·128	0·125
Time at end-point plus return movement time			
Younger	0·258	0·243	0·234
Older	0·408	0·391	0·340

fell in both age groups from the condition without delay to that with 0·1 second delay, but did not change appreciably from this to the condition with 0·2 second delay. The results thus indicate that part of the centre time—on average rather less than 0·1 second—was taken up by processes following the preceding movements, but that this was so in both age groups, and that when allowance is made for it the reaction time of the older subjects is still greater than that of the younger.

Comparing Table 4.10 with Fig. 4.6, it can be seen that the results tie up reasonably well with Singleton's original ones. The centre times for both younger and older subjects were shorter owing, presumably, to the 'direct' relationship between display and control. The 'end-point plus return movement' times were closely similar in the two experiments, so were the 'outward movement' times from the older group.

The only real difference was in the outward movement times for the younger subjects which were substantially shorter in Jeeves's experiment than in Singleton's. This may, perhaps, have been a result of the delay conditions during the practice period. A note-worthy feature of the results was that the delay conditions affected not only the centre times but also those for other parts of the cycle so that the times for all these became shorter as the delay increased. Why this 'spread of effect' should have occurred is not clear, but it would seem to imply the organization of the whole cycle as in some sense a single unit.

(c) *Does lengthening of reaction time with age depend upon the com-plexity of the subsequent responding action?*

It seemed at first sight possible that the increase with age of time taken at the centre points in Singleton's four- and two-choice experi-ments might have been due, at least in part, to the older subjects having greater difficulty than the younger in preparing a co-ordinated back and forth movement. A further experiment by Singleton with his 'simple lever apparatus' indicated, however, that the increase of reaction time with age was very little affected by the complexity of the ensuing action.

Subjects held the lever in the hand, and upon a neon light appear-ing moved the lever either with a single movement to the other end of the slot or with a double movement to the end and back again. The results, given in Table 4.11, show that the reaction times rose with age, and as Vince (1948b) found in a knob-turning task, those preceding double movements were, on average, slightly longer than those preceding single. This latter difference was, however, small and did not increase substantially with age.

(d) *Is the slowing proportional and capable of being described in terms of a lower rate of transfer of 'information'?*

The work surveyed so far would seem to make it at least plausible to suggest that many age changes of performance might be due to

TABLE 4.11. *Reaction times preceding single and double movements*

Means per reaction

	Age range				
	Twenties	*Thirties*	*Forties*	*Fifties*	*Sixties*
Reaction times preceding:					
Single movements . .	0·226	0·247	0·258	0·292	0·288
Double movements . .	0·237	0·265	0·279	0·298	0·299
Difference (D−S) . .	0·011	0·018	0·021	0·006	0·011

the rate of 'information' transfer becoming lower with age. Evidence is furnished by two experiments.

N. Welford obtained times for dotting alternately on two targets either 1 inch or 2 inches in diameter and either 1 foot or 2 feet between centres. Table 4.12 shows that the times taken, including,

TABLE 4.12. *Speed of 'dotting' between two targets as a function of target size and distance*

	1-ft. movements		2-ft. movements	
Age group	*2-in. targets*	*1-in. targets*	*2-in. targets*	*1-in. targets*
Mean time (in secs.) per movement including time spent on target				
Twenties	0·293	0·370	0·401	0·491
Thirties	0·355	0·435	0·443	0·547
Forties	0·455	0·544	0·568	0·656
Sixties	0·558	0·661	0·716	0·798
*Rate of information transfer in bits per second**				
Twenties	12·2	12·4	11·4	11·4
Thirties	10·1	10·5	10·3	10·2
Forties	7·9	8·4	8·1	8·5
Sixties	6·4	6·9	6·4	7·0

* Calculated according to Fitts's (1954) formula:

$$\text{Bits per movement} = -\log_2 \frac{W}{2A}.$$

where W = the target width and A = the length of the movement between target centres.

as did Fitts, both actual movement time and time spent at the end-points, agreed fairly well with Fitts's adaptation of Hick's law (see p. 33). The actual rate found for the subjects in their twenties was very close to that obtained by Fitts for his university student subjects. The rate declined substantially with age but remained relatively constant in each age group between the four conditions. The results of this experiment support the view that rate of information transfer declines with age.

The results, however, of a further experiment by Crossman and Szafran (1956) show a very different pattern.

Each subject held a pack of ordinary playing cards face down, turned them over one by one, and sorted them during different trials into red and black, the four suits, and the four suits separating court cards from the rest, thus providing two, four and eight categories. The subject was also timed sorting a pack alternately into two piles to provide a measure of time taken to perform the actual sorting *movements* without having to make choices or decisions on to which pile each card should be placed. For the two-, four- and eight-choice conditions we can thus think of the sorting time per card as comprised of two components: movement time as indicated by the time taken in the 'no choice' condition and choice time as indicated by the observed time per card less movement time.

The results are shown in Fig. 4.15. As is not unexpected from Leonard's and Singleton's experiments, the movement times of the 'no choice' condition showed little change with age. For the two-, four- and eight-choice conditions we might expect, if the rate of information transfer declined with age, that the choice time would rise proportionately as between the different age groups. Plotting time against log degree of choice as is done in Fig. 4.15, we should obtain a series of straight lines radiating from the 'no choice' time and gradually becoming steeper with age. The observed results clearly do not fall into this pattern. The over-60 group took substantially more time than the others in the two-choice condition. Age differences in the four- and eight-choice conditions were not, however, greater in proportion, but, surprisingly, of about the same *absolute* magnitude as those for two choices.

Crossman and Szafran point out that their results 'can be simply expressed by saying that wherever any choice or decision must be made, a constant time, increasing with age, is added to the normal choice-time' of young subjects for the degree of choice involved.

They further point out that this result is unlikely to have been due to factors such as older people taking longer to focus the eyes upon the cards since rather similar results were obtained in an experiment

signals in the brain, which would tend to obscure all differences between signals, but especially between those which could otherwise be dealt with most rapidly. They suggest this internal disturbance or 'noise' might be due to 'an increased rate of spontaneous firing of neurones or an increased likelihood for neighbouring neurones to excite one another'. We must consider their theory further in connexion with experiments on discrimination in Chapter VII.

Meanwhile, we may note two points. Firstly, their results are similar in some ways to those of Birren and Botwinick (1951) and Birren *et al.* (1954) who found that in adding tasks, even after full allowance had been made for the slower speed of older subjects at writing down figures, the proportionate age difference of time taken was greatest for the shortest task of adding two digits together and became steadily *less* as the number of digits increased. Secondly, from the practical standpoint the results have the surprising implication that older people may be *relatively* least slow at tasks involving somewhat elaborate choices. Everyday observation does, perhaps, furnish evidence which lends some support to this view.

The discrepancy between the results of N. Welford's and Crossman and Szafran's experiments is presumably due to different mechanisms setting the limits to performance in the two cases. In the latter, where the subject was required to interpret a 'code' of 'pips' on the cards, a symbolic translation was involved in relating display to action, while the actual motor task was simple, demanding only very low accuracy. The former task had a straightforward relationship between display and action, but demanded accurate central control of movement. Evidence that different mechanisms were involved is given by the rates of information transfer. The slope of the curves in Fig. 4.15 is a little over three 'bits' per second. The rates attained in the dotting task were all very much higher.

The complex nature of the mechanism involved is emphasized when we remember that information transfer is itself an overall measure combining together the effects of many different neural mechanisms and the times taken by several component actions. The point is strikingly illustrated when the dotting task results for 2-inch targets 2 feet apart and 1-inch targets 1 foot apart are analysed into times on the targets and times moving between them. According to Fitts's formula the times taken under these two conditions should be equal, and it can be seen from Table 4.12 that they were approximately so. Table 4.13 shows, however, that in all age ranges the movement times were longer and the end-point times were shorter when the targets were at the greater distance.

TABLE 4.13. *Analysis of the total times in Table 4.12 into times spent on targets and times moving between targets*

Age group	1-ft. movements		2-ft. movements	
	2-in. targets	1-in. targets	2-in. targets	1-in. targets
Moving between targets				
Twenties	0·237	0·289	0·338	0·398
Thirties	0·288	0·352	0·373	0·455
Forties	0·352	0·431	0·472	0·549
Sixties	0·440	0·509	0·591	0·650
On targets				
Twenties	0·056	0·081	0·063	0·093
Thirties	0·067	0·083	0·070	0·092
Forties	0·103	0·113	0·096	0·107
Sixties	0·118	0·152	0·125	0·148

It is possible that the results of both experiments could be explained in terms of 'noise' or randomness increasing with age in different central mechanisms. Fitts himself seems to favour such an explanation of his own dotting task results in terms of randomness in the central timing and control of movement. If this is true, N. Welford's results would seem to link with those of Miles's pursuit reaction task discussed on p. 62.

The slowness of the older subjects at the dotting task could not have been due to hand-tremor. This would have an effect equivalent to making all targets smaller by a constant amount. Had it increased substantially with age, the performance of the older subjects would, therefore, have been worse with the small targets than with the large. It can be seen from Table 4.12 that this was not so.

(e) *What is the reason for the disjointed performance of the older subject?*

The subjects in their sixties in both Leonard's and Singleton's experiments showed what was to an observer a 'jerky' performance as opposed to the more rhythmic flowing action by subjects in earlier decades. Singleton suggested that in his experiments this might have been due to their using the end-stops of the lever guides to arrest movement, thereby saving time over the movement itself but taking longer at the end-points. This explanation could not, however, apply to Leonard's experiment where there were no end-stops to be used in this way. Leonard himself suggested that the pattern of performance by older subjects closely resembled that of young subjects early in practice and that the reason why it appeared in older subjects was that they learnt more slowly and had not by the end of the experiment had sufficient practice to bring them to the same level of learning as the younger. He tried a pilot experiment in which three young subjects (aged 18, 20 and 23) and three older (aged 55, 59 and 60) had eleven trials spread over three days. On the first day the two groups were clearly separated, but by the end of the second day's trials the subject aged 55 was making scores which were closer to those of the young subjects than to those of the two remaining older ones. The scores of these two, however, showed no sign of joining those of the younger group. It is clear from Brown's figure-tracing experiment that absolute differences of performance between different age groups can be substantially reduced in the course of practice, but whether they can ever be completely eliminated in sensori-motor tasks, and if so, in what circumstances, is not known.

Another possibility which appears to provide a partial explanation is that the maximum size of 'higher unit' of performance which can be maintained as an integrated whole tends to fall with age. If this were so it would mean that older subjects would have to deal piecemeal with tasks which the younger could deal with as single entities. Certainly it was descriptively true that the rhythmical action by the older subjects was 'broken up', but it is unlikely to have been wholly because of the breakdown of 'higher units' if certain ancillary evidence is applicable. We have, for example, already seen that in the grid-matching experiment there were some indications that planning the cycle of action as a whole tended to increase rather than diminish with age.

Data having a more direct bearing upon the problem come from further results of N. Welford's experiment. In addition to trials made under the conditions set out in Table 4.12, each subject performed two runs, one involving movements of 1 foot and one of 2 feet, with a 1-inch target at one end and a 2-inch target at the other. As was expected, the overall results were intermediate between those obtained with two small and two large targets. What was not expected was that this would also apply to the individual movements and times spent at the end-points. It had been thought that the movement time

TABLE 4.14. *Times for 'dotting' between two targets of unequal sizes compared with those for two equal targets*

Means per response in seconds

	Time moving between targets			
	Moving to 2-in. target	Moving to 1-in. target	Difference between last two columns	Difference between moving over same distance between two 2-in. and two 1-in. targets
1-ft. movements				
Twenties . . .	0·269	0·273	0·004	0·052
Thirties . . .	0·326	0·346	0·020	0·064
Forties . . .	0·398	0·413	0·015	0·079
Sixties . . .	0·459	0·494	0·035	0·069
2-ft. movements				
Twenties . . .	0·366	0·379	0·013	0·060
Thirties . . .	0·434	0·451	0·017	0·082
Forties . . .	0·519	0·537	0·018	0·077
Sixties . . .	0·599	0·655	0·056	0·059

	Time on targets			
	On 2-in. target	On 1-in. target	Difference between last two columns	Difference between times on two 2-in. and two 1-in. targets for movements over same distance
1-ft. movements				
Twenties . . .	0·068	0·075	0·007	0·025
Thirties . . .	0·072	0·076	0·004	0·016
Forties . . .	0·113	0·113	0·0	0·010
Sixties . . .	0·136	0·138	0·002	0·034
2-ft. movements				
Twenties . . .	0·064	0·090	0·026	0·030
Thirties . . .	0·071	0·083	0·012	0·022
Forties . . .	0·096	0·103	0·007	0·011
Sixties . . .	0·145	0·140	−0·005	0·023

The figures in the third column are in all cases smaller than the corresponding figures in the fourth.

from a large to a small target would be the same as from a small to a small and from a small to a large the same as from one large to another, since we should expect the speed to have been dependent upon the size of the target to which the movement was directed. Instead, the times taken by movements in *both* directions tended to be intermediate between those for two large and two small targets. Similarly intermediate results were found for the times spent on the targets, indicating that these times were determined in part by the succeeding movements or target sizes.

These findings seemed to indicate that speed was being averaged over the different parts of the cycle in much the same way as was found by de Montpellier (1935) and as work by Wehrkamp and Smith (1952) and Denton (1953) has suggested can occur in other types of skilled performance. Further indications that this was happening came from an increase of errors made in moving to the small target under these conditions as compared with those when two small targets were used. If 'higher units' were breaking down in old age, we should expect the averaging effects to diminish and finally disappear as we went up the age scale. Inspection of Table 4.14 reveals that this did in fact appear to happen in the case of movement times, but did not for end-point times. It would seem that the pattern of performance changed with age and that some impairment of integration occurred, at least in the sixties, but that even in this group integration was not entirely destroyed.

A rather different line of explanation is suggested by the fact that the jerkiness of the older subjects' actions was due to their stopping at points where either some irrelevant change in the display occurred, such as a light going *out* in Singleton's four- and two-choice experiments, or where hitting end-stops would produce sounds, or where changes in the direction of movement would give rise to relatively powerful kinaesthetic impulses. It seems possible that the older subjects were slowed down by taking notice of these stimuli, whereas the younger could ignore them. This might occur for a variety of reasons, not mutually exclusive, of which we may mention three. Firstly, older subjects may not be able to exercise the same degree of perceptual selectivity as younger; secondly, they may not have the same ability to overlap the taking of decisions with the making of movements; and thirdly, they may need more sensory data for carrying out their task. A hint in favour of the first possibility is contained in the results of an experiment by Clay (1956a) which will be described in Chapter VIII. The second tendency was noted in Leonard's and in Singleton's first two experiments, but whether the non-overlapping of decision and movement was due to sheer inability to carry on the two activities simultaneously or whether uncertainty over the outcome of action made it necessary for older people to check results of one action before proceeding to the next, we cannot yet be sure. The third possibility, that more sense data are needed by older people, links closely with the results of several experiments which will be discussed in Chapter VII.

Conclusion upon speed and accuracy in relation to age

We may sum up the results surveyed in this chapter by saying that slowing of sensori-motor performance with age is due not to longer time required to execute movements *as such*, but to longer time needed to initiate, guide and monitor them, owing to a limitation in the capacity of central processes. The apparent discrepancy between this conclusion and Miles's results would seem to be due to two facts. Firstly, when one measures reaction times, as did Miles, in the classical manner, much of the 'work' of reacting can be done in anticipation of the actual signal, so that it is not included in the reaction time: what remains is very simple and well within the capacity of all except the oldest subjects. The tasks described here have been serial reaction tasks where the work of responding has had to be done wholly or almost wholly during the measured reaction time. They thus give a more accurate picture of the time taken by the reaction processes as a whole.

The second fact relates to Miles's motility measures. Even the simplest movement, such as winding a crank handle, involves the bringing into play, in the correct sequence, of different groups of muscles to move the hand along a prescribed path. The motility task is thus not a pure movement task but involves a great deal of central co-ordination and control.

The precise form and extent of slowing would seem to depend upon the nature of the task, and certainly cannot be wholly described in terms of a proportional increase of time taken over all tasks. In subjects over 60 there seems to be an added source of slowness due to difficulty in making decisions while executing movements, and this may be the cause of an inability to integrate series of actions into 'flowing' rhythmic wholes.

Where there is a choice open to them, older subjects appear rather consistently to shift the balance between speed and accuracy towards the latter. This has the effect of conserving action in the sense that less is wasted making and correcting errors. Such stress on accuracy does not, however, seem to be designed to conserve *energy* but rather to keep down the time taken to control action and make decisions. Since this time lengthens with age, we can see the care, caution and accuracy manifested by older people as likely to maximize their overall achievement and thus as a very reasonable and sensible course to adopt. Whether the choice is deliberately taken is another matter: almost certainly it is not in each individual performance, although perhaps if we could trace back in a man's or woman's history we should find them having consciously built up habits which have in the course of time become generalized and deeply ingrained so that they are used without any awareness of doing so.

V

SOME IMPLICATIONS OF SLOWING:
PACING, ACCIDENTS AND HEAVY WORK

THE research surveyed in the last chapter on the causes and nature of slowing with age has the implication that when the time for doing a task is limited older people will be at a disadvantage. They will either fail to complete the task in the time allowed or they will have to hurry and will in consequence make errors so that the positive relationship found, for instance, in Brown's experiments between accuracy and age will break down. On the industrial side we should, for the same reasons, expect work making demands for speed to cause difficulty to older people.

A number of experiments and studies in industry have confirmed these expectations. The industrial studies, rather surprisingly, soon showed that questions of speed are intimately bound up with problems of *heavy work*. The results of investigations made of heavy work in industry are conflicting and somewhat anomalous and the reason seems to be that timing characteristics as well as the muscular effort required need to be considered.

We shall in this chapter begin by discussing an experiment where the speed of work was *paced* in the sense that it was determined by the task and not by the subject, and shall then go on to consider industrial studies of both speed-stress and heavy work.

Experimental study of paced performance

If limitations in paced performance are due to limits of capacity to deal with data in a given time, we should expect the speed at which breakdown occurred in a paced task to bear a recognizable relationship to maximum speed attained at an unpaced task. A detailed comparison between paced and unpaced performance has been made by Brown (1957) in an experiment using the grid-matching task described in Chapter IV (p. 65). For this experiment the original apparatus was modified so that if the subject did not succeed in plotting the position correctly on the grid and making the ball move in 8 seconds it moved automatically and the subject had then to stop it and begin a fresh attempt to plot. The time chosen was such as to be comfortable for younger subjects although substantially less than the average time taken by older subjects in the former experiment. If the subject completed his plot correctly within the 8 seconds the ball remained stationary until the full time had elapsed, but a small red light came on to inform him of his success. The subjects worked at both the original and the new tasks for 10 minutes each, one group (A) doing the new 'paced' task first, the other (B) doing the original 'unpaced' task first.

The number of successes attained by the two groups combined are shown in Fig. 5.1. The scores for the unpaced task show performance to have changed relatively little with age up to and including the fifties and thereafter to have fallen by about one-third from the fifties to the sixties and seventies. The slight rise in the seventies was probably due to the subjects which were obtained at this age having been an unusually active and healthy group. The scores for the paced task remained very similar between the twenties, thirties and forties but thereafter showed marked declines to the fifties and again to the sixties. It seemed clear that the overall effect of pacing upon the performance of the subjects in their fifties and over was severe.

The fact that, on average, the scores for the paced task were lower than for the unpaced in every age range is in accord with a point made by Conrad and Hille (1955). Reaction times and movement times vary from one moment to another so that if we plot the times for individual cycles of a repetitive task we obtain a distribution with a hump around the mean and tails of quicker and slower times. If now each cycle must be completed within a rigidly prescribed time-limit any cycles in the 'slow' tail not finished in time will remain uncompleted and lead to errors. On the other hand, any cycles completed within the limit will lead to time being wasted. As the time-limit is shortened, or the average time taken by subjects becomes greater, so more of the 'slow' tail will fall outside the prescribed limit unless either the subject can in some way speed up the slow cycles, or the pacing is not quite rigid so that a slow time in one cycle can be redeemed by a quick time later.

The pacing in the present experiment was completely rigid so that the second alternative was excluded. A test was, however, made to see how far the subjects had managed to speed up their cycle times in the paced task. An 'expected paced' score was calculated by taking for each subject the proportion of cycles he completed unpaced in 8 seconds or less and multiplying by 75—i.e. the maximum possible

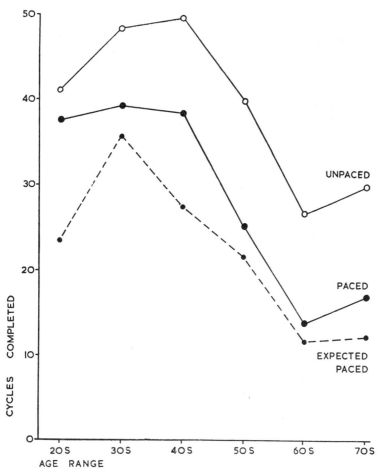

Fig. 5.1. Comparison of paced and unpaced performance.
Mean numbers of successes per subject

Open circles: unpaced.
Filled circles: paced.
Dotted line: 'expected' paced.

paced score. This gave the paced score that would have been attained if the distribution of cycle times in the paced task had been the same as the distribution in the unpaced. It can be seen from Fig. 5.1 that the actual paced score in each age range was on average a little higher than that expected, indicating that some speeding up had occurred. The differences were, however, small except in the twenties and forties.

The older subjects appeared harassed and often forgot to stop the ball during the paced task, even if they had already done the unpaced. The chief difficulty for them appeared to be that the short time-limit did not allow the meticulous counting of squares and checking position that was typical of an older subject's performance at the unpaced task: instead it required the quicker method of 'guessing' the correct position normally employed by the younger subjects.

It is very difficult to compare the effects of pacing in detail by comparing scores for the paced and unpaced tasks because the demands were so different that many of the possible scores are not really comparable between the two. Some objective indication that the older people were trying to hurry is, however, contained in their times to stop the ball given in Table 5.1. The sixties and seventies can be seen to have taken considerably less time to do this in the paced task than in the unpaced.

TABLE 5.1. *Comparison of paced and unpaced performances. Times to stop the ball in seconds per subject per cycle*

	Age range					
	Twenties	Thirties	Forties	Fifties	Sixties	Seventies
Paced task						
Group A (paced first)	1·15	1·26	1·50	1·30	1·84	1·89
Group B (unpaced first)	1·07	1·13	1·35	1·63	1·75	1·73
All subjects	1·11	1·20	1·43	1·47	1·80	1·81
Unpaced task						
Group A	1·20	1·08	1·50	1·30	1·97	2·34
Group B	1·07	1·30	1·53	1·71	2·65	2·73
All subjects	1·14	1·19	1·52	1·51	2·31	2·54
Difference (U−P): All subjects	0·03	−0·01	0·09	0·04	0·51	0·73

Some further indication is given by comparing the unpaced performance of Group A who did it after the paced task with that of Group B who did the unpaced task first. It can be seen from Table 5.2 that except in the seventies Group A were quicker but less accurate than Group B, taking a shorter time between stopping the ball at the end of one run and the first attempt to start it again, but making more

TABLE 5.2. *Comparison of performance by those doing paced task first and those doing unpaced first*

Means per subject

	Age range					
	Twenties	Thirties	Forties	Fifties	Sixties	Seventies
Time to first attempt in secs.						
Unpaced:*						
Group A (paced first)	7·7	7·1	5·9	8·7	11·7	13·6
Group B (unpaced first)	10·8	9·5	9·2	13·1	22·1	15·4
Difference (B−A)	3·1	2·4	3·3	4·4	10·4	1·8
Errors						
Unpaced:						
Group A	63·5	62·2	81·3	67·1	80·4	62·2
Group B	43·1	37·9	64·1	46·0	40·8	63·1
Difference (A−B)	20·4	24·3	17·2	21·1	39·6	−0·9
Paced:						
Group A	49·7	43·1	53·7	48·1	26·2	27·7
Group B	46·7	40·6	58·7	31·9	27·4	33·9
Difference (A−B)	3·0	2·5	−5·0	16·2	−1·2	−6·2
Successes						
Unpaced:						
Group A	45·6	50·4	59·4	45·1	31·6	32·8
Group B	36·4	46·6	40·0	34·6	22·0	27·3
Difference (A−B)	9·2	3·8	19·4	10·5	9·6	5·5
Paced:						
Group A	33·7	35·8	37·8	26·4	11·4	13·4
Group B	41·1	42·4	39·3	24·0	16·2	20·2
Difference (B−A)	7·4	6·6	1·5	−2·4	4·8	6·8

* 'Times to first attempt' in the paced task are not comparable with those in the unpaced.

errors. The *paced* performances of the two groups were on average more similar so that it would seem as if the difference of unpaced performance was due in substantial part to the effect of the paced task upon the unpaced and not only to practice.

It seems fair to say that in this experiment the pacing resulted in a serious fall of performance in the fifties which was a decade earlier than it occurred in the unpaced task. This is not to say that had the task been made less or more difficult the fall would not have occurred later or earlier, but the age at which it was observed is significant in view of the fact that it is in the early fifties that age difficulties at paced industrial tasks appear to become especially important.

INDUSTRIAL WORK UNDER TIME-STRESS

A. M. N. Shooter and R. M. Belbin in a preliminary study of 2,485 men and 736 women on 95 production operations in 24 firms found no clear age trends when the operations were divided according to type of work (machine-feeding, machine-operating, light assembly, inspection and heavy work), and no significant relation between age and length of cycle-time at machine-feeding operations. There was a clear overall tendency for the age distribution of the men and women paid by time rates to be higher than that of those paid by piece rates, but there were a great many anomalies when operations were scrutinized individually. This scrutiny together with the evidence from experiments suggested that a more fundamental classification could be made and clearer age trends seen if operations were divided according to the amount of *time-stress* they imposed. The operations were accordingly divided rather crudely but reasonably objectively into two categories thus:

1. *Operations in which there was time-stress*

(*a*) Operations where the work was *paced* in the sense that operatives were compelled to keep up with a machine or conveyor-line and to complete each cycle within a fixed average time. Operations were only placed in this class if failure to maintain pace led to serious errors of omission. They were not classed as paced when the operative could regulate the pace of work or if during any part of the cycle-time he was not actively engaged or acted in a purely supervisory capacity.

(*b*) Operations where although the pace was flexible there was *speed-pressure* exerted by piece rates paid either individually or to a small working group, except where there was some mitigating circumstance of the kinds given below.

2. *Operations in which time-stress was absent or in some way mitigated*

Under this head were included all operations paid at time rates or where group bonus payments were made to a large working group such as a whole shop. Operations paid at individual or small-group piece rates were also included if they possessed one or both of the following characteristics:

(*a*) The machinery or working group set a pace which was such as to permit or enforce frequent pauses in the work.

(*b*) The operation had to be carried out deliberately with special stress upon accuracy. This category included certain highly skilled trade and craft operations.

The age distributions of men and women on operations in these two classes of work are shown in Fig. 5.2. Although the distributions overlap, those for work involving time-stress are substantially lower, and include practically no men or women beyond the middle fifties. The objection can be raised to the data of Fig. 5.2 that many of the time-stressed operations may have been newly installed so that the men and women on them would not have had time to reach the higher ages. Operations known to have been started recently had been excluded from the sample, but the effect could easily persist for twenty or so years. To obtain some check upon this Belbin (1953) made a reclassification, including an extended sample of women's operations, according to whether or not *moves with age* were reported. These were taken to occur when men or women were moved to lower-paid work before retiring age because of failing performance, strain or difficulty not attributed to ill health. The classification was again crude and relied upon the accuracy of statements by supervisory staff, but within these limitations appeared to be stringent. Belbin's reclassification was found to give results which closely resembled those in Fig. 5.2.

Further examination of the characteristics of the operations revealed that moves with age were associated with *pacing* and with conditions demanding *continuous bodily movement and activity* although not necessarily heavy physical exertion. The association is strikingly shown in Table 5.3. What is the nature of the demand

TABLE 5.3. *The relationship between operations from which there were moves with age and those on which pacing and continuous bodily movement and activity occurred*

	Moves with age	No moves with age
Operations involving both pacing and continuous bodily movement and activity	10	1
Operations involving pacing without continuous bodily movement and activity	3	3
Operations involving continuous bodily movement and activity without pacing.	6	7
Operations involving neither continuous bodily movement and activity nor pacing	0	77

made by 'continuous bodily movement and activity' we cannot say on the present evidence. At first sight it seems likely to result in physical exhaustion, although if this were so we might expect older people to be less tolerant of heavy work than, as we shall discuss

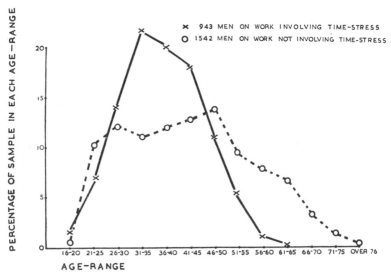

FIG. 5.2*a*. Age distributions of men on operations with and without time-stress

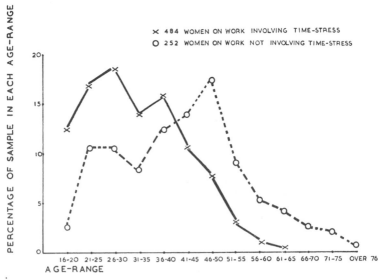

FIG. 5.2*b*. Age distributions of women on operations with and without time-stress

later, they appear to be. It seems possible that the essential demand is for the sensori-motor control of body movement, and that the difficulties shown by older people are again due to slowing of such control.

This table and Fig. 5.2 taken together imply that in the original sample, operations involving *speed-pressure* as opposed to pacing had young working groups from which no moves with age were reported. There seem to be two possible reasons why this might be so, each of which would merit further study. Firstly, it may have been that moves were in fact made which were at least partly conditioned by age but were attributed to other causes. Secondly, the operations may have been recently established and have recruited entirely young labour. In this latter case it would seem important to try older people on them as a test of the correctness of the recruitment policy. Even if such an experiment failed it would be worthwhile re-examining some of these operations after ten or twenty years to see whether men and women placed on them when young could continue to a relatively late age.

Perhaps the most striking feature of these results is the rather sudden fall around the age of 50 in numbers employed on operations which are difficult for older people. This was especially true of paced operations and would seem to be analogous to the sharp fall of performance between the forties and fifties in Brown's paced task.

ACCIDENTS

Slowness is almost certainly the cause of many, perhaps most, accidents to older people. King and Speakman (1953) reviewing the literature on industrial accidents in relation to age point out, however, that accident statistics are often difficult to interpret because if older people tend to do different work from younger they will be exposed to different risks. Even where people of different ages are doing nominally the same work small differences may still substantially affect the degree of risk. The difficulty can, however, sometimes be largely overcome by a more detailed treatment of the nature and causes of accidents or by correlating accidents with other variables. A full discussion of the relationship between accidents and age will not be attempted here: readers interested in this problem will find the main work and problems outlined in King and Speakman's paper.

The most direct evidence of a relation between slowness and accidents among older people comes from a study by Whitfield (1954) among coal miners. A group of men with high accident records were each individually matched with two other men of similar age and normal mining occupation, one with an average and one with a low record of accidents. Data were taken for each man on medical history and present medical state and tests were made of visual and auditory acuity, the former by Snellen cards with varying degrees of dark adaptation, the latter by a differential threshold test. A battery of perceptual, cognitive and memory-function tests were also given together with two tracking tasks, the Craik 'triple-tester' and an intermittent tracking task by Davis (1949).

TABLE 5.4. *Correlations comparing accident group with other coal miners*

Measure	Age group			
	20–27	*33–45*	*42–51*	*53–66*
Visual acuity . . .	−0·211	+0·183	+0·485*	+0·073
Auditory acuity . . .	−0·061	−0·147	+0·266	+0·555*
Stated weight . . .	+0·533	+0·341	−0·051	−0·035
Physique	+0·401		−0·124	
Directions test . . .	−0·312*		+0·100	
Visual-cognitive tests . .	−0·452*	−0·415	+0·368*	−0·032
Tracking tasks . . .	+0·046	−0·158	−0·449*	−0·232

A positive correlation means that the accident group performed *better* than the others.

An asterisk indicates statistical significance beyond the 5 per cent. level.

The relevant portion, for our present purpose, of the results is given in Table 5.4. The correlations in this table show, rather surprisingly, little relation between acuity and accidents in any age group—the only two significant correlations are contrary to what might be expected and are in the direction of the accident-prone men having better acuity. In respect of other characteristics younger and older accident-prone men tended to be very different. The younger tended to be heavy, with powerful physique, and to perform poorly on the perceptual, memory and cognitive tests, but to show little or no impairment on the tracking tasks. The older accident-prone men showed average or above-average performances at the perceptual and cognitive tests but tended to do worse at the tracking tasks.

Whitfield points out that 'if an accident is considered as a failure to make an adequate response to a hazardous situation' it could arise either because of '(a) failure to appreciate the demands of the situation . . . to perceive the hazard or to decide what, if any, response ought to be made, or (b) . . . failure adequately to produce the appropriate response, even though the hazard has been perceived and the appropriate course of action initiated'. He suggests that his younger accident-prone subjects tended to fail in the first respect and his older in the second.

Discussing explanations for his results Whitfield recognizes the possible influences of such factors as selection due to the most accident-prone men leaving, and changes in recruitment over the years. He points out, however, that the data support a more direct explanation which also carries practical implications about methods of accident prevention. The older accident-prone men, he suggests, are those with good or at least normal perceptual and cognitive ability who are deficient in motor control. When young this may not be serious and in any case adequate compensation may be possible by anticipating hazards before the situation becomes pressing. As age advances, however, deterioration of sensori-motor performance gradually takes place and eventually a point is reached at which it is too slow to deal with an emergency. As regards the young accident-prone men, their carelessness—one might say stupidity—combined with a physique and level of activity better than average leads them to take risks they fail to appreciate. With age, however, their activity wanes and in consequence they cease to expose themselves to the same risks as formerly.

An analysis by King (1955b) of nearly 2,000 accidents sustained by agricultural workers showed that whereas the overall accident rate varied little with age, the causes of accident, nature of injury and part of the body injured varied substantially. The causes are set out in Table 5.5 from which it can be seen that the greatest increases with age are in falls. The increase of deaths from falls with age is well known from such sources as the Registrar-General's Statistical Reviews, information from some of which, together with American data, has been summarized by King and Speakman (1953). The high incidence of non-fatal falls by *old* people has been noted by Sheldon (1948) and by Droller (1955). The latter has produced evidence to show that such falls are not associated, as has sometimes been supposed, with vertigo or with visual defects. He did, however, find a substantial relation between falls and extensor plantar reflex from which he concluded that they were due to 'involutionary changes in the central nervous system'. We do not know whether this is the explanation of the substantial increase in the number of falls in middle age shown both in King's sample and in the Registrar-General's statistics, but whatever the ultimate cause the immediate

TABLE 5.5. *Causes of agricultural accidents*

Cause	Number of cases	Percentages of each kind of accident by age groups					
		15–20	*21–30*	*31–40*	*41–50*	*51–60*	*61–80*
Increases with age							
Falls from heights or machines	252	7·6	8·4	10·5	14·5	19·2	16·4
Falls through slipping or tripping on ground .	201	3·8	6·3	9·4	13·4	11·0	16·4
Hit by falling or moving object	339	14·0	15·7	13·9	17·6	21·4	21·3
Decreases with age							
Caught in machine . .	202	13·4	11·8	11·5	9·1	7·9	6·6
Injury inflicted by own tool	184	13·4	11·8	10·7	5·8	6·6	9·3
Continued activity . .	127	4·5	9·2	7·9	6·2	2·8	4·4
Starting an engine . .	98	12·7	7·9	4·1	4·5	1·3	1·1
No significant change with age							
Moving heavy objects .	103	3·2	4·8	6·8	4·2	7·5	1·6
Knocked against, or trod on, object . . .	90	6·4	3·6	5·3	4·9	3·4	3·8
Action of animals* . .	79	1·3	3·9	4·3	4·2	5·3	2·7
Trapped, other than in machine . . .	48	1·3	3·1	1·9	2·7	1·6	3·8
Miscellaneous . . .	127	9·5	6·0	7·7	4·7	6·0	6·0
Cause not specified . .	141	8·9	7·5	6·0	8·2	6·0	6·6
Total . . .	1,991	100	100	100	100	100	100

* Some cases in which animals were involved were classified under 'Hit by falling or moving object'. This group constitutes the remainder.

one in the majority of cases is almost certainly failure to take rapid enough correcting action when thrown off balance either by the vagary of some internal mechanism or by an external agent. It is reasonable to suppose, as Sheldon has suggested in a private communication, that at least much of the increase of falls with age is attributable to slower sensori-motor control. The same could be said of the only other category of accident in King's table which showed a significant increase with age, namely: 'Hit by falling or moving object.'

Of the causes of accident in King's sample which declined with age 'Starting an engine' was almost certainly due to the fact that tractor drivers tend to be young men (King 1953). Avoidance of sinovitis and other ailments due to 'Continued activity' perhaps reflects greater caution and experience by older men while avoidance of becoming 'Caught in a machine' or of 'Injury inflicted by own tool' are probably the result of greater accuracy by older people in the manner evidenced by the experiments discussed in Chapter IV.

Before leaving the subject of accidents one further point needs to be made regarding the nature of the slowness that may cause them. Anyone familiar with road-safety posters will have met the term 'thinking time' for the reaction time between the occurrence of an emergency and the initiation of action to deal with it. The time is usually assumed to be wholly occupied by perception of the events which constitute the emergency and by organizing the responding action. According, however, to the 'intermittency' principle outlined in Chapter II, there will be, in addition to the time for perception and organization of response, the time required to finish the perception and organization of the response already in progress when the emergency occurs and to switch over from the one to the other. The additional time may be appreciable and, in that reaction times increase with age, will increase proportionately among older people.

The tendency noted by Brown (p. 69) for older people to plan ahead more than younger raises the question of whether this delay may not in fact increase *dis*proportionately with age. There is no definite evidence on this point, but it would seem possible that, in spite of the shorter span of 'motor tactics' shown by older people in the sense that a series of actions does not seem to be as easily welded into a rhythm as it is by younger people, they tend to lay down a longer 'strategy' ahead. If so, they are committed by any decision to a longer series of actions, and if their attention is once engaged by some extraneous event it may take a disproportionate time to return to the main task. This possibility came to the author's attention as a possible explanation of a number of road accidents which are sustained by older people and seem to be due to their deciding upon a course of action and then carrying it through in spite of a change in the traffic conditions. If a tendency of this kind could be demonstrated the danger could probably be greatly reduced if older people were made aware of its existence.

HEAVY WORK

One of the commonest assumptions about the employment of older people is that heavy work is unsuitable for them. This view would appear to accord well with the physiological findings that maximum instantaneous muscular strength, exercise tolerance and rate of recovery from exertion all show declines with age (Cathcart *et al.* 1935; Fisher and Birren 1947; Simonson 1947; Shock 1947; Cullumbine *et al.* 1950; Hugh-Jones 1952), but it would appear to be at variance with the records of work in industry upon which older people are actually employed (Industrial Welfare Society 1950; Thomas and Osborne 1950).

The pioneer study was made by Barkin (1933) during the depression in the United States between the two world wars. His results in this field have been well summarized by Belbin (1955) as follows:

Barkin presented data on the type of work in which people of different ages tended to be found in industry. Industrial work was divided into five main groups: hand work, body work, machine work, clerical work and supervisory and technical work. Barkin observed:

'The most striking fact presented by a study of the persons engaged at various types of work is that the percentage of persons at body work increased with advancing age, particularly after 35 years of age. While 21·3% of the persons 30–34 years were employed at such work, this percentage rose to 25·6 for the age group 40–44 years, to 28·7 for the age group 50–54 years, to 34·3 for the age group 60–64 years, and to 37·5 for the age group 70 years and over.'

Body work was defined as 'that type of work which is performed by the application of bodily strength or by the use of large tools demanding bodily movements'. In a further analysis operations were divided into three grades according to the degree of physical exertion imposed—great, medium, and slight. The smallest percentage engaged on work requiring great physical exertion was in the youngest age group (5·4%), the percentage increasing with each demi-decade up to 18 in the 40–44 age group and thereafter declining by not more than 1% per demi-decade up to the age group 70 and over where the percentage fell to 12·4. Even more striking were the results which Barkin obtained for those newly hired.

'The group where the older person as a class possesses the greatest hold,' he observed, 'is that in which the job demands great physical exertion. Approximately 26% of all the persons hired for such jobs were 40 years and over. The others follow in inverse proportion to the degree of physical exertion which is needed. Twenty-five per cent. of the men added to jobs grouped as requiring medium physical exertion were beyond 40 years of age. The proportion, however, for those requiring slight physical exertion was only 15%. . . . Among the women workers the largest percentage of older females hired in any one single class is also to be found in the jobs requiring great physical exertion (13·3). The other two classes follow in the same order as for the males, medium (12·6%) and then slight (9·7).'

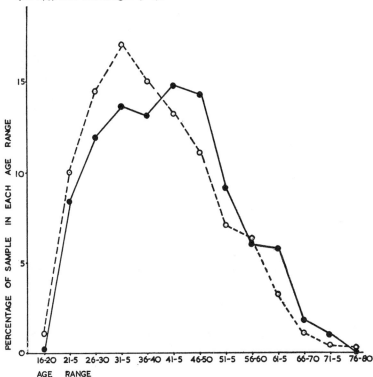

FIG. 5.3. Age distributions of men engaged in a sample of heavy and light operations

Filled circles: 1,240 men on heavy operations.
Open circles: 853 men on light operations.

Barkin's sample covered both production and non-production work. Shooter and Belbin, studying only production operations, found that the age distribution of men on those classed as heavy in the sense that they required the lifting and moving of heavy objects and strenuous exertion, was at least as high—indeed a little higher— than that for other operations. Their results are shown in Fig. 5.3 which may be compared with the analysis of the same data in terms of time-stress in Fig. 5.2. A similar picture emerges from an analysis by Belbin (1955) of information contained in the 1951 Census. We should note that all these findings are from studies of the actual jobs on which people are employed and not from surveys of whole industries. They are thus not subject to the possible fallacy that although the proportion of older men in heavy industry is higher than in light they may nevertheless be employed on the lighter jobs.

These results would seem inevitably to mean that at least a substantial proportion of older people can do at least a substantial proportion of heavy jobs to a standard which makes it economic to employ them, and that for the people engaged on them these jobs do not make demands which they are physiologically incapable of meeting. This does not, however, imply that heavy work in general is suitable for the large majority of older people. Data by Richardson (1953) which will be discussed shortly show that older people on heavy work are to some extent selected, and it may well be that experience and skill sometimes enable an older man to do a heavy job with less effort than a younger. The results in Figs. 5.3 and 5.2 taken together would seem to imply, however, that the demands for heavy muscular exertion may often be less taxing to older people than demands of many light jobs for speed.

One possible argument against this last conclusion is that heavy operations tend to be those which have been long established and that new recruits have been placed on the newer, more highly mechanized and lighter operations, leaving the heavy operations with a relatively old labour force. A close study by Belbin (1955) indicates, however, that this is unlikely to be the sole explanation. The study was made in certain departments of a firm manufacturing batteries where the men periodically changed jobs to minimize the risk of lead poisoning. The jobs were graded by the firm's time-study department according to the degree of physical exertion required into five grades ranging from I 'very heavy' to V 'light', and the percentage of work done by men of various ages on each grade was computed. The results, given in Table 5.6, show clearly that the heaviest jobs had the highest proportion of work done by older men.

The measure of work used in computing Table 5.6 was the number of job cards produced by each man on each job and suffered from the disadvantage that the number of hours represented by the cards varied within wide limits. As a check, therefore, the actual numbers of hours worked was calculated for all the men over 55 and for a sample aged 25–35 with results given in Table 5.7. It can be seen that practically all the very heavy work was done by the older men and all the light work by the younger.

Evidence of a different kind and import is contained in a study by Richardson who interviewed 489 men over the age of 50 in two foundries and a coal-mine. He found in the latter that as one passed

TABLE 5.6. *Percentage of work done by older workers according to degree of physical exertion required*

	I	II	III	IV	V
Number of operations in each grade .	4	4	11	12	3
Number of persons who worked in each grade	35	63	283	312	90
Percentage of work done by under 50's .	35·8	81·7	71·1	73·5	89·5
Percentage of work done by age group 50–54	23·5	14·2	17·7	13·8	10·5
Percentage of work done by age group 55–59	23·4	3·9	9·1	7·5	0
Percentage of work done by age group 60+	17·3	0·2	2·1	5·2	0

I = very heavy.   V = light

TABLE 5.7. *Hours spent on work graded according to physical exertion (to nearest hour)*

No. in sample	Age group	I	II	III	IV	V
22	55–65	2,311	2,312	16,707	14,436	0
22	25–35	73	5,572	17,917	13,203	503

from the fifties to the seventies there was a significant change in the proportions of men on heavy, medium and light work in the direction of older men being on lighter jobs. He found, further, that in all three establishments about 60 per cent. of the men interviewed had at one time in their lives changed to lighter work. The frequency of change appeared to be low up to the thirties, to rise a little in the forties, and to increase sharply thereafter. It was clear from the changes in the foundries where the skill in the work could be graded that these moves involved a great many of the men concerned in a reduction in the skill of their jobs and were therefore presumably made only for serious reasons. The figures are given in Table 5.8.

Two significant points emerge from the reasons given for these moves to lighter work. The first is that although 62 per cent. of the men who changed stated that the reason why they did so was illness or injury, these were often of a minor nature from which the men had recovered quickly and completely. 'It seemed', as Richardson put it, 'that many men carried on in heavy work under an increasing strain until a "trigger-factor" such as illness or injury supervened and

TABLE 5.8. *Numbers of men transferring to lighter work in two foundries, classed according to degree of skill*

Age at interview	Skilled	Semi-skilled	Unskilled
50–59			
Before transfer	51	23	16
After transfer	25	15	50
60–69			
Before transfer	40	18	15
After transfer	15	8	50
70–79			
Before transfer	5	2	..
After transfer	1	3	3

the decision to change to lighter work was made.' Other factors precipitating change appeared to be the sudden death or illness of a fellow heavy worker, the closing down of the colliery at which they had worked necessitating a change of *place* of work, or the falling vacant of a desired job with light duties.

The second point was that when the men were asked what features of their work had caused them difficulty as they grew older the commonest reply was the adverse effects of speed. Richardson states: 'Indeed the most important component of "light" or "lighter" work, as these terms were used by the men interviewed was opportunity to control the pace of work and the distribution of rest pauses.' The heavy jobs were undoubtedly very strenuous, especially when combined, as most of them were, with piece-rate payment schemes, and the lighter work to which the men moved was often such as would still be regarded as heavy in a wider survey of industrial jobs. We may, therefore, reasonably suppose the desire to regulate the pace of work was, at least in many cases, for physiological work reasons rather than due to slowing of sensori-motor performance.

Conclusion on heavy work and time-stress

Richardson's findings and those from other studies of heavy work would seem, taken together, to indicate that either physiological work capacity or sensori-motor capacity can act as limiting factors to performance as age increases. Which does so would seem to depend on the demands of the task which limit its application to people of any age. Many jobs do not, of course, make high demands of either sort but are limited by other factors such as level of skill which in turn depends on training, experience and intellectual power. Among the heavy jobs it is those which are strenuous in the sense that they demand a continued effort without intermission that appear to cause most difficulty to older people. Those where occasional or discontinuous heavy muscular effort is required do not seem to be avoided by older people, at least by those who are healthy. The physiological demands of these jobs are, of course, almost certainly lower than of those demanding continual effort.

We may suppose that where the physiological demands or the speed of a job are going to set the limit to performance they are commonly adjusted to suit men in the late twenties or thirties. Men in their forties manage by greater skill and experience or by working more continuously or by some other means to maintain adequate standards in the face of some fall in physiological capacity or slowing of sensori-motor performance. They do so, however, under an increasing strain and eventually a point is reached where some precipitating factor such as a slight illness decides them—often with encouragement from home or job-mates—to change to less arduous work. The move may often be attributed to the event which has precipitated it, although the real cause lies in slow changes with age which have been gradually accumulating over many years. The crucial age in the case of time-stressed work appears to be in the late forties or early fifties, and in the case of strenuous physical work in the fifties or early sixties.

When the change comes it may sometimes, as Le Gros Clark (1954; 1955) has shown for the building industry, be to a similar job under less severe conditions, as when building tradesmen move to maintenance work. This is often a very satisfactory arrangement: it means that they do less in any given time but where work is spasmodic and very varied, as it frequently is in maintenance, an older man may not achieve appreciably less than would a younger. Where such a move is not possible it is important to recognize that a change from very strenuous work must be to lighter work which does not at the same time impose time-stress. It would, for example, be inappropriate to transfer miners in late middle or old age to light assembly work in a factory. At the same time, moves with age from light time-stressed work appear sometimes to be made successfully to work which is slower but actually heavier. The heaviness is not so severe as to make the work strenuous, and the slower performance required once more restores the ability to match demand with capacity.

Perhaps the most fundamental point which emerges from the studies of heavy work is the need for a definition of the term 'heavy'. Work at present called heavy seems to be of many kinds. We have already presented evidence that a distinction should be drawn between maximum instantaneous effort and integrated effort over time, and that the latter seems to impose a more severe limitation with age than does the former. On the other hand, some heavy work seems to be so classed mainly because it is dangerous, demanding either physical fitness and maintenance of balance such as when working at heights, or vigilance as when handling dangerous materials or working in a hazardous environment. Again, it may be that sometimes 'heaviness' lies in 'mental' demands for responsibility or sensori-motor speed. It is probable that heavy work as usually conceived means work which 'takes it out of you' in any of several ways, and that it is not really correct to think of all types of heavy work as belonging to a single class. Assessment and measurement of work in terms of demands such as those listed here would greatly clarify what is at present a confused area of ageing research. They would open up the way to a much more precise specification of work suitable for older people, and suggest ways in which some of their existing difficulties could be removed.

VI

TRANSLATION PROCESSES

THE evidence surveyed in the previous chapters suggests that the difficulty for older people in many sensori-motor tasks lies in what we have termed translation processes. Translation of one kind has been studied many years ago in relation to age by means of 'substitution' tests. The subject's task in these was to substitute one set of symbols for another according to a more or less arbitrary code. Results such as those of Willoughby (1929) in Fig. 6.1 have shown

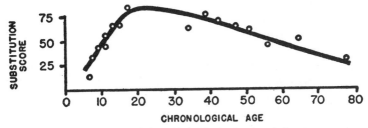

FIG. 6.1. Scores for digit-symbol substitution in relation to age

substantial falls of performance from young adulthood onwards. In the present chapter a series of experiments will be discussed which have specifically explored the effects at different ages of complications in the relationship between display and control and the insertion of intervening 'steps' or judgements between perception and responding action. Such complications appear to have effects, sometimes small, sometimes profound, upon the performance of older people which are not attributable to either perceptual or motor limitation. They are likely also to be of considerable practical importance since complication of the relationship between display and control appears to be a very common result of replacing hand work by mechanized operation in industry.

We may begin with an experiment by Szafran, in which the subjects were required to throw loops of light chain about 3 inches long at a target flat on the floor 8 feet away. The target was made of strips of fibre board, intersecting in 'egg-box' fashion to form forty-nine (7 × 7) 3-inch square open-topped boxes. The edges of the centre box were painted white to act as a 'bull's-eye' and all slanted forwards so that the subjects could see into them and observe where the chains fell.

Each subject threw fifty chains under each of three conditions which were presented in different orders to different subjects to balance practice effects:

A. In this, the simplest condition, the subjects threw directly at the target. The task thus presented a straightforward static display and required an action which, while involving highly complex timing and co-ordination of movement and posture, was familiar and did not require any great muscular effort.

B. The display was essentially the same as in condition A, but the motor performance was complicated by requiring the subjects to throw over a horizontal bar set 32 inches from the ground and $5\frac{1}{2}$ feet away. The target could be seen uninterruptedly beneath the bar.

C. Both the visual display and the motor performance were complicated by requiring the subjects to throw over a screen of the same height and at the same distance as the bar in condition B. The screen hid the target from view, so that it could be seen only in a mirror placed behind it. In this condition, the target was turned round so that the subject could still see into the boxes and obtain knowledge of the results of his throwing by looking in the mirror. The effect of this arrangement was to present the subject with the same motor task as condition B, but to require him to perform it in relation to a display which had its 'far-near' dimension reversed, and which was seen at a place other than that to which he had to direct his aim.

The results were scored not only in terms of time and of distance from the 'bull's-eye' on the 'far-near' and 'left-right' dimensions separately, but also in terms of the position of each chain thrown in relation to the one before. This latter scoring gave an indication of over- and under-corrections and thus some indication of the method whereby the achievement in the time and accuracy scores was attained.

Fig. 6.2 and Tables 6.1 and 6.2 indicate that with throwing *direct* and over the *bar* no significant deterioration of achievement or change of method took place. Similar results for direct throwing had been obtained in an earlier experiment by Gillian C. Webb with subjects ranging from the late 'teens to the seventies—most of them the same as those who acted in the grid-matching experiment (p. 66). It would appear that either the capacities demanded both by direct throwing and by the more complicated motor task of throwing over the bar are unaffected by age or that adequate compensation is made for any deficiencies. Evidence that some such compensation was occurring was shown in the way subjects approached the tasks.

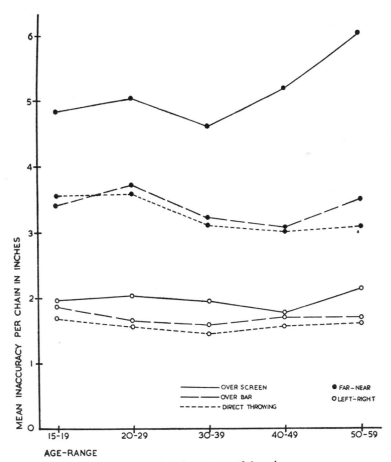

FIG. 6.2. Mean inaccuracy of throwing

The only substantial rise of inaccuracy with age was on the far-near dimension when throwing over the screen.

Those in their 'teens and twenties tended to adopt a somewhat happy-go-lucky manner, and while seeming interested in doing their best, did not appear to make any great effort to do so. Those over 30 tended to show a much more concentrated and careful performance.

TABLE 6.1. *Mean times to throw 50 chains*

Seconds per subject

		Age range				
		15–19	*20–29*	*30–39*	*40–49*	*50–59*
Condition of throwing						
Direct . . .		156	140	153	143	147
Over bar . . .		155	142	153	148	149
Over screen . .		154	151	165	159	169
Ratios						
Bar/direct . .		0·994	1·01	1·00	1·03	1·01
Screen/bar . .		0·994	1·06	1·08	1·07	1·13
Screen/direct .		0·987	1·08	1·08	1·11	1·15

TABLE 6.2. *Percentages of error due to under- and over-corrections in throwing*

Condition of throwing	Type of correction	Age range				
		15–19	*20–29*	*30–39*	*40–49*	*50–59*
Far-near dimension						
A (Direct) .	Under	20	21	21	21	18
	Over .	37	31	34	38	34
B (Bar) .	Under	18	21	25	17	22
	Over	35	36	28	36	38
C (Screen) .	Under	*32*	*33*	*36*	*39*	*41*
	Over	*21*	*21*	*15*	*15*	*12*
Left-right dimension						
A (Direct) .	Under	27	22	23	26	21
	Over	22	18	20	18	24
B (Bar) .	Under	25	26	25	25	22
	Over	22	25	23	21	25
C (Screen) .	Under	*29*	*33*	*25*	*27*	*22*
	Over	*20*	*22*	*22*	*23*	*27*

In the screen condition the percentage of error due to under-correction on the far-near dimension tended to rise with age but the percentage due to over-correction tended to fall. These trends were reversed on the left-right dimension. No consistent trends were observed in the direct and bar conditions.

The results for throwing over the screen showed more striking changes with age. As regards accuracy, the left-right dimension—which did, of course, remain unreversed by the mirror—was little affected. On the far-near dimension, however, inaccuracy was very much greater in all groups of subjects and, relatively to that in other conditions, rose continuously with age, as shown in Table 6.3. There was a similar rise with age in the times taken, as set out in Table 6.1.

TABLE 6.3. *Ratios of errors made under three conditions of throwing. Far-near dimension only*

Ratio	Age range				
	15–19	*20–29*	*30–39*	*40–49*	*50–59*
Bar/direct	0·96	1·04	1·04	1·03	1·14
Screen/bar	1·42	1·36	1·44	1·69	1·72
Screen/direct . . .	1·36	1·41	1·49	1·74	1·96

Considering accuracy and time together it is clear that the complication of the display-control relationship resulting from the screen and mirror caused more difficulty to the older subjects than it did to the younger. As in other experiments, however, it seemed that some compensation was attempted. This was done by making less correction for error on the difficult far-near dimension and more on the left-right dimension which was easier to comprehend. It can be seen from Table 6.2 that on the far-near dimension the percentage of error due to under-correction rose and the percentage due to over-correction fell with age, indicating a kind of 'rigidity' on the part of the older subjects in that they were tending to throw successive chains to the same part of the target. The opposite trends were shown, although less consistently, on the left-right dimension. The trends are summed up in Fig. 6.3 which shows strikingly the pattern of corrections changing with age.

Lowering of performance by older people at tasks involving eye-hand co-ordination via a mirror, has also been shown, although in less detail, by Snoddy (1926) and by Ruch (1934). The former attributes it to the older subjects learning the required new co-ordination more slowly than the younger. The latter regards the mirror as introducing a conflict with previous habits which impairs the performance of older subjects more than that of younger.

Both these factors doubtless play a part, especially if the attainment of rapid co-ordination over a long period of practice is considered, but for short-duration tasks such as Szafran's they would seem to miss the core of the problem. Anyone who has tried a mirror task will almost certainly have found that initially, and at least for a considerable period of practice, he has not really built a co-ordination which translates *directly* from what is seen to what is done.

There is hesitation and usually some considerable effort of imagination to, as it were, 'turn the display round mentally', or a conscious effort to use a 'rule of procedure'. The mirror does, in short, require the insertion of some additional process or stage in the translation

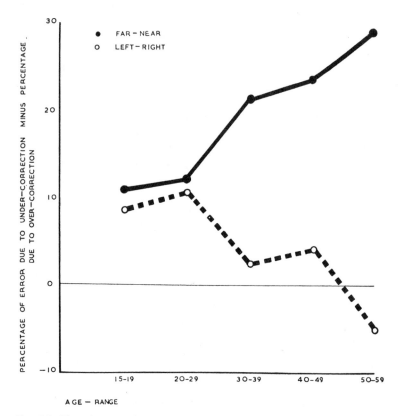

FIG. 6.3. Throwing over the screen. Differences between the percentages of error due to under- and over-correction

On the far-near dimension the percentage of error due to under-correction became progressively greater than that due to over-correction as age increased. The opposite tendency was shown on the left-right dimension.

from display to action and the fundamental question would seem to be why such an extra stage causes difficulty for older people and whether some types of stage cause more difficulty than others.

What little further work there is on this problem in relation to age is as yet mainly exploratory. It may conveniently be described under four heads:

(a) Attempts at a more precise localization of the difficulty in mirror-image reversals.

(b) Translation from one sensory mode to another.

(c) Simple spatial transpositions other than mirror reversals.

(d) The combination of two translations in the same task.

(a) Further work on mirror image reversals

Some evidence regarding the extent to which difficulty in mirror tasks results from the need to run counter to an established *motor habit*, is contained in the results of the figure-tracing experiment described in Chapter IV. From Fig. 4.4 (p. 73) it can be seen that the older people tended to take longer than the younger when first confronted with the task of tracing reversed figures after normal ones. Observation of the subjects confirmed that part at least of the difficulty did lie in the upsetting of previous habits of movement. The younger subjects tended to treat the reversed figures as nonsense shapes and to trace them as such. The older treated the reversed figures for what they were and often seemed to hesitate before beginning each, as if to get clear what movement to make.

The extra time taken to trace the reversed figures was, however, relatively small. It was certainly much less than the extra time taken to *write* reversed figures as compared with writing them the normal way round. The results for the writing stages of the figure-tracing experiment, which were given in Table 4.5 (p. 74), show that the times to write reversed figures, even after tracing them five times, were still some two or three times as long as the times required to write them the normal way round, and that the increase of time was much greater among the older subjects.

It seemed likely, when considering the results of this experiment, that the important difference between tracing and writing lay in the fact that in the former the subject had a definite visual display laid out in front of him that he could follow but in the latter he was required to construct, as it were, his own imaginary display, and it was the need to effect a mirror image reversal of the display in imagination that was the source of difficulty for the older subjects. Such a difficulty would be well in line with the results of a number of intelligence and other similar tests such as Raven's Matrices, where for some items the subject's task is to effect a spatial transposition in his head. Foulds and Raven (1948) have shown substantial declines with age on this test (see p. 229).

Additional evidence pointing in the same direction is contained in a series of experiments by Szafran (1953). The groups he used were small, but the results seem clear enough. The series consisted of four experiments.

1. In the first, subjects were required to move a pencil along a groove $\frac{1}{8}$ inch wide, pressed into a metal plate, seen via a mirror in front of them. The plate was hidden from view by a screen. The groove followed a wavy pattern with fourteen reversals of direction. In the instructions the task was compared to 'driving a motor along the road as quickly as possible without getting off the road'. It was not possible to record the errors made in the sense of the number of times subjects left the groove, but any such errors were likely to increase somewhat the time taken, owing to the need for the subject to return to the groove before proceeding. The times may therefore be regarded as a reasonably accurate indication of overall performance. They are set out in Fig. 6.4(a) and show that the older subjects, although tending to be slower during the first few trials, quickly arrived at approximate equality with the younger. The groove in this task did, of course, provide a means to guide the subject's hand by 'feel', without reference to what could be seen in the mirror, and to the extent that this was so, it was not really a mirror task at all. The equality of the older and younger subjects was probably due to this fact.

2. In the second experiment the groove was replaced by a wavy track about 1 inch wide, drawn on paper. The results, shown in Fig. 6.4(b), indicated that this resulted in a substantial slowing of performance, especially among the older subjects. Part of this appeared to be due to 'blockages', the subject being unable to decide for an appreciable time which way to move. These were commoner among older subjects, especially during the early trials, but tended to disappear with practice.

3. The plates used in the figure-tracing experiment (p. 71) were presented to the subjects so that they could be seen via a mirror, direct vision again being screened. The plate was positioned in such a way that the normal figures were seen reversed and the reversed figures were seen normal way round. As in Brown's original experiment, errors were indicated by a buzzer when the stylus ran over the boundaries of the figures on to the plate. The results, shown in

Table 6.4, indicate that there was some, although not very much, difference between the age groups in respect of speed, but that the forties and fifties made substantially more errors, with both normal and reversed figures, than the twenties and thirties. There was, however,

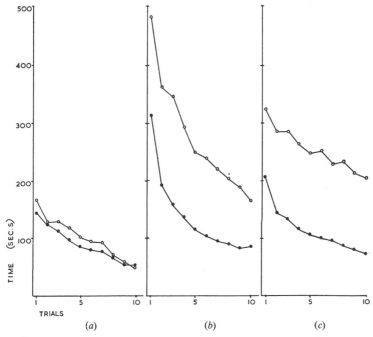

FIG. 6.4. Times taken over three mirror tasks as a function of practice and age. Means per subject

(a) Following groove. (b) Following track on paper. (c) Writing figures to appear normal in mirror.

Filled circles: twenties and thirties.
Open circles: forties and fifties.

very little difference in either age group between normal and reversed figures. The tracing of familiar and unfamiliar figures hardly enters here, because in order that the figures should appear right way up in the mirror, they had to be traced upside-down by the subject. What *is* indicated is that for a tracing task it makes little difference whether the display takes a familiar form or not. Taking this result, together with that obtained in Brown's original experiment, we see that the reversal of either display or responding action, did not by itself account for much lowering of performance with age. The difficulty for older people would seem to be attributable clearly to the relationship between display and action.

Comparing this experiment with the previous one, the difficulty appears to have resulted in one case in an increase of time and in the other an increase of errors. What is the cause of this difference is not clear, but as we have seen in previous chapters, the two tend, in circumstances such as these, to be inversely related.

TABLE 6.4. *Figure tracing in mirror. Times and errors*

Means per subject

Figures seen in mirror	Unreversed			Reversed		
Trials	1	2	3	1	2	3
Times in seconds						
Twenties and thirties .	200	156	127	196	149	128
Forties and fifties . .	211	179	141	200	158	146
Errors						
Twenties and thirties .	3·0	2·3	1·7	3·4	2·3	2·1
Forties and fifties . .	13·8	8·0	6·8	14·3	9·1	8·5

4. In the last of this group of experiments, the subjects were required to write on a sheet of paper, screened from direct view, the figures, 1 2 3 4 5 6 7 8 9 X, so that they appeared normal when seen in a mirror in front. The task did, of course, differ from that of the third experiment in that the subjects had to create their own display in imagination, instead of merely tracing one provided. As in Brown's previous experiment, the lack of display resulted in the task becoming very much more difficult, especially for older people. The results in Fig. 6.4(c) show the older subjects at a relatively severe disadvantage, taking on average about twice as long as the younger.

It should be noted as an incidental finding, that the learning curves in Fig. 6.4 give little support to Snoddy's (1926) contention that the shape of the learning curve for older people is radically different from that for younger.

The results of these four experiments, together with those of Brown's original Figure Tracing study, are summed up in Table 6.5. It can be seen that of the four tasks for which there was no mirror or the mirror could be ignored two—writing normal way and following the groove—showed relatively little rise of time with age, one—tracing—showed a greater rise of time but with a compensatory fall of errors and only one—reversed writing—showed a substantial rise of time. This last is, as we have seen, different from the others in that the figures had to be 'turned round' in the subject's imagination in

TABLE 6.5. *Ratios of scores by subjects in the forties and fifties to those by subjects in the twenties and thirties in five experiments*

	Times	Errors
Tasks not involving or not requiring the use of a mirror		
Brown's Figure Tracing Experiment:		
Writing figures normal way	1·13	..
Writing figures reversed	1·60	..
Tracing figures	1·37	0·51
Following groove with stylus	1·12	..
Tasks requiring the use of a mirror		
Following track on paper	2·00	..
Drawing figures so that they are seen normally in mirror.	2·20	..
Tracing figures:		
Seen unreversed in mirror	1·10	4·09
Seen reversed in mirror	1·07	4·09

order to guide his action: in other words, a mirror image reversal was in fact required. The other four tasks in which reference to the mirror was required all showed a substantial rise with age in either time or errors. Within these four, such comparisons as can be made reveal relatively minor differences. Thus the two figure-tracing tasks using the mirror show practically identical age differences, and the rises with age in the two other tasks are very similar. It would thus appear that although the change with age was shown in different ways for the different tasks—in times for two and in errors for two—little age-change resulted from the differences within either type of task. These were essentially attributable to the *display*, such as reversing the figures to be traced or having an imagined display as opposed to a track to follow. The evidence thus indicated that the change of performance with age in mirror tasks is due mainly to the need to effect an 'imaginary reversal' in order to 'normalize' the relationships between display and control and is to only a limited extent due to the disturbance of motor habits or to any purely perceptual factor.

(b) Translation from one sensory mode to another

An experiment by Szafran, involving the relating of visual to kinaesthetic data, indicates that some difficulty may upon occasion arise from this source, although its importance is probably small compared with other factors. The experiment required the subject to move his hand horizontally over a distance of 12 inches to an end-stop and back again to the starting-point, blindfolded. The subject was seated at a table, holding a pencil in his dominant hand, and made his movements under each of two conditions. In one of these, after the completion of each movement, the experimenter moved the subject's hand in a circle over the table and then placed it again at the starting-point. In the other condition, after completion of each movement the subject lifted his blindfold, noted how far his previous movement had been in error, and himself returned to the appropriate starting-point. For some subjects, the starting-point was opposite the midline of the body and the movement was made towards the dominant side. For others, the end-point was opposite the midline, and the movement was made inwards from the dominant side and out again.

The results are set out in Table 6.6. In the first condition, which

TABLE 6.6. *Making hand movements 'blind' with and without 'knowledge of results'*

Mean errors and times per subject per movement

	Age group		
	18–29	*30–49*	*50–69*
Errors in inches			
Without knowledge of results . . .	0·85	0·83	0·99
With knowledge	0·59	0·63	0·95
Difference	0·26	0·20	0·04
Times in seconds			
Without knowledge of results . . .	4·1	3·6	4·2
With knowledge	4·0	3·7	4·6

The first movement in the 'With knowledge' condition was, for obvious reasons, not scored.

did not permit 'knowledge of results', the older subjects were a little less accurate than the younger, but the difference was small and not significant. In the second condition where visual knowledge of results was obtained, the young subjects showed markedly better performance than in the first, whereas the performance of the older subjects was relatively little changed. This could not have been due to a practice or a fatigue effect, since about half the subjects took the conditions in the order stated and the other half performed them in the opposite order. It appeared that the older subjects were less able than the younger to make use of the visual knowledge of results given in the second condition. This was not apparently due to the older subjects forgetting what corrections to make, but rather to their tending to over-correct at one attempt their error on the previous attempt. Szafran points out that the subjects, after testing, indicated that they tended to rely entirely on 'feel' in the first condition, but experienced a good deal of visual imagery in the second. It seemed fair to conclude that the difficulty the older subjects found in making adequate use of the ability to see the extent of their errors, was due to their being unable to translate accurately from visual to kinaesthetic terms.

(c) Simple spatial transpositions

An experiment by Kay (1955a) indicates that the need to effect a simple spatial transposition may sometimes cause difficulty for older people, although again the effect would seem to be small. His subjects sat at a table and were confronted with a box containing a row of twelve small light bulbs and another box containing a corresponding row of twelve morse keys. One of the lights was on and by pressing one of the keys the subject could put it out, whereupon another would come on and could be put out by pressing another key, and so on. The experiment was presented under three different conditions. (a) The lights were placed directly above the keys and the keys and lights were connected so that the correct key was always the one immediately below the light that was on. (b) The task was the same as in condition (a) except that the lights were placed on the table 3 feet away from the keys. (c) The box containing the light bulbs was turned end to end, still at 3 feet distance.

The times taken and errors made in the various arrangements of this task are shown in Table 6.7. In the first condition there was a small but fairly consistent rise with age in time taken, but no errors appeared in any age group. Condition (b) showed a substantial rise of time in the oldest two age groups coupled with a fall in the number of errors. This result is somewhat difficult to interpret, as we do not know how much increase of time is compensated by any given fall in errors. It would seem that the change in the tempo and accuracy of performance is an indication of the first beginnings of difficulty for older people, although it certainly cannot be said to have been at all serious.

The third condition (*c*) did cause a more definite fall of performance, at least in the oldest age group where there was a fairly substantial rise of time taken with no corresponding fall in the number

TABLE 6.7. *Times and errors at a spatial transposition task by Kay*

Means per subject per run of 30 responses

Age range	Condition		
	a	*b*	*c*
	Times in seconds		
15–24	22·8	38·4	75·9
25–34	23·9	37·7	86·5
35–44	23·4	38·6	76·6
45–54	24·3	37·6	85·9
55–64	25·5	44·8	92·9
65–72	26·9	47·5	126·7
	Errors		
15–24	0	5·5	9·1
25–34	0	4·2	10·1
35–44	0	3·9	8·3
45–54	0	4·5	10·6
55–64	0	3·5	7·8
65–72	0	2·4	8·2

of errors. On the whole, however, it would seem that none of these simple spatial transpositions caused a marked deterioration of performance with age among the groups tested.

(*d*) *The combination of two translations in the same task*

Although inter-sensory translations and simple spatial transpositions do not appear to cause much difficulty to older people when each is required alone, experiments by Szafran show that they do so to an appreciable extent when they are combined, and a further experiment by Kay has shown that spatial transposition, when combined with symbolic translation, can cause very marked deterioration of performance among older subjects.

Two experiments by Szafran are relevant in this connexion. In the first, the subject sat at a table which had two levels, one 7 inches above the other. On the top level were ten disks, numbered and arranged at distances of 5 to 14 inches from a disk marked '0' at the edge. The lower level had a drawing-pin directly under this last disk. The subject could not see his arm as a black cloth was attached to the edge of the upper level and was tied round his neck. The arrange-

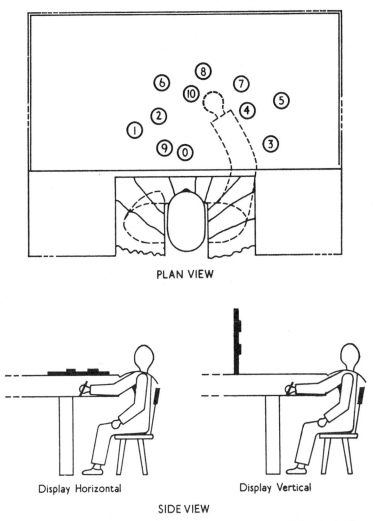

PLAN VIEW

Display Horizontal   Display Vertical

SIDE VIEW

FIG. 6.5. 'Double table' apparatus used in transposition experiment by Szafran

ment is shown in Fig. 6.5. The subject held a pencil in his hand and was required to move this from the drawing-pin on the lower level as a starting-point, over the distances indicated by the positions of the numbered disks from 1 to 10 in turn, returning to the '0' between each.

The task was done under two conditions. In the first, the upper level display was flat, like the lower level, so that the subject's task was easily conceived as that of placing his pencil at a point judged to be directly below the indicated disk in the upper level. In the second condition, the upper level was placed vertically, but the same horizontal hand movements were required. It can be seen that in both conditions a translation from a visually observed distance to a movement made without observation was required, but that in the second condition, the subject had in addition to this visual-kinaesthetic translation, to make a spatial transposition of the indicated distance from the vertical display to the horizontal responding movement. About half the subjects performed the task with the display first horizontal then vertical and half with the conditions presented in the opposite order. The results are given in Table 6.8 and show that with

TABLE 6.8. *Times and errors with two relationships between display and control in Szafran's 'double table' experiments*

Means per subject per ten movements

	Age range		
	Twenties	*Thirties and Forties*	*Fifties and Sixties*
Time (in seconds)			
Display Horizontal . . .	71	89	84
Vertical . . .	68	77	81
Total error (in inches) irrespective of sign			
Display Horizontal . . .	11·7	12·0	12·8
Vertical . . .	18·6	19·7	25·2
Difference (V–H) . . .	6·9	7·7	12·4
Ratio V/H	1·59	1·64	1·97

the display horizontal there was little rise of error with age and no very consistent rise of time taken. When the display was vertical, however, there was a consistent and substantial rise with age in both respects and it seems clear that an appreciable difficulty for older subjects arose in this second condition which was absent in the first.

Szafran's further experiment made use of the same two-storied table, together with the boxes, one of light bulbs and one of keys, used by Kay, arranged in the manner shown in Fig. 6.6. The lights were, however, obscured by a ground-glass screen, so that the subject, in judging their position, could not simply number them off from one or other end of the row. He was also prevented from counting the

morse keys by being required, instead of pressing them directly, to move a small handle mounted on a horizontal bar. Pressing a button on the handle actuated the key directly underneath. Once again the subject's arm was hidden from view by a cloth attached to the upper level of the table and tied round his neck. The subject was given initial practice to get the 'feel' of the apparatus, and then was required to make a series of movements to extents indicated by lights on the display, under two conditions—one with the display placed horizontally on the table—the other with the display vertical. The detailed procedure was as follows:

The light appeared at the left-hand end (or the bottom) of the display, with the subject's hand holding the handle at the extreme left-hand end of the rod on which it was mounted. Upon the subject's pressing a button on his control handle, the light jumped to the right (or upwards). The subject's task was to make a smooth movement of the same distance and on completion to press the button again. If the movement was correct to within $\frac{1}{2}$ inch, a buzzer rang, and the light jumped to a new position. The subject then returned to the starting-position and made a fresh movement of the extent indicated by the new light. If the movement was more than $\frac{1}{2}$ inch too long or short, the subject had to return to the starting-position and try again, continuing to make trials until he was successful in making the light move. He worked under one condition until he had made the light move fifty times, and then transferred, after a short rest, to make a similar series of 'trials' in the other condition. After each ten correct trials had been made, the subject was told his score in terms of the number correct on the first attempt and the maximum number of extra movements required when the first attempt was unsuccessful.

The experiment was on a small scale with only thirty-two subjects spread evenly over the age range of twenties to sixties, half receiving the first condition and then the second and half receiving the conditions in opposite order. There appeared, nevertheless, with the display vertical, a significant correlation between the number of movements correct at first attempt and age, the older subjects tending to have fewer successes of this kind than the others.[1] With the display horizontal, there was no detectable trend with age.

Age changes on both these experiments were, however, small com-

---

[1] This was a partial correlation obtained with score in the condition with the display horizontal and time per movement (which was correlated negatively with success) held constant.

pared with those found by Kay (1954) combining spatial transformation with a symbolic translation. The same apparatus was used as in his former experiment, with the addition of an index card carrying the numbers 1 to 12 (one for each light/key) in random order. The layout for two of the three conditions used is shown in Fig. 6.7.

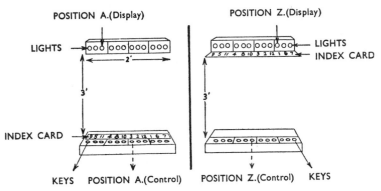

FIG. 6.7. Layout of apparatus in Kay's (1954) experiment combining spatial transposition with symbolic translation

The subjects were given the following instructions:

1. Think of the lights as being numbered 1 to 12.
2. When the light goes on, decide which number it is.
3. Find the number on the card.
4. The correct key to hit is the key in line with the number on the card.

The task was performed with the index card in three different positions. In condition (1) it was immediately above the keys, as shown on the left of Fig. 6.7. In condition (2) it was half-way between the keys and the lights, and in condition (3) it was, as shown at the right of Fig. 6.7, immediately under the lights.

The instructions applied equally to all three conditions yet surprisingly the conditions varied widely in difficulty. The times taken and errors made under each are set out in Table 6.9. Comparing the figures in this table with those in Table 6.5, it can be seen that the addition of the card and the symbolic transformation it involved added greatly to the difficulty of the task in all age ranges. The times required to make twenty responses under the easiest condition (1) are substantially longer than those required to make thirty responses under the second condition of the previous experiment. What is more, the changes with age in both times and errors are greater and more consistent. The rise with age is clear in condition (1) but is more striking in condition (2) and even more so in condition (3).

TABLE 6.9. *Times and errors in Kay's (1954) experiment*

Means per subject per run of 20 responses

Age range	Condition (1)	Condition (2)	Condition (3)
		Times in seconds	
15–24	56·4	70·8	84·8
25–34	54·2	71·7	111·6
35–44	62·0	85·7	137·1
45–54	64·1	96·3	174·7
55–64	73·7	124·8	229·3
65–72	84·7	198·7	445·3
		Total errors	
15–24	1·2	2·9	4·0
25–34	1·3	3·2	8·5
35–44	2·6	4·5	13·6
45–54	2·6	8·5	23·5
55–64	3·6	7·3	33·6
65–72	3·1	15·0	47·9

The reason for condition (3) being more difficult than (1) cannot have been due to lack of knowledge on the part of the subjects, as the three conditions were always performed in the order 1, 2, 3; nor can it have been due to fatigue, because all subjects, having completed condition (3) returned to condition (1) and showed a tendency to improve performance over their first attempt. It would appear that the difference between the conditions must lie in the fact that (1) does not really require the subject to align across the gap between the lights and keys, whereas condition (3) does require him to do so. The gap in (1) is crossed by the use of the number taken from the light and found on the index card. With (3), however, the subject has not only to find the number on the card, but having done so, he must align the number with the key. Condition (3) does in fact combine the intermediate steps required both by condition (1) and by condition (b) in Kay's previous experiment.

A study of the errors made and remarks by subjects after the experiment, indicated that they were attempting, albeit unconsciously, to simplify this double task which attached to condition (3) and to a less extent also to condition (2). The analysis given in Table 6.10 of the errors made, showed that a proportion, increasing with both difficulty and age, was of a kind which reduced the task in condition (3) to the simpler tasks in condition (1) and condition (*b*) of the previous experiment. Thus the older subjects in condition (3) tended

TABLE 6.10. *Analysis of errors in Kay's (1954) experiment*

Age range	Condition (1)	Condition (2)	Condition (3)
Errors due to associating index-card with lights and not keys.			
15–24	0·6	0·2	1·0
25–34	0·8	0·7	1·8
35–44	0·5	0·8	4·4
45–54	0·3	1·7	7·6
55–64	0·2	1·7	11·6
65–72	0·4	5·0	15·6
Errors due to omission or double use of card			
15–24	0	0·4	1·3
25–34	0·3	0·7	2·9
35–44	0·5	0·7	5·0
45–54	0·4	2·2	8·5
55–64	0·4	2·1	11·4
65–72	0·5	5·2	22·6
Other errors			
15–24	0·6	2·3	1·7
25–34	0·2	1·8	3·8
35–44	1·6	3·0	4·2
45–54	1·9	4·6	7·4
55–64	3·0	3·5	10·6
65–72	2·2	4·8	9·7

sometimes to imagine the *keys* instead of the lights as numbered, and pressed the key corresponding to the number on the card opposite the light which was on. In this way, they avoided the need to align across the gap in condition (3), crossing it, as in condition (1), by means of the number on the card. Alternatively, they often simply pressed the key opposite the light which was on, as in condition (*b*) of the previous experiment. Their reasons for doing this could have been of two different kinds. Either they ignored the card altogether, or more likely, as Kay himself reports, they used the card twice, imagining the lights as numbered, finding the number on the card, and then imagining the keys as numbered and pressing the key corresponding to the number on the card. They thus again avoided the double task of making both symbolic translation and spatial alignment. There is, as we have said, no suggestion that such simplifications of the task were carried out deliberately. It would seem rather to be an example of one way in which older people may unconsciously react to a task which is too difficult for them.

Part of the cause of the difficulty of condition (3) appeared to be that when the numbers on the card were close to the lights the subjects found themselves tending to associate the two together. As one put it: 'The lights and the numbers on the card are close together; when a light comes on it seems to mean the number immediately below it.' Kay notes that this procedure is contrary not only to the instructions but to the way in which the subjects had themselves previously done the experiment in condition (1).

This type of explanation does, perhaps, receive some support from an experiment by Clay (1956a) in which confusion was found to be greater among older subjects in a task requiring the adding of numbers in close proximity to others which had at the time to be ignored. It seems hardly capable, however, of accounting alone for the very substantial changes of performance found by Kay. The types of error made suggest that subjects found difficulty stemming directly from the requirement to make two 'translations' in order to relate display to control. The precise nature of the difficulty is not certain, but two possibilities arise from a consideration of the type of error which resulted in the subject pressing the key directly opposite the light which was on. If the older people were merely omitting to use the card in condition (3), their behaviour would be consistent with the view that the *number* of translations or 'stages' between display and control was the operative factor, and that their purpose was to reduce this number. If, however, the tendency noted by Kay in some cases for them to use the card twice was general, a different view would be required, because the actual number of intermediate stages would then be the same as in the correct performance of the task. A possible reason why the double use of the card tended to replace the correct procedure, is that it involved only one *type* of translation, whereas the correct method required two different types, one in the use of the card, and the other in making the alignment. On this view, it would not be mere number of stages but their lack of consistency or uniformity that would be the cause of the difficulty for older people. Such a question would seem eminently suitable for further experimental study.

The important point to note is that taking the results of Kay's two experiments together, the fall in performance by older subjects is relatively small for either symbolic translation or the alignment task taken separately, but very great indeed when both are required together. Adding the one difficulty to the other appears to have produced a degree of change with age in performance which was far greater than would have been predicted from the study of either

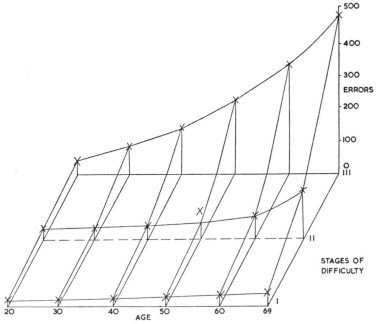

FIG. 6.8. Graphical representation of Kay's (1954) results relating performance to difficulty of task and age

difficulty on its own. It is tempting to compare Kay's results with those of Lashley (1929) relating performance to brain injury. Lashley found that in easy tasks performance was little affected by amount of brain injury and that with small amounts of injury difficult tasks were only slightly impaired. When difficult tasks and substantial injury were combined, however, the performance was severely affected. Kay's results shown in Fig. 6.8 follow essentially the same pattern if for 'brain injury' we substitute 'age'. The fact that a substantial loss of brain cells occurs progressively from early adulthood to old age, suggests that this similarity may be more than superficial, although this is not to say that the data have any bearing upon

Lashley's theories of 'mass action' and 'equipotentiality' of brain tissue which were hung upon his original findings. What is assumed here is a statistical view that loss of cells will affect the probability of sound functioning of many different processes.

From the practical point of view Kay's experiment provides an example of how adding one complication to another in a task may result in a quite disproportionate fall of performance among older people. At the same time, however, it implies that removal of one source of complexity from among many might, in at least some instances, cause a disproportionate improvement of performance and thus bring a seemingly impossible task within the capacities of older people.

As we have said, translation processes are interesting in relation to the use of mechanical aids in industry. These, while they reduce the physical effort demanded, also tend to introduce indirect or symbolic relationships between display and control in place of the straightforward ones existing when there is direct handling of objects or the use of simple hand tools. It would seem very important, if such mechanical aids are to be used easily by older people, that their operation should be kept as straightforward as possible in the sense that readily grasped and consistent principles should underlie the relationships between signals and responding action, and between controls and their effects.

VII

PERCEPTION

'There is more in vision than meets the eye'

SOME gross difficulties of perception in old age are clearly due to optical defects which beset the eye with advancing years and to analogous physical deficiencies in other sense organs (see, for example, Covell 1952; Friedenwald 1952). It is well known that some of these deficiencies begin in middle age, so that, for instance, substantial loss of power of accommodation has usually been sustained by the eye as early as the middle forties. It is often assumed that such changes underlie, and are indeed the sole cause of any deterioration of perceptual function in middle and old age. Evidence, however, is such as to indicate that these factors are not the only ones concerned: changes in central brain mechanisms are also important. Even when peripheral organs do lie at the root of changes in perceptual function, the manner in which they produce these changes may not be simple or direct. More or less elaborate functional systems are involved in even the simplest act of perception and must be taken into consideration in the study of performance at perceptual tasks.

Researches on perception in relation to age would seem to divide reasonably clearly into two groups, although the exact division between them is inevitably somewhat arbitrary. They are: (*a*) sensory discrimination, and (*b*) more complex meaningful perception.

(*a*) SENSORY DISCRIMINATION

An important experiment by Weston (1949) has indicated that loss of visual acuity with age may be more severe than is revealed by the tests commonly used by ophthalmologists. He gave a group of subjects, with ages ranging from 20 to 45 years, sheets of Landolt rings with instructions to cancel with a pencil each one having the break in a certain direction. The rings were of three different sizes, having gaps subtending 4·5, 3, and 1·5 minutes at the observer's eye, and of four different contrasts, 0·97, 0·56, 0·39 and 0·28, all on different sheets. They were presented at six different illuminations ranging from 0·5 1m./ft.^{2} to 512 1m./ft.^{2} Measures taken were the number of rings correctly cancelled in a given time and the number of errors made—usually omissions. Allowance was made for the time taken by the motor part of the task as opposed to the visual discrimination part by deducting the time taken to deal with sheets of rings where those to be cancelled were clearly marked in red, thus requiring no fine visual discrimination. Each subject did the tasks twice, with an interval of five years between tests, so that the experiment was, in fact, of the combined cross-sectional and longitudinal type.

The twelve subjects were all able to read the Jaeger I test type for near vision, correcting glasses being worn if necessary, and were closely similar for far vision as indicated by reading the Snellen test charts. There was thus approximate equality between the ages and adequacy at all ages on these tests of visual acuity. Nevertheless, as is shown in Fig. 7.1, there was a definite fall with age in performance at cancelling the Landolt rings, even in the case of the largest rings with the best contrast at the highest illuminations. Smaller size of ring, poorer contrast or lower illumination each singly made some difference to performance which became larger with age. In combination, their effects increased sharply from small differences among the youngest subjects to profound decline among the oldest.

Weston points out that from these results it would appear that although high levels of illumination can bring closer together the performances of younger and older people on fine visual tasks, there is no level of illumination at which their achievements could be made equal. He discusses his results in the light of previous work on visual acuity and notes that the declines shown by his subjects on a timed task are much greater than on the untimed tasks used previously. Since the times he used already made allowances for the motor actions of cancelling, the lengthening with age of time taken must imply a slowing somewhere within the processes concerned with vision and perception.

Following Hecht and Mintz (1939), visual acuity is generally agreed to be a facet of brightness difference discrimination, the limits of acuity being set by the subject's capacity to discriminate adjacent areas reflecting different amounts of light into the eye. It is clearly reasonable on this basis that difficulty should arise under conditions of poor contrast and dim illumination. More difficult to understand is the question of speed which Weston's experiment brings into the field of visual acuity measurement.

If loss of acuity were entirely a matter of the resolving power of the eye we might expect to find a threshold above which discrimination was possible and below which it was not. Weston's experiment is not entirely straightforward to interpret because both time and error scores were affected by the variables he studied, and we cannot be sure how much time should be regarded as equivalent to any given

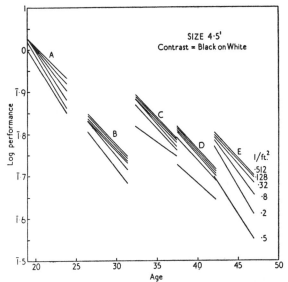

FIG. 7.1. The index of performance was arrived at as follows: From the gross time taken was deducted the time required to cancel rings clearly marked in red. The number of rings cancelled was expressed as a fraction of those which would have been cancelled had no omissions (which were almost the only errors) been made. The net discrimination time was divided by this fraction to give a corrected time corresponding to that which would have been taken for a completely accurate performance. The reciprocal of this corrected time is the index of performance of which the logarithm is plotted on the ordinate of the figure

number of errors. In so far as slowness did occur, however, and did increase with age we may as well ask what was its nature and how the extra time was spent.

This is a question which studies of vision have largely avoided facing. The explanation is almost certainly contained, however, in a formulation and experiments by Gregory and his co-workers following, and very substantially expanding, a theory put forward by Tanner and Swets (1954). We have to think of a visual signal as represented in the retina, the optic tract, and the visual centres of the brain in terms of frequencies of nerve impulses superimposed upon a certain amount of random nerve-cell activity, or 'noise', as it is often termed. This 'noise' will be inevitably added to the signal, and the problem for the subject's 'discrimination mechanism' is to distinguish the signal-plus-noise from noise alone, or a change from one level of signal-plus-noise to another. This is, of course, impossible in terms of a 'point' source of stimulation operating instantaneously. Either a very substantial number of nerve fibres must be involved, implying that the stimulation extends over an appreciable retinal area, or there must be integration over a period of time. In either case, the discrimination mechanism seems, as it were, to carry out a statistical difference test between the number of nerve impulses produced by one signal level and that produced by another, and the difference threshold represents the amount of signal change required to pass this test at a level of confidence acceptable to the subject.

Following the work of Hartline (1934) it is commonly assumed that the frequency of nerve impulses in the optic tract is more or less directly related to the logarithm of the intensity of the stimulus falling upon the subject's eye—the retina is assumed to effect a log transformation between stimulus and nerve impulse frequency.

The difference threshold is traditionally formulated in terms of the Weber fraction $\Delta I/I = $ constant, where $I = $ the intensity of the background and $\Delta I = $ a just noticeable increase of intensity. Gregory (1956) has pointed out that in so far as the Weber fraction is constant it seems that, if the log relation between intensity and nerve impulses holds, the difference threshold depends upon a constant absolute increase in the frequency of impulses resulting from ΔI at all levels of I. The Weber fraction is well known to hold for several sensory functions over a considerable stimulus range, but to break down at low intensities. Gregory (1955, 1956) and Gregory and Cane (1955) have suggested that this breakdown can be accounted for by the fact that owing to the presence of 'noise' the Weber fraction should be written

$$\frac{\Delta I}{I+k},$$

or, taking the area of the signal and the background against which it is viewed into account,

$$\frac{\Delta I}{I+k} = \text{constant} \sqrt{\left(\frac{I}{A_1}+\frac{I}{A_2}\right)}+C$$

where $k = $ 'noise' expressed in the same terms as I; A_1, and $A_2 = $

the areas of the background and the test patch, and C is a constant. This formula they find to fit reasonably well with observed data. A somewhat similar formulation could doubtless be arrived at incorporating integration time as a variable.

This approach makes the differential threshold depend upon four factors:

(a) *The areas to be compared.* Applied to problems of acuity, this would connect difficulty with fineness of detail in the display and would explain why small detail in very small test objects is frequently more difficult to see than the same detail in larger objects: it would, for example, explain why vernier acuity is dependent upon the lengths of the lines involved.

(b) *The signal to noise ratio in the subject.* This would seem to be dependent upon two distinct classes of factor: firstly, opacity of the eye media, narrowing of the pupil and any other factors tending to lower the level of stimulus reaching the retinal nerve cells, together with any randomness of action in the sensory cells of the retina itself; secondly, scattering of light in the eye together with losses and randomness in the optic pathways and brain. The difference between the two groups can be ascertained from the fact that in the ratio $I\Delta/I+k$ the first group determines the magnitude of k, while the second affects the magnitude of $\Delta I/I$.

(c) *A 'gating function'*—that is to say a minimum level of difference below which any neural activity is ignored. Some such threshold is necessary if the subject is not continually to be regarding peaks of 'noise' in his visual system as 'signals'. This 'gating function' is detectable in experiments in terms of the number of times a subject reports a signal as present when in fact there is none. It can undoubtedly be influenced considerably by the subject's attitude, one individual in one set of circumstances being prepared to risk a number of 'false positives', another in different circumstances trying studiously to avoid any, even at the expense of not responding to weak signals which are in fact present.

(d) *Integration time*—that is to say the time over which the 'sample' of incoming data is taken. This can compensate to a considerable extent for poor 'signal to noise' ratio as well as for restricted area of test patch and background. Two types of integration should probably be distinguished in this connexion. Firstly, the integration time of the mechanisms of the eye itself, and secondly, and more important for our purpose, the accumulation of data on a much longer time-scale by longer viewing time coupled with storage of data centrally in the brain.

Experiments by Gregory and others, of which we shall consider two, have enabled the effects of these various factors to be assessed separately in relation to age and have in particular shown that optical defects in the eye are unlikely to be the sole cause of poorer

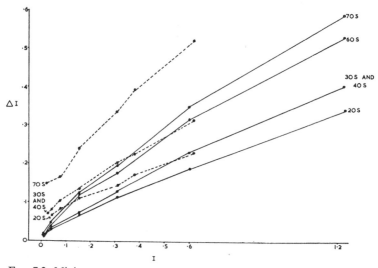

FIG. 7.2. Minimum perceptible increases of intensity of a patch of light as a function of background illumination

Dotted lines: patch illuminated in brief flashes
Solid lines: patch illuminated continuously

differential sensitivity in older people. The method of the first experiment was to flash a spot of light for about 0·057 second on an illuminated background and to ask the subject to report when the spot was seen. The intensity of the spot and of the background could be varied independently and the spot was sometimes absent in order to provide a measure of the extent to which the subject was giving 'false positive' judgements. The second experiment, by Gregory and Kendon, presented instead of flashes a steady illuminated spot which the subject adjusted so that it was just visibly brighter than the background.

The results of both experiments are given in Fig. 7.2. It will be seen that the curves relating ΔI to I in the *second* experiment radiate from a common point of origin and that the slope is greater among the older subjects than among the younger—in other words, $\Delta I/I$ rose with age. This result cannot have been due to opacity of the eye media, smaller pupil size or other factors reducing effective illumination of the retina. These would not have steepened the slope but would merely have shifted the curves upward by a constant amount at all values of I. They would have increased k but since they would have affected both ΔI and I in equal proportion, the ratio $\Delta I/I$ would have remained constant.

The curves for the first experiment may be interpreted as showing a rise of k with age in just this very way, together with a rise of slope in the older subjects.

The rise of slope with age in both experiments might at first sight be thought to have resulted from the tendency to emphasize accuracy found among the older subjects in experiments reported in previous chapters—in other words, from a higher 'gating function'. Had this been so, however, we should have expected fewer 'false positives' to be given by older subjects than by younger in the first experiment. In fact the accuracy of the different age groups was substantially similar so that the higher slope would seem to indicate the operation of either or both of two factors increasing with age, namely either scattering of light in the eye or alternatively 'noise' or loss of signal in the visual pathways and brain. How much of the effect is to be attributed to each factor cannot be decided on the present evidence. In favour of the first may be cited the lower tolerance to glare shown by older people. Evidence for the latter comes from experiments by Crossman and Szafran to be described later, where scattering of light in the eye would not have provided an explanation. We may further note in this connexion that recent work (see Obrist 1954) on electroencephalograph records of old people has shown a lowering of the general level of activity and slowing of the dominant rhythms, but some relative rise of what appears to be fairly fast random activity. Such evidence is consistent with the finding that in middle and old age the number of functional brain cells is substantially reduced. Many die and are replaced with non-nerve tissue while the weight of the brain becomes less (Appel and Appel 1942; see also O'Leary 1952). Apart from the fact that shortly before they are destroyed, these cells tend to show considerable random activity, the mere loss of cells would serve to bring about some lowering of the 'signal to noise' ratio, as the lower number of brain cells would result in less averaging of the random activity.

Gregory, in a private communication, has pointed out that the theory that 'signal to noise' ratio diminishes with age can also account for the well-established finding that critical flicker frequency—the speed at which 'on' and 'off' in a continuous temporal sequence can just be seen as a flicker rather than a steady light—falls with age as it does with almost all other sources of perceptual difficulty or impairment such as dim illumination, fatigue or damage to the visual area of the brain (Brozek and Keys 1945; Misiak 1947; Oshima *et al.* 1954). The rise of nervous activity following the onset of light is not instantaneous but builds up over an appreciable time, so that, very broadly speaking, a rapidly flashing light is represented as a rising and falling level of nervous activity with the difference between 'peak' and 'trough' gradually becoming smaller as the frequency is increased. Flicker fusion in these terms can be thought of as occurring at the point at which the brightness difference between peak and trough is too small to be distinguished, and this is a function of differential brightness threshold. Any lowering of signal to noise ratio will make the difference between peak and trough required for flicker to be seen greater, and thus cause the frequency at which fusion occurs to be lowered.

The reason for the lower slope and elimination of k in the second experiment is probably that, having the light on all the time instead of being forced to judge from brief flashes, subjects could compensate for poor 'signal to noise' ratio both in the eye and more centrally by integrating data over a longer time. In part this integration may represent a longer summation time in the basic physiological mechanisms of vision, but almost certainly it is largely due to a demand for more data by higher-level perceptual processes. In so far as this latter is the case, these findings link with others to be discussed later.

If the theory that older subjects are integrating data over a longer time is correct, we may well ask why such integration was not even more effective. The probable answer is that there is a limit to effective integration time, because any such integration implies the storage of information in a system which is of limited capacity and is itself 'noisy'. We shall see in Chapter VIII that this view could also explain certain findings in the seemingly remote field of complex problem solving.

The possibility of compensating, at least partially, for poor 'signal to noise' ratio by means of longer viewing time would seem to tie up well with Weston's results: we may assume his older subjects were slower because they were taking a longer integration time in order to offset their poorer 'signal to noise' ratio, whereas in the test with Jaeger types and Snellen charts, relatively little difference with age appeared because no account was taken of time. In this connexion we may note two parallel observations regarding the discrimination of lengths of line. The first is an experiment by Birren and Botwinick (1955*b*) who measured the times taken by subjects to indicate which was the longer of each of a number of pairs of lines. They found the time taken by older subjects to respond was longer for all pairs but became progressively more so when the lengths to be compared differed by 10 per cent. or less. Their results are shown in Table 7.1 and may be contrasted with Galton's (1885; see also Ruger

TABLE 7.1. *Mean times (in seconds) taken to discriminate between two lines of different lengths*

Age group	Percentage difference in length of lines											
	1	*2*	*3*	*4*	*5*	*7*	*10*	*15*	*20*	*30*	*40*	*50*
61–91 .	1·41	1·29	1·22	1·14	1·10	0·94	0·88	0·77	0·78	0·77	0·76	0·77
19–36 .	0·94	0·86	0·83	0·77	0·78	0·67	0·63	0·60	0·59	0·60	0·57	0·59
Difference (older minus younger)	0·47	0·43	0·39	0·37	0·32	0·27	0·25	0·17	0·19	0·17	0·19	0·18
Difference as percentage of younger	0·50	0·50	0·47	0·48	0·41	0·41	0·40	0·28	0·32	0·28	0·33	0·31

and Stoessiger 1927) classical data on bisection and trisection, in which accuracy and not time was scored. Galton's results are set out in Table 7.2. They show that although mean error rose from the twenties to the fifties and beyond, the errors were at all ages remarkably small, and the rise with age was of an order which could easily be

TABLE 7.2. *Percentage error made when bisecting and trisecting lines. Galton's data*

Age group:	*10–19*	*20–29*	*30–39*	*40–49*	*50–59*	*60–69*	*70–79*
Error of bisection .	0·91	0·80	0·84	0·89	0·98	0·91	0·47
Error of trisection .	1·37	1·18	1·14	1·24	1·25	1·31	1·28

The 'lines' were wooden rods 15 ins. long. Judgements were registered by sliding the rods into position against pointers.

attributed to factors such as the motor task involved in registering judgements.

Three important consequences follow from the experiments on visual discrimination that have been surveyed so far. Firstly, from the practical standpoint untimed tests such as Snellen charts and Jaeger test types, as normally used, are not sensitive instruments for detecting loss of acuity in middle and old age; time required to read them should be taken into consideration. Secondly, if this general approach is correct for vision, there would seem likely to be analogies in the case of the other senses. Gregory has, for instance, obtained evidence that hearing losses associated with nerve deafness, from which many older people suffer, can be explained in terms of lowering of the 'signal to noise' ratio. High levels of external noise have relatively less effect on hearing by people with this form of deafness than they do upon the hearing of those whose auditory sensitivity is normal, a fact which raises the possibility that older people may be, on average, relatively *less* affected than younger by having to work under high levels of noise. Thirdly, it is obvious that any means that can be adopted for improving 'signal to noise' ratio without overloading the subject's sensory mechanisms, are likely to give proportionally greater benefit to older people than it is to younger. Such measures would probably not be able to bring the performance of older and younger to equality, but they might serve to bring them very much closer together.

Above-threshold discrimination

Birren and Botwinick's results indicate that for discrimination well above threshold values age changes are substantially independent of the fineness of the discrimination required. Such changes as there are might therefore result from the fact that some *choice of action* must inevitably be made in order to register judgements of discrimination.

Further evidence in amplification of this point is contained in three experiments in which discrimination was incorporated into different types of sensori-motor task. The first is an exploratory experiment by Cherns intended to simulate an inspection operation. The subject sat facing a screen from behind which a series of sixty rectangular aluminium blocks, 13 cm. in length and of widths ranging from 5 to 7 cm., appeared one at a time on a horizontal runway. The subject had to judge whether each block was 'up to standard' on two criteria: the width of the block—blocks greater or less than 6 cm. wide were to be rejected; and the accuracy of a design of four holes, one of which varied in position relatively to the others in some blocks—blocks in which this hole was not in the correct position were to be rejected.

Examples of a block correct in both respects, of a block which was too narrow (5·2 cm. wide) and of a block showing an error of pattern were displayed on the screen above the runway throughout the experiment. The subjects were required to indicate their acceptance or rejection of each block by pulling or pushing respectively a lever on the right-hand side of the apparatus. The words 'Accept' and 'Reject' were clearly marked in large white letters at the appropriate ends of the slot in which the lever moved. The blocks could be made to appear either at regular intervals or on each pressing of the lever. The task could thus be carried out at a speed either 'paced' by the apparatus or determined by the subject himself. Each subject was given the series of blocks three times—once at his own speed, once at 3 seconds per block, and once at 5 seconds. Half the subjects in each age range had their first run at their own speed, half at 5 seconds per block. When the experiment was first designed it was expected, on the ground that speed and accuracy were likely to be compensatory, that older subjects would show less accuracy when working at a speed determined by the experimenter than when allowed to work at their own speed. Inspection of the results did not, however, reveal any marked difference of performance between these two conditions —probably because the speeds were set too low to impose any great speed pressure. Accordingly, for comparing the accuracy of the various age ranges, the three runs were combined.

The percentages of blocks of each width accepted are shown in Fig. 7.3 and indicate some change of accuracy with age, although very little until the oldest group is reached. This group accepted a surprisingly high proportion of large blocks. Why they should have done this is not clear, but the difference of width between these very large blocks and the standard was obviously too great for their acceptance to be due to defects of the peripheral visual mechanism. It was thought at first that it might have been because the sample 'error-block' displayed on the screen in front of the subject was narrower than the standard, and that the older subjects had been forgetting the instructions and tending to reject only blocks which were too narrow. This explanation seems to be excluded, however,

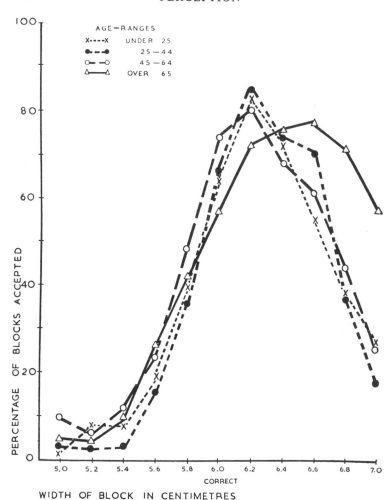

FIG. 7.3. Percentages of blocks accepted during three runs

because the same result was obtained in a brief check experiment in which nine subjects over 65 were given one run at their own speed with a sample error-block much too wide (6·8 cm.) displayed on the screen.

Although accuracy, except in the highest age range, was very similar over the experiment as a whole, some differences associated with age did appear in the time taken to deal with the first few blocks.

The mean times taken during their first run by subjects for whom this was at their own speed are shown in Fig. 7.4. Those for the first few blocks rose sharply with age, accompanied among the oldest

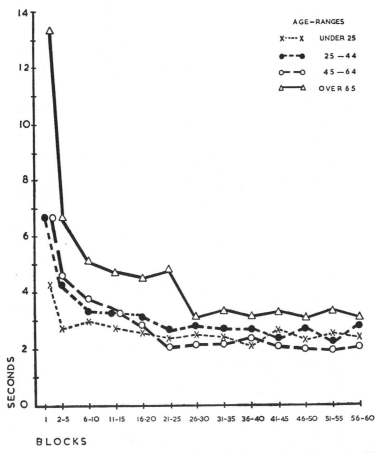

FIG. 7.4. Mean judgement-times per block during first run by subjects who did this at their own speed

subjects by slightly greater accuracy. When the first run was paced there was a slightly greater tendency among the older subjects to let blocks go by without recording judgements. This tendency continued among the oldest subjects on paced runs after the first, but otherwise there was no sign of slowness once the first run had been completed. The older subjects thus appear to have taken a little longer than the younger to settle to the experiment, although the effect was fleeting. Whether the initial slowness was due to a difficulty of discrimination as such, or to some other feature of the task, it is not possible to say.

The second experiment we shall mention on above-threshold discrimination is a card-sorting task by Crossman and Szafran (1956) in which the subjects sorted packs containing equal quantities of cards bearing two alternative numbers of irregularly arranged dots, e.g. 8 and 12. Subjects held packs face downwards, turned the cards up one by one, and were instructed to sort them as fast as possible without making errors. Very few errors were in fact made. The performance was timed by a stop-watch and the times for varying difficulty of discrimination from one dot as opposed to four, up to eight dots as opposed to ten, are shown in Fig. 7.5. Comparing this with results for sorting into various numbers of categories set out in Fig. 4.15 on p. 101 we see that the times for the easiest discrimination are similar to those for two-category sorting. Making finer discriminations caused the sorting time to rise a little in all age groups, but, surprisingly, slightly less among the older subjects than among the younger.

This result was confirmed in a further experiment by Crossman and Szafran in which the subjects sorted a row of twenty small aluminium canisters into two categories by weight. There were again equal numbers in each of the two categories. The weights in the various series were in the ratio of 0 to 8, 2 to 8, 4 to 8, and 6 to 8. The time taken to sort the whole row was measured by stop-watch. From Fig. 7.6 it will be seen that again the time taken rose a little as the difficulty of discrimination became finer, but that again the older subjects were, if anything, relatively better at the finer discriminations than at the coarser. Crossman and Szafran point out that these findings, although at first sight contrary to the results of the experiments by Gregory and his co-workers, are not in fact so but that both can be explained in terms of signal to noise ratio becoming lower with age. They suggest:

We may imagine that the process of discrimination is carried out by the brain in the following way. The presented signal is compared with a remembered representation of each possible alternative and the one to which it most closely corresponds is selected. The comparison must be

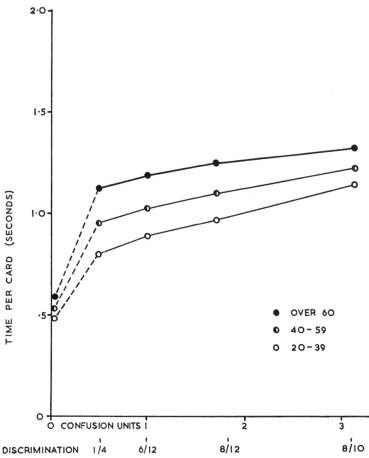

FIG. 7.5. Times taken to sort cards into two categories as a function of the degree of discrimination required

The 'confusion units' were calculated according to the formula given by Crossman (1955), namely:

$$\text{confusion units} = 1/(\log_2 x_1 - \log_2 x_2),$$

where x_1 and x_2 are the two magnitudes being compared—in the present case the numbers of dots on the cards

in the nature of a statistical test between several 'hypotheses' made on the basis of an incoming stream of samples. The difficulty of deciding between the hypotheses depends (Crossman 1955) on the ratio between them; the more different the signals are, the easier being the discrimination; a longer integration time is needed to discriminate finer differences. Now the characteristic of our ageing effect is that very different ('easy') are more affected than similar ('difficult') ones. If we suppose that a random disturbance is added to all signals before discrimination, exactly this effect would be produced, for the ratio would be little altered if nearly unity, but

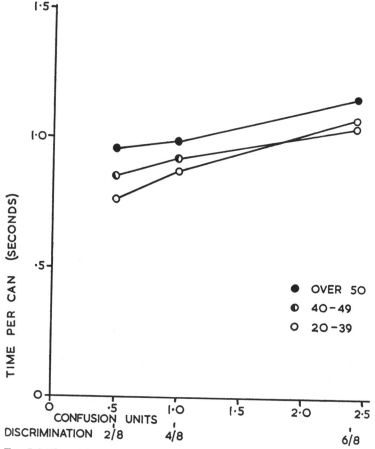

FIG. 7.6. Times taken to sort small canisters into two categories by weight as a function of the difference of weight between the categories

much altered if near zero. We postulate, in effect, an increasing level of 'internal random noise' in the brain, which tends to obscure all differences between signals or states.

Crossman and Szafran's results do not, at first sight, agree with those of Birren and Botwinick on p. 161, although in fact no conflict is involved. The range of discrimination over which older subjects took disproportionately long to judge lengths of line was from 1 to 10 per cent. These discriminations are all finer than any used by Crossman and Szafran and seem to be near threshold. On the other hand, the easier discriminations in the sorting experiments were beyond the range studied by Birren and Botwinick. Over the range common to the three experiments age differences were in all cases stable. It thus appears that although older people are slower than younger at discrimination tasks, there is a wide range over which the difficulty of discrimination is not related to age changes in performance.

(b) MORE COMPLEX MEANINGFUL PERCEPTION

(i) *The perception of ambiguous figures*

The experiments surveyed so far have been concerned with perception in tasks where the limitations lay in the strictly visual demands or in making simple judgements. We turn now to experiments which have attempted to study more complex perceptual tasks laying stress on the application of material from past experience to present sense data. These tasks do not lend themselves to such precise treatment as do those of simple sensory discrimination, and the results are in consequence less clear cut. This is, however, an inevitable feature of the material and the techniques at present available.

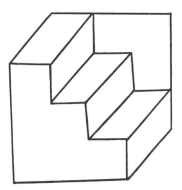

FIG. 7.7. A reversible perspective drawing

This can be seen either as a 'staircase' or as an overhanging stepped cornice

Ambiguous figures, such as that shown in Fig. 7.7, have been part of the 'stock in trade' of experimental psychologists for many years. Their interest lies in the fact that when looked at steadily they show spontaneous alternations between one 'organization' and another, in the present case between a three-step staircase and an overhanging cornice. Precisely what happens when such reversals take place is not certain, but the change of perceptual organization has clearly nothing to do with the objective stimuli, but with the central mechanisms interpreting these and giving them meaning. Attempts have been made to use the frequency of reversal in such figures as an indicator of mental deterioration (Cameron 1936; Eysenck 1952). Miles (1934) studied the effect of age upon perception of a different type of ambiguous figure produced by rotating a vane in a beam of light so that the shadow was projected on to a ground-glass screen. This shadow could be perceived in several different ways. Miles found little change with age either in the number of different ways in which the shadow was seen or in the frequency with which one interpretation gave way to another. Eysenck, however, using a reversible perspective cube figure, found some tendency towards slowing of reversals amongst older subjects although there was doubt in his groups as to whether this was due to age itself or to his older patients being in poorer mental condition—his subjects were neurotics and there may have been a tendency for the degree of neuroticism to have been greater among the older subjects.

This complication did not apply to an experiment by Speakman who showed the diagram in Fig. 7.7 and asked the subjects to watch and report if they saw any change. If no reversal was reported within 2 minutes, the nature of the change was described and an attempt was made to get them to achieve it. All subjects, except one, saw the change before 5 minutes had elapsed. Results from the one who did not were not used.

When two or three changes had been seen, the figure was then covered up and the subject instructed that it would be shown again and that he should watch it for 1 minute and report each change as it occurred. After a rest of 1 minute he was asked to repeat the procedure, but this time trying to prevent the reversal taking place.

The times taken to the first change during the practice period are set out in Table 7.3, from which it will be seen that from the twenties onwards there was a clear tendency for the time to first change to rise. The number of changes recorded during the two subsequent periods of 1 minute are also shown in Table 7.3. The spontaneous reversal rate shows a clear fall with age from the twenties onwards, but the rate when subjects were trying to prevent reversals is fairly similar at all ages. These findings would seem to imply that if, as has sometimes been suggested, spontaneous reversals of this type are the result of some kind of central fatigue, such fatigue does not increase with age.

The slowing of the spontaneous reversal rate was, however, substantial, and Speakman carried out a series of control experiments in an attempt to understand more clearly the reasons why this should have occurred. It seemed possible that some of this slowing might have been due to factors such as decreased pupil size with age resulting in less light entering the eye. It would be reasonable to expect slowing of the reversal rate under these conditions on the analogy of the lowering of critical flicker frequency in dim illumination. The

TABLE 7.3. *Perception of the reversible figure shown in Fig. 7.7*

	Age range				
	10–19	*20–29*	*30–39*	*40–49*	*50–65*
Time to first change (number of subjects):					
60 seconds or less	12	8	5	6	0
61–120 seconds	3	2	4	1	4
Over 120 seconds	15	0	1	3	6
Mean number of reversals reported during 1 minute without special instructions— i.e. 'spontaneous' reversal rate . .	16	23	17	16	13
Mean number of reversals reported during 1 minute when trying to prevent reversal	9	13	13	9	12

The decline with age from the twenties to the sixties in the spontaneous reversal rate was significant at the 2 per cent. level.

same figure was accordingly exposed to a fresh group of subjects, both under the original conditions where it was illuminated by a 100-watt lamp in a shade 1 foot from the figure and under conditions where the lamp was only 15 watts. Half the subjects were given the weaker lamp first, and the other half the stronger. The decreased illumination was found to produce a significant decline in spontaneous reversal rate of about 13 per cent. This, however, was less than a third of the decline between the twenties and the over-fifties in the original group. The diminution of pupil size in the same age range would, according to the figures of Birren *et al.* (1950), have been only about 50 per cent., in other words, much less than the reduction of illumination. Decrease of pupil size would therefore appear not to be a sufficient explanation of the slowing of spontaneous reversal rate with age. It is, of course, possible that other peripheral eye defects should be considered as well as pupil size.

No relationship between reversal rate was found with a number of other measures which may be briefly listed:

1. Pulse rate.
2. Body temperature.
3. Speed of turning over cards one by one from a pack.

4. Speed of dotting a pencil on a sheet of paper for 30 seconds.
5. Forward digit span.
6. Critical flicker frequency measured at an 'on–off' ratio of approximately 1/1. The subject viewed a 2-inch square ground-glass test patch in an elongated blacked-out viewing box illuminated from behind by a 5-watt neon lamp.
7. Blink rate, obtained by counting the numbers of blinks made by the subjects viewing the diagram in the main experiment.

The only relationship, other than illumination and age, which turned out to be significant was that between parent and child among seven cases where scores for both were obtained.

If this result is valid it would appear to mean that reversal rate is dependent upon some relatively fundamental factor which is either inherited or substantially influenced by early upbringing. Since in a perceptual task of this kind experience is likely to play little part, the factor is presumably inherited. The change with age may, it would seem, be attributed, at least tentatively, to a change in this factor, although its precise nature remains obscure.

(ii) *Identification of objects*

Verville and Cameron (1946) presented subjects with incomplete pictures consisting of disconnected patches which, when viewed as

FIG. 7.8. Example of incomplete pictures
used by Verville and Cameron

a whole with the gaps filled in by the subject's imagination, could be seen as objects. An example is given in Fig. 7.8. Each picture was projected on to a screen and shown until it was named correctly, when it was removed. They found clearly marked differences between a group of college students from 16 to 23 years of age and a group of adults from 35 to 56 years of age in the time taken to identify the pictures correctly. It is quite clear that the difficulty for the older subjects in this case lay not in fine visual discrimination but in the interpretation of the picture and the identification of the object represented in it.

These results and those of experiments on problem-solving which will be outlined in the next chapter, suggested that part at least of the difficulty for older people might be in synthesizing data to form an integrated whole. As we have mentioned in Chapter II, all perception involves some integration of information over an area and over a period of time. To study this type of synthesis, a series of experiments was carried out by Wallace (1956) in which complete designs and pictures were mounted upon a band moving downwards behind a narrow horizontal slit, so that the whole display was scanned from bottom to top but only part was visible at any one time. Two groups of subjects, one in the twenties and one in the sixties and seventies, were shown displays of four types: (a) simple geometrical figures, (b) more complex block figures, (c) representational silhouettes and (d) pictorial line drawings. An example of each type is given in Fig. 7.9. Each display was shown with the narrowest slit (0·1 inch) and if it was not identified it was shown again with the slit 0·2 inch wide and so on by successive tenths up to 0·5 inch, when, if it was still unidentified, it was not tried again. The pictures were about 3 inches high and the band moved at about 1 inch per second so that the widths of the slit in inches corresponded approximately to the length of time in seconds that each part of the display was exposed. The results of this experiment are shown in Fig. 7.10. The older subjects were fairly similar to the younger in their achievements with the simple geometrical figures and the representational silhouettes, showed greater differences with the more complex block figures and very marked differences with the line drawings. Clearly the first two types of display were, relatively, somewhat easier for the older subjects than was the third and much easier than the last.

The experiment was repeated, using line drawings only, with two groups of subjects each ranging from the twenties to the sixties, in order to determine the point at which the age changes became marked. The results are shown in Fig. 7.11. In both groups the twenties, thirties and forties gave fairly similar results, but a decline appeared between the forties and sixties. The two groups differed in educational and occupational status. Group 1 consisted of naval ratings, men employed at a government training centre and pensioners from a factory employing mainly unskilled and semi-skilled workers. Group 2 consisted of those in administrative positions in industry and of university teachers and research workers. It can be seen that, except in the twenties, the successes when the largest aperture had been reached

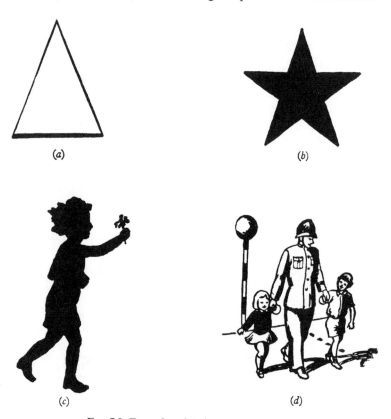

(a)

(b)

(c)

(d)

FIG. 7.9. Examples of designs used by Wallace

were, in each age range, greater among the subjects of higher occupational status, although the differences were not significant. This result may be compared with those obtained from very much larger numbers, with ages ranging from the late teens to 55 years of age, on a series of tests by Pacaud (1955a, b). She found clear differences with education in tests of intellectual, memory and learning functions and noted that in each case the difference between educational levels in performance was either the same for both older and younger or a large difference among younger subjects was reduced among older.

We may ask what is the cause of the profound changes with age shown in Wallace's experiments. Clearly, it cannot be a matter of fine visual acuity in the traditional sense. Many of the subjects were shown the pictures, or others like them, out of the apparatus, and all

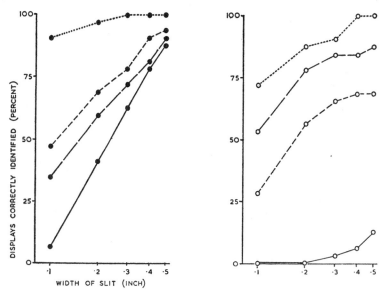

FIG. 7.10. Identification of different types of design as a function of aperture

Filled circles: subjects in their twenties
Open circles: subjects in their sixties and seventies
Dotted lines: geometrical figures (a)
Short dashes: more complex block figures (b)
Long dashes: representational silhouettes (c)
Continuous lines: pictorial line drawings (d)

were able to identify them easily. Any subject who complained of difficulty in actual seeing was rejected and all those who normally wore glasses did so. Nor did the difficulty appear to be due to the speed of the belt. It is true that in control experiments where displays were shown stationary all at once for a limited time, performance by subjects of all ages, especially older subjects, was relatively better, but another control experiment in which the width of the slit was kept constant at 0·3 inch and the exposure time was varied in successive presentations from 0·1 second to 0·5 second by varying the speed of the band, yielded results if anything slightly better than those of the main experiments. This was so in spite of the fact that initially the band was running at three times its normal speed.

One of the difficulties with the method of exposure used in these experiments was that slit width and exposure time varied together if band speed was kept constant. A series of control experiments were accordingly undertaken in which an attempt was made to

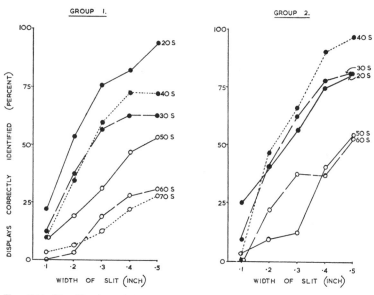

FIG. 7.11. Identification of line drawings as a function of age and occupational status

separate these two variables. Two of these have already been mentioned. Others involved giving a series of exposures keeping both aperture and band speed constant. These experiments, taken together with the earlier ones, indicated that two factors were important: (*a*) the amount of the display seen at once, especially at the first presentation, and (*b*) total viewing time over a series of exposures. Five sets of results for two age groups—twenties and sixties—are shown in Fig. 7.12. There are considerable irregularities, but there seems to be a clear tendency for the percentage of displays correctly identified to rise with the time for which they were viewed, in such a way that for any given amount of picture seen at once, the percentage of correct identification is a linear function of the logarithm of the cumulative viewing time. It would seem that subjects in their sixties can be expected to attain about the same percentage of correct identification as subjects in their twenties, if allowed to see the display for about fifteen to twenty times as long.

The influence of the amount of the display seen at once, especially on the first exposure, is also evident. The results with a constant slit

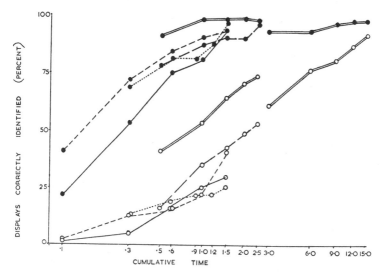

FIG. 7.12. Identification of line drawings as a function of cumulative viewing time (in seconds) and with different amounts of display seen at once

Filled circles: subjects aged 18–29.
Open circles: subjects in their sixties and seventies.
Single continuous line: aperture increasing as in Wallace's first two experiments (Figs. 7.10 and 7.11).
Long dashes: repeated exposures with fixed aperture of 0·5 inch.
Dotted line: repeated exposures with fixed aperture of 0·3 inch.
Short dashes: exposures with fixed aperture of 0·3 inch but with speed adjusted to give the same exposure times as with increasing aperture in Wallace's first two experiments; i.e. first exposure at three times normal speed, last at ⅔ normal speed.
Double lines: designs exposed all at once in a tachistoscope.
It can be seen that, on the whole, the conditions shown by the continuous lines, where the designs are first shown with an extremely narrow aperture, yield the poorest results, and the tachistoscope in which the designs are exposed all at once, yield the best. All, however, tend to show percentage of correct identification as linearly related to log cumulative exposure time.

width of either 0·3 or 0·5 inch tended to be a little better than those for the slit gradually increasing from 0·1 inch, while the results with the tachistoscope, in which the whole picture was seen at once, are clearly superior. The point was further confirmed in an additional experiment where slit width and band speed were varied together so that exposure time was kept constant at 0·3 second. Each subject viewed some displays starting with an aperture of 0·1 inch gradually increasing, and others with an aperture of 0·5 inch gradually decreasing. The results given in Fig. 7.13 show that the second condition gave greatly superior results. Among the younger subjects it did

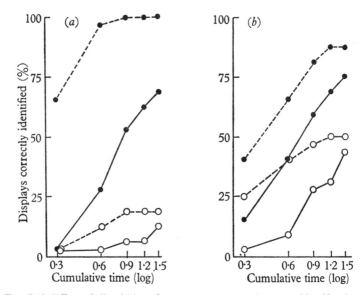

FIG. 7.13. Effect of slit width at first exposure upon subsequent identification of designs. Exposure time held constant

(a) Filled circles: subjects aged 18–29
    Open circles: subjects aged 65–75

(b) A group of somewhat higher occupational grade:
    Filled circles: subjects aged 25–38
    Open circles: subjects aged 42–54

In both (a) and (b) the continuous lines are for a series of exposures in which slit width was increased from 0·1 inch to 0·5 inch by steps of 0·1 inch. The short dashes are for a series of exposures starting with a slit width of 0·5 inch and decreasing to 0·1 inch. In both series speed was adjusted so that exposure time was kept constant at 0·3 second

so from the first exposure: among both younger and older a difference persisted right to the last exposure. Why the early exposures should be so important is not clear, but is in line with other results from the same experiments, to be discussed later, and also with other experiments such as that of Kay (1951) (see p. 242) and of Szafran and Welford (1950). Taking the results of these experiments as a whole we may say that with more complex displays there appears to be a sharp rise of difficulty in identification after the age of about

50, although if such displays are seen whole, and for a sufficient length of time, they can be identified as accurately and well by older people as by younger.

We may well ask what is the precise nature of the difficulty for older people. It seems likely that two factors are operative, one associated with the fact of seeing only part of the display at any one time, the other with the results of restricted viewing time. As regards the former, perception tends to be selective and also economical (Attneave 1954; Hochberg and McAlister 1953). The seeing of objects as coherent wholes reduces the amount of information that it is necessary to carry in order to perceive and remember the object, although this economy may be obtained at the expense of detailed accuracy. The prerequisite of such economy is, however, that the object can be seen as an 'articulated' whole, so that the overall form can be recognized. The very narrow slit made this impossible, and a wider slit, although better in this respect, was still far from allowing the same degree of articulation as when the display could be seen all at once. Viewing through the slit, a subject could achieve articulation and select the data upon which to identify the object and reject what was redundant only by carrying temporarily in some kind of short-term memory almost all the data presented. We shall see in Chapter IX that the capacity for this seems to be reduced in old age. It is reasonable to suppose, therefore, that part of the difference of performance between older and younger subjects in Wallace's experiments was due to the manner of presentation resulting in the temporary overloading of their capacity for short-term memory. In this respect, the difficulty as regards perception was peculiar to the set-up of the experiment. The danger of such overloading would, however, seem likely to apply in all cases where the display rapidly changes, especially where the data are presented for a short time and then removed.

The requirement by the older subjects of longer viewing time would seem clearly to imply a slowing in the processes of identification. This might, on the face of it, be due to attitudinal factors such as extra care and stress upon accuracy that older subjects have shown in experimental tasks outlined in previous chapters. It is, however, difficult to say whether such attitudinal factors, even if they do operate, are the primary cause of the requirement of longer viewing time, or whether they represent a shift in the manner of performance in the face of other changes of the organism which set a premium on economy of action.

It is also possible that the requirement of longer viewing time could result directly from the increased experience of older people in either of two ways. Firstly, such increased experience would widen the range of possible identifications and thus make more laborious the task of arriving at any particular one. Following Hick's (1952*a*) work relating choice reaction time to degree of choice, we should expect the time taken to make identifications to become longer as the range of experience increased. Secondly, even if the total range of experience does not become greater with age, some parts of it may become relatively more prominent than others and thus, so to speak, 'set' the observer towards particular types of identification in preference to others. The fact that the representational silhouettes in Wallace's first experiment were more easily identified by the older subjects than were the objectively simpler block figures, may well be an example of such a 'set', resulting from an interest in persons and living objects rather than abstract forms. The experiments by Crossman (1953) and Hyman (1953) make it reasonable to expect that the result of such 'sets' would be to make certain classes of object identified quickly, but to make other classes take a relatively long time.

Closer inspection of the evidence makes it doubtful, however, whether these are the basic causes of the age changes Wallace observed. One striking result she found was that subjects, when told that their identification was wrong at one exposure would often nevertheless repeat it at the next. Subjects of all ages did this to some extent but the older groups tended to do so more than the younger. There was also a considerable tendency among older subjects to repeat for succeeding displays the type of identification they had made for a previous display. Wallace quotes the following example: 'An older subject gave this series of responses; to the arrow (type *b*) "shaped like a fan", followed immediately as a response to the star (type *b*) by "same as the fan but opens out like a tent", and then for the next stimulus, the triangle (type *a*) "a tent—a triangle". The same subject, with the series at fixed aperture, gave these responses: having identified the yacht (type *c*) correctly, responded to the monk (type *c*) as "someone signalling on a steamer", and to the next simulus, a man carrying a pile of records (type *d*), "something on the sea, a lighthouse".'

The same tendency was noted by Verville and Cameron who pointed out, for example, that "some subjects, after correctly identifying the first picture as a frog, continued to name animals for one or more succeeding pictures'. It is just conceivable that these results could arise directly from the fact that increased experience may make the task of identification more laborious than older subjects are willing to undertake, but it seems more reasonable to view them as due to the older subjects finding the actual process of search among possible categories of identification more difficult. In this connexion we may view them in relation to those of an experiment by Birren on verbal facility. Subjects were required to write down as many words beginning with a stated letter as they could in a period of 2 minutes. Birren found that the number of words written rose to the thirties and thereafter declined. A separate determination of writing speed indicated that this was not a limitation. An example of the results is given in Table 7.4.

TABLE 7.4. *Numbers of words written in 2 minutes*

Example from Birren (1955)

	Age range							
	16–19	20–29	30–39	40–49	50–59	60–69	70–79	80–89
Words beginning with C.	20·7	22·0	25·2	20·0	16·0	8·4	5·6	5·6
Writing speed . .	45·2	48·0	47·1	38·0	29·4	22·0	16·5	15·2

A similar finding was obtained by Speakman, who asked his subjects to name as many 'things' or nouns as they could within a period of 1 minute. His results are shown in Table 7.5, from which

TABLE 7.5. *Numbers of 'things' named in 1 minute*

Means per subject

	Age range				
	20–29	30–39	40–49	50–59	60–65
Number of subjects . .	10	10	10	8	4
'Things' named . . .	52·7	48·4	48·4	43·6	35·0

it appears that there was a clear slowing with age. From a study of the actual replies made, it appeared that subjects of all ages tended to start by naming things in their immediate environment and then, having seemingly exhausted the possibilities of this, turned to objects not immediately present (cf. Jung 1918). The actual objects named, especially in this second stage, tended to follow the lines of subjects' interests. Subjects of all ages also tended to make 'runs' of associations, either of the type described by Jung as coexistent (e.g. door, panel, hinge, key) or co-ordinate (e.g. apple, pear, cherry, currant). These would seem to be similar to the runs of identifications noted by Verville and Cameron and by Wallace. It was unfortunately not possible to record in sufficient detail to be sure whether the length and frequency of these runs increased with age. It did, however, seem clear that there were no gross qualitative differences in the replies given by older and younger subjects.

Birren's and Speakman's tasks were in a sense the complement of perceptual identification. Instead of the subject being required to find terms from his past experience in order to match a presented display, he had to produce as quickly as possible all available terms which belonged to a particular category. The analogy between these experiments and perception may at first seem far-fetched, but is in many ways similar to the relation between perception and imaging studied by Bartlett (1932).

A direct test of whether older people have more difficulty than younger in changing from one category of identification to another has been made by Korchin and Basowitz (1956) who showed subjects a series of drawings which started with a clear picture of a cat and changed progressively into a dog. They found that subjects in the twenties and thirties abandoned the identification 'cat' sooner than did those in the sixties and beyond, and also gave their judgements faster. Some doubt must, however, attach to their results because their young subjects were of substantially higher educational grade than their older. This objection does not apply, however, to the results of a somewhat similar experiment by O'Doherty. Subjects were shown a series of ten cards on each of which was a boldly drawn design. The first and the last of each series portrayed readily identifiable objects. The intermediate cards formed a gradual transition from the one to the other. O'Doherty found that when the designs on the first and the last cards were of closely similar category, e.g. Jug—Teapot, there was little difference in the point at which young and old recognized a new object. When, however, the two objects were of different category, e.g. Mouse—Car, older people achieved identification of the new object much later in the series than did the younger. Both young and old recognized at about the same point in the series that the identification of the first card was no longer appropriate. The young quickly went on to recognize the new, whereas the older made identifications for several cards within the same general category as the first card. For instance, in the series mentioned they named various animals. Examples of O'Doherty's results are given in Table 7.6.

TABLE 7.6. *Changes in category of identification as a function of age and of degree of change required*

Number of subjects changing at each card

	Card in series of 10 at which change occurred								
	3	4	5	6	7	8	9	10	No change by 10th card
Categories very different: Mouse—Car									
Point at which old identification is abandoned:									
Older (mean age 76·2)	4	1	4	..	2	2	2	..	..
Younger (mean age 23·6)	1	5	10	4	3	2	..	..	..
Point at which correct new identification is achieved:									
Older	..	..	..	1	..	5	3	5	1
Younger	..	..	1	8	10	6	..	..	..
Categories closely similar: Jug—Teapot									
Point of change (old identification abandoned and new achieved at some point by all subjects):									
Older (mean age 73·0)	6	8	3	3	1	..	..	..	..
Younger (mean age 21·6)	2	3	6	2	..	..	..	..	..

How much change with age in ease of identification can be attributed to attitude or experience and how much must be assumed to be due to more basic organic causes, is obviously of practical importance in so far as the former is more amenable than are the latter to prevention or cure by suitable training or retraining.

(iii) *Building and maintenance of perceptual frameworks*

It has already been mentioned that perception includes temporal integration as one of its essential aspects. One facet of this is the building and maintenance of spatial frames of reference in terms of which we maintain orientation in the world around us and are able to find our way about. Incoming data from various sources, mainly from the eyes but also from other senses, are organized together over a period of time to provide a framework immediately available for the co-ordination of posture and movement, the guidance of action and the localization of any fresh data about events in the environment.

It is well known that in extreme senility gross losses can occur of both temporal and spatial orientation, indicating that such frames of reference are gravely impaired. Noticeable changes of this kind are usually absent in middle and normal old age, but it would seem, nevertheless, that some changes can be detected. Little is known beyond a few bare facts, and we shall discuss here only one exploratory experiment by Szafran (1951). The method of the experiment has already been briefly described in Chapter IV (p. 75). The subject was required to locate targets arranged round him at approximately arm's length, under two conditions: (a) with full ability to view the targets, and (b) wearing dark goggles which hid them completely and allowed sight only of a display of light bulbs indicating which target should be aimed at. The subject's task involved translating from the display of lights to the targets, the spatial arrangement of which in condition (b) had to be carried in the subject's memory from previous sight of the apparatus as a whole. The subjects were given time to look at this before the experiment started, and it was originally intended to give half of them the conditions in the order (a) (b), and half in the reverse order. This latter was, however, found to be impossible for older subjects and had to be abandoned because without previous experience of condition (a) they were completely lost in condition (b). It seemed that some actual practice at the first condition was necessary for them to establish their framework for use in the second.

Any difficulty of building or maintaining a spatial framework should show in longer time taken or, in the case of severe impairment, in location of the wrong targets. The results showed that few errors of this kind were made, and were not related to age. There was therefore no *gross* impairment of spatial framework among the older subjects. The times taken for the various component actions of the task are shown in Table 7.7. Taking those for condition (a) first, we see there was little change with age, although the subjects in their fifties were slightly slower over each component than were those younger. Clearly no serious difficulty, such as might have arisen from motor factors setting a limit to performance, arose under this condition in any of the age groups tested. A striking difference, as one turns from condition (a) to condition (b), is in the time taken over 'search', that is to say, between first making contact with the target and finding the 'bull's-eye'. This 'search' time would seem to be a function of the efficiency—or rather the inefficiency—of the subjects' spatial framework in giving accurate guidance to their initial aim and directing subsequent attempts to locate the 'bull's-eye' if the first attempt was unsuccessful. The time taken by this component was substantial at all ages, and showed a rise of more than 100 per cent. as between the twenties and the fifties.

TABLE 7.7. *Analysis of cycle times in Szafran's 'cockpit' experiment*

	Age range			
	Twenties	Thirties	Forties	Fifties
Between the occurrence of the signal and first making contact with the target:*				
Without goggles	1·74	1·96	2·10	2·33
With goggles	2·32	2·42	2·76	2·84
Between first making contact with the target and finding the 'bull's-eye':				
Without goggles	0	0	0	0
With goggles	16·28	17·15	22·58	35·96
From first contact with the bull's-eye to the beginning of the return movement:				
Without goggles	0·47	0·73	0·57	0·91
With goggles	0·97	1·06	1·63	2·49
Return movement from bull's-eye to plate:				
Without. goggles	0·93	0·96	0·93	1·00
With goggles	1·20	1·38	1·58	1·60
Total cycle times:				
Without goggles	3·14	3·65	3·60	4·24
With goggles	20·77	22·01	28·55	42·89

* These times are further analysed in Table 4.6.

The longer time between contact with the 'bull's-eye' and the beginning of the return movement in condition (*b*) was due to the fact that in order to be sure they had located the 'bull's-eye' correctly, subjects had to check the display lights which signalled that the target had been touched by the corresponding light coming on, whereas in condition (*a*) they could see directly when their aim had been correct. Again we find a substantial rise with age in time taken. Inability to see the targets also resulted in the subjects sometimes not realizing when they had found the 'bull's-eye', so that having entered it they would leave again and continue to search. The percentage of times this happened rose from 29 in the twenties to 33 in the thirties, 51 in the forties, and 75 in the fifties.

More detailed indications about the difficulties encountered in this task were obtained by watching the subjects at work. In condition (*a*) all of them watched their hands and the stylus until contact had been made with the bull's-eyes. In condition (*b*) the necessity to check the display made a different behaviour more appropriate, namely watching the display and reaching for the target without turning the head. Subjects of all ages tended, however, at the beginning, to turn their head and shoulders and thus reinstated the postural and kinaesthetic data of condition (*a*). The young subjects tended to abandon this turning sooner than did the older, and much of the difference in their performance was doubtless due to this fact. The essential point is that the older subjects seemed unable to do without this additional postural and kinaesthetic information.

The very striking results of one subject provide evidence that the maintenance of orientation without vision under condition (*b*) is something that can be learned and transferred from one situation to another and that doing so can completely override the normal age trend. It was not known before the experiment that this subject had had considerable experience in photographic dark rooms. For obvious reasons his results were not included in those of the experiment as a whole. He was 49 years of age and by all standards the most efficient performer of all those tested. His times for initiation of response and for outward movement were similar to those of his own age group, but he was strikingly different in 'search', at which he was quicker than the mean of the twenties, and in time to react to finding the bull's-eye, for which he took about the average time of the twenties. His well-formed frame of reference was shown by the fact that he hardly ever looked away from the display of lights.

The tendency of older people to seek additional data

It might have been inferred from the foregoing experiments on perception together with the tendency noted in previous chapters for subjects, especially older subjects, to make the best use of opportunities available to them, that older people would tend actively to seek additional sensory data on which to base perception and action. In fact, it was the observation of such behaviour that led to the undertaking of experiments on perception. An early indication is contained in an anecdote recounted by Miles (1933). 'When the late Charles W. Eliot of Harvard was about 84 he told me that the chief change he noticed in his powers as he grew older was that he had to give direct visual attention to the performance of manual habits. He said: "If I lift a glass of water I must now keep watch on it or the glass may slip from my hand. A few years ago, the hand itself would entirely take care of such a matter.'''

An experimental study of the problem has been made by Szafran who noticed in the throwing experiment outlined in Chapter VI a difference between the behaviour of older and younger subjects in picking up chains when throwing over the screen at the target seen in the mirror. When throwing direct or over the bar, subjects of all ages tended, while picking up each chain, to look away from the target towards the stand on which the chains were hung. When throwing over the screen, however, many tended to keep their eyes fixed on the mirror and to pick up the chains by 'feel'.

On the basis of observations made when throwing over the screen the subjects were divided into those who always or almost always looked while picking up the chains, and those who seldom or never did so. The results of classifying the subjects in this way are shown in Table 7.8, from which it will be seen that the tendency to look for

TABLE 7.8. *Behaviour of subjects when picking up chains to throw over the screen in Szafran's first experiment*

	Age range				
	Teens	*Twenties*	*Thirties*	*Forties*	*Fifties*
Number of subjects who: Seldom or never looked while picking up chains . .	9	10	9	6	5
Always or almost always did so	3	2	15	12	13
The latter as a percentage of the whole age group .	25	17	62	67	72

the chains when picking them up increased strikingly between the twenties and the thirties. This was an unexpected result, and it was decided therefore to carry out an additional experiment which would permit more accurate observation and recording of the frequency with which subjects did or did not look. A new group of subjects, half in the twenties and half in the thirties, were taken, and each was required to throw two groups of fifty chains over the screen. One group had to be picked up in a regular pattern on a board, the layout being such as more or less to compel a subject to look towards the board each time he picked up a chain. The other group were handed by the experimenter to the subject one by one as he threw, so that there was no need for him ever to take his eyes off the mirror—all he had to do was to hold out his hand and the experimenter placed a chain in it. To balance practice effects, half the subjects in each age range threw their first fifty chains picking them up from the board

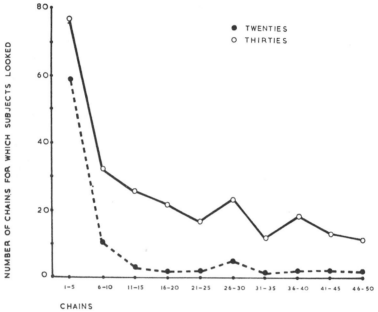

Fig. 7.14. Numbers of chains for which subjects looked when there was no need to do so

The percentages of subjects who looked less than five times in all were almost exactly the same as those for subjects of the same age groups in the former experiment who were classed as 'seldom or never looking'.

and their second having them placed in the hand by the experimenter. The other half received the treatments in the reverse order.

The experimenter stood to the side of and slightly behind the subject, and noted for each chain whether the subject looked for it or not.

As was to be expected, the subjects in both the age ranges looked away from the mirror almost every time when picking up the chains from the board. The results obtained when the chains were handed to the subjects were, however, very much less uniform. They are shown in Fig. 7.14, from which two points emerge. Firstly, the subjects in both the age ranges tended to look away from the mirror towards their hands when receiving the first few chains of the series. This tendency, however, rapidly diminished, indicating that as the subjects became familiar with their task they gave their main attention to the reflection of the target in the mirror, and carried on the task of receiving the chains with reduced sensory cues—that is to say they were doing by 'feel' alone what they were before doing by 'feel' supplemented by vision. Secondly, the results strikingly confirm those of the former experiment in that the subjects in their thirties did, on the average throughout the series, look round more frequently when receiving the chains than did those in their twenties. The tendency appeared to be fairly general. No subject in the twenties looked round more than nine times in all or twice after the first ten chains, as against some 35–40 per cent. of the subjects in their thirties.

Similar trends were subsequently observed (Szafran 1955) in other performances, as, for instance, in Leonard's experiment outlined in Chapter IV: both younger and older often looked at the control, but the former tended to do so while carrying out movements, whereas the latter tended to look before initiating movements. Szafran himself in a factory made a film study which showed that older women operatives tended to look at what they were doing more than younger in various manipulative tasks. In a less formal manner, Schonfield watched people posting letters, and reported that those who appeared to be over 35 years of age tended to look at the envelopes more often than people who appeared to be younger before placing the letters in the box—behaviour which colleagues exasperatingly confirmed in themselves. It is perhaps relevant to add that Shooter found at a Post Office training school that visual aids and practical demonstrations of apparatus were regarded as specially helpful for older trainees.

It would seem that looking at what one is doing serves either or both of two functions. Firstly, it provides information for the guidance of action, and secondly, it enables checks to be made upon the occurrence of action or upon some point of accuracy such as the presence of stamps upon letters. It would seem that older people tend to require more of such information than do younger. Thus in Leonard's case both young and old made some visual check on their action, but the older tended to guide with vision a movement which the younger could guide by 'feel' alone. It is reasonable to believe that the same causes lay behind looking in Szafran's experiments also. Several subjects in his second experiment, on being questioned afterwards, complained that when the experimenter put the chain into their hand it made them feel hurried and lacking in a 'confidence' which turning round to look seemed to restore. The tendency to check upon action is of course similar to the tendencies noted in other experiments, particularly the grid-matching experiment outlined in Chapter IV.

Detailed consideration of Szafran's experiments and of the remarks made by the subjects suggested that two other factors, both of which would seem to merit further study, may have made some contribution to his results. The first is a possible restriction of the visual field which has been noted by Ferree and Rand (1930) to occur with increasing age. If this happened to any substantial extent, the possibility is raised that some visual guidance of the hand in picking up the chains was needed by younger and older subjects equally, and that the younger were able to do this by peripheral vision 'out of the corner of their eye', whilst the older were not. Part of the interest of this possibility derives from the question of whether the loss of visual field is a direct cause of looking or is in fact itself the result of lower perceptual efficiency leading to the data of peripheral vision becoming ineffective.

The second possibility arises from remarks made by a few of Szafran's subjects who maintained that they preferred to look away from the target because prolonged fixation of one point resulted in the field of vision 'becoming blurred' or their 'seeing everything double and shaky'. As one of them said: 'It is, I think, an obvious and well-known fact that looking at one point for a while is bound to tire one's eyes. It is always easier to look at, and to see, a fresh point, even if this point was looked at and seen before.' Such remarks indicate that at least in a few cases prolonged fixation induced some perceptual disorganization or fatigue. The possibility has to be considered that this arises more easily in older subjects than in younger.

Conclusion on perception

The evidence upon changes of perception with age is still somewhat scanty, but it seems very clear that difficulty of visual perception in later middle and old age is not solely due to readily observable and commonly recognized changes in the eye. The neural mechanisms lying behind the eye, including the central processes involved in object identification and maintenance of frames of reference, undoubtedly play an important part. The tests of visual acuity in common use do not fully reflect the magnitude of the changes that occur with age.

While the avoidance of very fine discrimination under conditions of poor contrast or low illumination can substantially improve conditions of perceptual work for older people, the evidence implies that this is not enough. Attention must be paid to the ease with which objects to be perceived can be identified and to viewing time. Of assistance in this respect would appear to be the confining of objects to relatively few categories and presenting them under conditions where they can be seen all at once. Looking at the problem another way, it would appear that perceptual conditions can be improved for older people by providing additional sensory data or producing conditions under which the information required is minimized. Again, more time for inspection allows greater cumulation of information, stronger 'signals' can avoid difficulties of near-threshold discrimination, more continuous opportunities for observation can avoid temporary overloads upon the subject's capacity for short-term retention. In many cases, data from other senses can be called into play, such as the supplementing of touch by vision or of vision by kinaesthesis. The use of such additional information may slow performance, but there would seem likely to be an appreciable zone over which time lost in this way would be more than offset by a rise in the accuracy or quality of the resulting perception and action.

VIII

PROBLEM SOLVING

'Can you do Addition?' the White Queen asked. 'What's one and one and one and one and one and one and one and one and one and one?'
'I don't know,' said Alice. 'I lost count.'
'She can't do Addition,' the Red Queen interrupted.

LEWIS CARROLL

THE characteristics of tasks included under the heading of 'Problem Solving' cover a wide range. Some appear essentially to involve the classification of material such as blocks of different shapes and colours according to one or more rules, or the discovery of the least or greatest number of rules that can bring about a given type of result. Others involve building up a 'set' or expectation in the subject and then seeing how easy or difficult it is to divert the subject's behaviour to a different line. We shall not, in the present chapter, attempt to deal with these types of problem but will confine our attention to work which does in a sense represent an extension of that surveyed in the last two chapters. The concept put forward in Chapter VI of intermediate steps between signal and response is similar on a shorter time-scale to the analysis of thinking and problem solving as step-wise processes by Bartlett (1950). The tasks we shall consider all had this feature as one of their main characteristics. In each case the subject was required to organize several different pieces of data together in order to answer certain pre-determined questions or to arrive at a specified end result. The tasks thus set problems in what Bartlett has called 'interpolative' rather than 'extrapolative' thinking. They were also, as is perhaps obvious but will appear more clearly later, akin to perceptual tasks demanding the building and maintenance of a frame of reference in the sense that they all involved the 'holding-together' simultaneously of a quantity of data to form a coherent 'scheme', without which a solution could not have been arrived at except as a result of a very unlikely accident.

Perhaps the most crucial and at the same time the most elusive feature of problem solving is that it always involves what, for want of a better term, we may call *manipulation of data in the abstract*. In some tasks, the apparatus permits the moves leading to a solution to be made by physically moving counters or other objects or by drawing lines or writing notes. Such actions are, however, seldom if ever done blindly and at random; always, or almost always, they follow imagined moves, the anticipated results of which have already been considered by the subject. Their part would thus seem not to represent the spearhead of the attack upon the problem by the subject, but rather the registration and consolidation of what has been done. Any problem-solving task thus involves the subject in anticipating ahead of his actions to some extent, and it is easy to see that there is a certain minimum distance over which this must be done if any progress is to be made at all. Just what this minimum distance is depends very greatly upon the nature of the task, and the amount of data that must be handled in making such an anticipation would seem likely to be an important variable in determining the degree of difficulty of any problem. The terms 'distance' and 'amount' must be used with caution in this context owing to the coding of data and the organization of perception and action into higher units as discussed in Chapter II. The amount of data from the subject's point of view may be different from that determined by simple objective counts of features in the display, or of the detailed actions required. If these can be grouped together and dealt with, as it were by standard sub-routines, the amount of data from the subject's point of view will be very greatly reduced.

We should expect, from what is known of the results of intelligence tests, that the requirement of handling data in the abstract would be a serious difficulty for older people. Why this should be so is, however, not at all clear. The problem lies in the fact that we have no precise understanding of what manipulation of data in the abstract really means. We need, therefore, to try to go behind this concept and analyse it in terms of other mechanisms which are known, from other evidence, to change with age.

We shall take first an exploratory experiment by Allan in which subjects were presented with a series of statements between which there were certain connexions or inconsistencies according to the rules of formal logic. The subjects were required to make a written statement in which they drew deductions or pointed out fallacies. The task thus differed in an important way from many tests in demanding the construction of an answer instead of merely the choice of one of a number given.

When designing the statements and the method of the experiment an attempt was made to overcome two criticisms levelled against studies of ageing using material such as intelligence tests: firstly, that the test-items are of such a nature that older people regard them as trivial and not worth serious effort, and secondly, that they bear a resemblance to examinations given in schools, and therefore discriminate against subjects in proportion to the length of time since they have left school. This second objection has more force in America than in this country because school examinations of the 'quiz' type are commoner there than they are here. Two of the four sets of material are shown below:

Set B

1. A right action is an action that will bring about at least as much good, or, failing that, will avoid at least as much evil as any other action open to the agent at the moment of acting.
2. A good man is a man who always does what seems to him, after due consideration, to be right.
3. It is always wrong to tell a lie or break a promise.
4. Suffering in itself is undoubtedly evil.
5. In some cases it seems obvious that the only consequence of telling the truth or of keeping a promise will be to cause more suffering than would result from the opposite behaviour.

Instructions

Read carefully the statements printed on the sheet and answer the following questions.

Questions

(i) Are these statements compatible one with another?
(ii) If not, what is the least number that must be rejected to yield a completely consistent set?
(iii) Write out such a list, containing the fewest possible rejections, and state briefly wherein lies the incompatibility between those you reject and those you retain.

Set C

1. The diversion of labour to the production of machinery and other forms of capital goods is an essential step in the industrialization of a non-industrial country and must cause a temporary fall in the standard of living of the labouring classes of the country concerned.
2. People who are not familiar with an industrial economic system will never voluntarily submit to a reduction in their standard of living simply on the promise of better things to come.
3. There are only two ways of surmounting this obstacle in the path of industrialization: (i) by borrowing from abroad in order to keep up the standard of living at home; (ii) by making illegal the forming of trade unions and strikes and so making the workers wholly subject to the heads of industry.
4. Only after industrialization had advanced to a high level of efficiency in various parts of the world was it possible to adopt the expedient of borrowing.
5. No Communistic government wishing to industrialize can hope to obtain such loans.

Instructions

Using the facts stated on the sheet, state any conclusion or conclusions you think are justified by them and explain briefly how your conclusion or conclusions follow from the facts.

Each subject was given one of the four sets of statements to work at in his own time, returning the answers a few days later. In view of the nature of the material, subjects were not required to append their names to the answers.

The clearest finding that emerged from the results was that, although the older subjects seemed as capable as the younger of giving answers *of some sort* to the problems, they did so in a different way. In particular, they tended not to draw logical deductions based strictly on the statements as given, but to introduce supplementary premises or to confine themselves to comments upon the statements.

Examples of answers in which the required deductions were drawn are:

Schoolteacher, aged 32, in answer to question (iii) of set B:

According to statement 5 a lie would in given circumstances cause less suffering, therefore (statement 4) would be less evil than the truth, and would (statement 1) be a right action. Under these circumstances a good man in doing right would tell a lie. As statement 3 states it is always wrong to tell a lie it must be rejected.

Housewife, aged 45, in answer to question (iii) of set B:

Statements 1, 2, 4, and 5 on the question sheet are compatible with each other, but 3 must be rejected because if a case arises such as that in statement 5, surely a good man as qualified in 2, will not tell the truth or hesitate to break a promise, because to do so would cause unnecessary suffering (4), and being a good man he naturally wishes to carry out statement (1).

Clerk, aged 34, in answer to set C:

The first conclusion justified from the facts stated is that, while a non-Communist state would meet no insuperable obstacle in the path of industrialization, it would be impossible for a Communist state to become industrialized. The fact that people unaccustomed to an industrial economic system would not accept a reduction in their standard of living, necessary to achieve industrialization, can only be surmounted in two ways. These are both open to a non-Communistic state, provided a sufficient amount of industrialization has occurred in other parts of the world to permit of a loan. A Communistic state would be unable to effect such a loan, however, and is thus faced with the alternative of suppressing trade unions and strikes and making the workers subservient to the heads of industry, which is incompatible with Communistic doctrines. If it adopted this course it would cease to be a Communist state.

A second conclusion is that the first states to become industrialized must have done so by a policy of repression as, with no other states industrialized loans were impossible.

Examples of answers of the purely commenting type are:

Extra-mural lecturer, aged 46, in answer to question (iii) of set B. (The subject rejected statements 1, 2, and 4 in answer to question (ii).)

The rightness or wrongness of an action must, as I think, be determined by its end-result. Thus a good man is the one who does what is right according to thel ight he possesses. Experience has taught me that to adhere absolutely to the truth or even to a promise may lead to suffering— personal suffering, and moreover suffering to other people. This is contained in statement 5. Regarding 4, I might add that suffering is evil, though in some cases it may be a form of discipline which can result in some kind of good. Even so, I find it difficult to justify it. I am forced to regard it as an evil which ought to be eradicated.

Industrial welfare officer, aged 49, in answer to set C:

Regarding paras. 1 and 2, people will not co-operate unless they are educated to appreciate (1) the actual position as it applies to the individual and the nation as a whole; (2) unless the leaders are quite frank and can be trusted to give them a square deal, before, during, and after a national crisis.

There must be an incentive to work, to regard work not as a painful necessity but as a pleasure, or a means of obtaining satisfaction unobtainable in any other way.

Regarding para. 3. (1) Borrowing from abroad is a short-term expedient which tends to confuse the issue, creates a wrong impression among the workers, and makes the borrower subject to the financial dictatorship of the country lending the money, restricts the market and leads to a state of distrust, &c. (2) The making illegal of trade unions and strikes is the best way to foment unrest, workers suffering from frustration will find an alternative outlet for their emotions, will not co-operate with the heads of industry, and will listen to the worst if it offers some redress for their suppressed opinions.

Regarding para. 4. 'Borrowing' as we now understand it only becomes possible when the majority of the major countries have adopted a monetary standard. 'Bartering' has been in universal practice ever since history has been recorded, and no doubt existed before.

Regarding para. 5. Communistic governments had and do obtain loans.

The results of classifying the answers into those drawing deductions from the material and those which consisted solely of comments about the statements, are set out in Table 8.1. They show a substantial association between age and commenting for each of the four sets of statements used.

In seeking to explain these results several widely different possibilities were considered, of which three may be dismissed with reasonable confidence. Firstly, the younger subjects tended to be of a somewhat higher occupational grade than the older and it seemed possible that this might have influenced the results. Reanalysis of the answers by occupational grades, as shown in Table 8.2, made it clear,

TABLE 8.1. *Classification of subjects into those who drew deductions and those who only commented upon the material*

Set	Age range	Subjects who drew deductions	Subjects who made comments only
A	Under 35	10	6
	Over 35	1	9
B	Under 35	13	6
	Over 35	3	18
C	Under 35	25	4
	Over 35	13	15
D	Under 35	5	6
	Over 35	0	8

TABLE 8.2. *Relationships between age, occupational status and drawing deductions. All four sets of material combined*

Occupational status	Age range	Subjects who drew deductions	Subjects who made comments only
University teaching and research	Under 35	28	7
	Over 35	8	10
Professional and managerial .	Under 35	24	11
	Over 35	8	27
Others, mainly clerical and secretarial	Under 35	1	4
	Over 35	1	13

however, that this was not the sole explanation. The association between age and the tendency to comment on the material rather than draw deductions, was present in each of the three grades. Secondly, it seemed possible that some of the older subjects might have been busier in their everyday lives than were the younger, and in consequence had been less willing to take trouble over the experiment. Examination of the answers failed to reveal any obvious signs of perfunctoriness or carelessness, and remarks made by many of the subjects confirmed that they had been by no means indifferent to the task. As an additional check, however, the mean lengths of answer were calculated, with results shown in Table 8.3. Clearly

TABLE 8.3. *Numbers of words in answers to logical problems*

Means per subject

Set	Subjects under 35	Subjects over 35
A	209	184
B	147	198
C	102	94
D	190	197

there was no substantial or consistent tendency for the older subjects to produce shorter answers than the younger. This evidence makes it clear that the actual writing of an answer was not the limiting factor for the older groups. Thirdly, it seemed conceivable (although un- likely) that a number of subjects who failed to draw the required deductions *misunderstood the instructions* given on the papers. This, however, again cannot give a sufficient explanation of our results. Not only would the number of subjects involved be improbably large, but several, in their answers, gave definite evidence that they had understood the instructions, but found difficulty in carrying them out, e.g. a schoolteacher, aged 57 commenting on C: 'I find this work difficult because I am inclined to question several of the statements, instead of accepting them and drawing the conclusions, if any, which may be justly derived from them.'

We may defer consideration of more positive attempts at explana- tion and turn now to another problem-solving task, similar in many ways, which formed part of an experiment by Speakman (1954) on incidental learning in relation to age. On 3 May 1951 the colours of most British stamps were changed. The former colours and designs were retained, but the colours were assigned to different values, except in the case of the threepenny, which was unchanged. The previous association between colours and values on the lower denomination stamps had continued without a break since 1912. Speakman removed the numbers indicating the values of the $\frac{1}{2}d.$, $1d.$, $1\frac{1}{2}d.$, $2d.$, $2\frac{1}{2}d.$, and $3d.$ stamps (which were all of the same general design) and presented subjects with the six stamps on a card, asking them whether they could identify the values of the stamps at present in use. They were then reminded that the colours had been changed, and asked if they could remember what values the stamps would have borne before the change was made. If the subject had been able to identify all the values in the new series, the experiment was then discontinued. If not, he was informed of the fact and given an additional 'clue card' on which were mounted the numbers indicating values in both the old and new series. The card thus bore eleven numbers on little patches of coloured background—two for each value of stamp except the threepenny, for which there was only one, and two values for each colour except mauve, the colour of the threepenny in both the old and new series.

Speakman explains the use of the clue card as follows:

A subject could use it in either of two ways: he could either use it simply as an aid to memory, or he could, if he knew certain of the stamps, use it to deduce logically the values of the rest. In practice some 90 per cent. of the sample were able to identify either the old or new values of the red and green stamps; working on these two premises it was possible to deduce all the other values as follows: (a) If the old value of the red is 1d., then the new value of the red must be 2½d., and the new value of the blue must be 1d., and the old value 2½d. (the same information could have been deduced from knowledge of the old or the new value of the blue stamps); (b) If the old value of the green is ½d., the new value of the green must be 1½d., the new value of the orange must be ½d., the old value of the brown must be 1½d., the old value of the orange must be 2d., and the new brown also 2d. (the same information could have been deduced from knowledge of the old or new values of either the orange or the brown stamps); (c) Since there is only one mauve 3d. disc, this stamp must have been the same in both old and new series. To subjects with a fair knowledge of either the new or the old values the process was considerably less complicated than this, since they had merely to identify the one value in each colour pair belonging to one series, and, by elimination, the second number of the pair must belong to the other series. By contrast, subjects only knowing one or two of the new series and no old values had a more difficult task in identifying the new, since the process involved more than one deduction for each identification.

The main results of this experiment are set out in Table 8.4. The scores for recall do not concern us here, but will be considered in Chapter IX. The important point to note for our present purpose is that the younger subjects benefit more from the clue card and there is a steady decline in the benefit derived from it as one goes up the age scale. Speakman points out:

From the comments and behaviour of the subjects, it seemed that the older people responded to the clue card in a different way from the younger. Thus while many of the younger subjects found logical analysis easier than trying to create order among a mass of partly remembered meanings, older subjects seemed to find it easier to pick out visually those colour-value bonds which seemed most 'appropriate'. The result was that whereas the younger people seemed to regard the clue card as a useful aid, many of

TABLE 8.4. *Recall of stamp values and the improvements resulting from giving a logical clue*

Means per subject out of six

	Age group					
	20–29	*30–39*	*40–49*	*50–59*	*60–69*	*70–86*
Number of old values correctly recalled . .	4·8	4·7	4·3	3·0	2·3	2·2
Number of new values correctly recalled						
Before clue card given .	3·4	2·9	1·9	2·2	2·5	2·4
After using clue card .	5·5	5·1	4·2	4·1	3·9	3·4
Actual gain after using clue card as a percentage of possible gain . .	81	71	56	50	40	28

those over 60 quite obviously regarded it as merely another complication in a problem that was already difficult enough. This was exemplified in an 83-year-old woman who had made a reasonable score on identification of the stamps, but when she was shown the clue card and its functions had been explained to her, commented: 'Now this is really difficult, I shall never be able to sort them all out.'

Many older subjects tended to make judgements that 'felt right' and then either tried to twist data to fit or to ignore data when they did not fit. Compare, for example, the comment of a 26-year-old clerical worker who by logical deduction had identified the new value of the brown stamp as 2*d*., and who said with some surprise: 'It doesn't look right, but it must be', with that of a 69-year-old woman who identified the new value of the orange as 2*d*. and the old as ½*d*. (the reverse of the real position), having previously identified the modern green as 1½*d*., which was correct. When it was pointed out that this identification made two ½*d*.'s in the old series, she retorted: 'You're not trying to tell me I'm wrong, are you?' and she emphatically reiterated her previous response. Some three weeks later she approached the experimenter's wife in the street and, commenting on this experiment, mentioned this incident, and said: 'but I was right about it after all!'.

It was also common for older people who did not use logic to identify two 2*d*.'s or two 2½*d*.'s in their response and seem to be unaware of it. If and when this was pointed out it was in several cases rationalized into an apparently logical framework by the introduction of a 'deus ex machina' of which the most frequent was: 'Of course, there are really two in circulation.' Many of the older subjects in fact seemed to lack the ability to carry on significantly connected trains of thought of the type necessary to solve this problem; that is to say, later responses did not seem to be evolved in meaningful relation both to the immediate situation and to earlier responses, but seemed independent in sole response to the immediate stimulus.

The numbers of subjects given the clue card and the numbers using it to make logical deductions are shown in Table 8.5. In computing the actual and possible gains from using the card it was borne in mind that since older subjects remembered fewer of the old values, the type of deduction required of them would have tended to be of the more complex variety, so that they might have had in fact a more difficult task than the younger. The results were therefore tabulated omitting the few cases where the more complex processes would have been required. It appears from Table 8.5 that the efficiency of logical

TABLE 8.5. *Results on new series with clue card after removal of situations requiring more complex deductions. Analysed by stamps, but omitting 3d. mauve, which all subjects identified*

	Twenties	Thirties	Forties	Fifties	Sixties	70–86
(a) Users of logic						
Number	6	6	5	4	1	0
Total possible gains	16	17	15	13	4	. .
Total actual gains	14	15	14	9	2	. .
Actual as % of possible	87	88	93	69	50	. .
(b) Non-users of logic						
Number	4	4	7	7	8	8
Total possible gains	12	11	22	16	22	15
Total actual gains	8	4	5	5	9	5
Actual as % of possible	67	36	23	31	41	35

deduction among the subjects who used it rose slightly from the twenties to the forties and declined sharply thereafter. Improvement, as a percentage of possible improvement, was higher for the subjects who used logical deduction than for the subjects who did not, in all age groups.

Taking the results of Allan's and Speakman's experiments together we see that, in both, the older subjects were tending to apply to the material knowledge and opinions which they brought with them to the experimental situation, and it looks as if they were often in a sense unable to get away from these to a more strictly logical treatment. Many of Allan's subjects who were given credit for having answered correctly, inserted one or two comments obviously deriving from such opinions or knowledge, in an answer which was otherwise strictly in the manner required. Many others seemed to make no attempt to consider any logical conclusions, and their answers consisted only of disconnected remarks about individual statements, in which they gave information and expressed their views. Many of the remarks of Speakman's older subjects appeared to be equally unconnected with the logical requirements of his experiment.

The question arises as to how far this kind of answer resulted from *interference* with thinking by the firmer, better-structured opinions and increased information that go with age, and how far it represented a secondary effect of *inability to organize complex material* in a logical manner. It must be remembered that in one sense the commenting type of answer in Allan's experiment was 'better' than that demanded by the instructions since the material was more closely linked with the rest of the subject's experience. One may suspect also that social pressures often operate against an incisively logical approach to everyday problems, so that a more factual method of dealing with them would tend to become habitual and to be used even in situations where it was inappropriate.

On the other hand, any inability to draw conclusions from the data is likely to give rise to the commenting type of approach observed by Allan, or the illogical treatment observed by Speakman, for one of two reasons: firstly, it enables some response to be made to the data, even though this is less than optimal; secondly, inability to deal with the material in the way demanded may result in failure to control emotionally toned opinions which are thus left free to obtrude in the answers.

Further experiments indicate that although interference by experience brought from the past may have some deleterious effect upon thinking among older people, it could hardly be the whole explanation, and some reference to a more fundamental disability is required.

An experiment by Bernardelli achieved some control of experience by presenting an electrical problem, simulating those involved in fault-finding by radio-service engineers, to subjects with no previous electrical knowledge. The task was derived from one developed by Carpenter (1946) and the apparatus consisted of a number of small boxes each with six terminals on top connected underneath by resistances. The subject was given a box, together with a resistance

meter and a circuit diagram which showed the connexions between
the terminals in the box, but did not indicate which terminals in the
diagram corresponded to which on the box. The subject's task was to
deduce which terminals corresponded to which, by means of readings
taken on the meter. The usual method was to take readings until one
or two of the easier terminals had been identified, and then to use the
information thus gained as a guide to taking further readings which
would identify another terminal and so on. The experiment consisted
of an initial training period in which one box was used, followed by

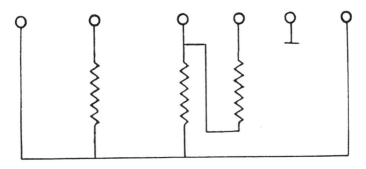

EACH RESISTANCE —\/\/\/\— = 1000 ohms

FIG. 8.1. Circuit diagram of the boxes used in electrical problem experiment

a test period in which four boxes had to be solved. The circuit
diagram of all five boxes was the same, but the arrangement of the
terminals was different in each case. The circuit is given in Fig. 8.1.

The results for the training stage of the experiment will be left
aside until Chapter X. There was no doubt that the task was difficult
and some subjects in each age range failed to deal with the first box
presented. The proportion who so failed was about the same in both
age ranges, but little weight can be placed upon this result as the
older subjects were on average probably of somewhat higher intellectual level than the younger. The data do, however, permit a type
of age comparison which is rather different from that usually carried
out between matched representative samples. The subjects in the two
age ranges who completed all four boxes in the 'test' part of the
experiment provide two groups who show approximately equal
achievement and by examining them we are able to compare the
manner in which an older and a younger group attained the same
achievement. The results are set out in Table 8.6, where it can be seen

that the numbers of terminals correctly identified were closely similar for both age groups but that the older took a much greater time and substantially more meter readings to achieve this result.

TABLE 8.6. *Performances at electrical problem experiment*

Means per subject

	Age range	Boxes			
		1st	*2nd*	*3rd*	*4th*
Terminals correctly identified	Younger Older	5·61 5·08	4·59 4·92	5·38 5·55	5·63 5·95
Difference: older minus younger . . .		−0·53	+0·33	+0·17	+0·32
Difference: as % of mean of younger .		−10	+7	+3	+6
Time taken (*in seconds*)	Younger Older	253 465	260 418	117 254	125 227
Difference: older minus younger . . .		+212	+158	+137	+102
Difference: as % of mean of younger .		+84	+61	+117	+82
Readings taken on meter	Younger Older	20·4 28·4	27·0 34·4	14·2 20·0	17·8 22·8
Difference: older minus younger . . .		+8·0	+7·4	+5·8	+5·0
Difference: as % of mean of younger .		+39	+27	+41	+28

In seeking reasons for these results, two points appear to be important: firstly, the longer time taken by the older subjects for each meter reading indicates that they were having difficulty in giving meaning to them, and secondly, the large number of readings taken by the older subjects means that some readings were being taken more than once. This appeared to be mainly due to their being forgotten, several older subjects complaining that they 'could not hold the readings in their heads'. These two points would seem to be closely interdependent. The solution of a problem of the type used in this experiment appears to demand the bringing together of information, some of which is used at once, while the rest is being 'carried' in some form of short-term memory ready to be brought into play when required. Slowness in dealing with any part of the problem will place a strain upon the short-term memory and will cause pieces of information such as meter-readings to be forgotten so that they have to be taken again. On the other hand, any failure to carry information satisfactorily will have the effect of reducing the quantity of data that can be applied simultaneously to the part

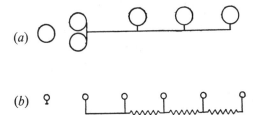

FIG. 8.2. Diagram given to subjects in the 'horses'
problem and its electrical equivalent

(a) Diagram given to subjects
(b) Electrical equivalent

of the problem being dealt with, and at least slow down a solution if not prevent it altogether. It seems therefore that any slowness in organizing data will produce an apparent inefficiency of short-term memory, and any deficiency in short-term memory will impair the ability to organize data.

The difficulty of controlling the electrical knowledge possessed by subjects made the foregoing task of limited application. An attempt was accordingly made by Clay to devise a task which was essentially similar but was cast in other terms, so that no electrical knowledge was required. The subject was presented with a box on which was a row of press-button switches, numbered 1 to 6, and a row of four red lights numbered 0, 3, 6 and 9. With this box the subject was handed the diagram shown in Fig. 8.2(a) and the following instructions:

The diagram represents the photo finish of a horse race.

Each ○ = a horse

One horse has passed the winning post. Two horses are at the post and the distance between these two and the rest of the field is measured in lengths.

Each |____| = 3 lengths

The buttons on this box are numbered from 1 to 6. There is one button for each horse on the diagram.

The problem is to find which button correponds to each horse.

You can do this by pressing any two of the buttons simultaneously. If both the horses they correspond to have not passed the winning post, one of these four lights will go on. The number under the light indicates the distance between the two horses in lengths. Continue to do this until you have identified a horse.

When you have identified a horse, write the number of the corresponding button in the ◯ on the diagram.

All horses must be identified.

The connexions in the box were such that the 'distances' between the 'horses' represented the resistances connected between the push-button switches and the numbered lights indicated the amounts of resistance involved. An essentially similar task, although with a different pattern of connexions and with instructions in terms of traffic on a road, was also prepared.

The subjects were chosen so that those of different ages were of comparable educational background, all being somewhat above average in this respect. Each was given both tasks—half in the order 'horses' followed by 'cars' and half in the reverse order. Having read the instructions for the first box, eight out of the 114 subjects refused to attempt to solve the problem. All these were over 40 years of age. They made excuses such as 'they were never any good at puzzles' and it seemed clear that their refusal was due to their being unable to see either an immediate solution or any obvious method of tackling the problem. Such refusals might at first sight have appeared to indicate unwillingness on the part of the older subjects to undertake the task in the first instance. This is almost certainly not so, however, as all had been keen volunteers and the accuracy of those who did undertake the task was shown to fall progressively with age.

The results, shown in Table 8.7, indicated a clear difference between the fifties and the thirties in the numbers of errors made. The forties appeared, as they did in Brown's grid-matching experiment described in Chapter V, to be a transitional group, benefiting substantially from practice in that they moved from a position near that of the fifties in the case of the first box, to one about the same as the twenties and thirties in the second. Numbers of readings taken showed, as in the electrical problem, an upward trend with age. In this case the thirties appeared as a transitional group, reducing their readings from a number nearly equal to that of the forties on the first box, to one about the same as that of the twenties on the second. Times showed a straightforward rise with age as regards time spent actually taking readings, but a curious irregularity as regards time spent otherwise—presumably interpreting readings—especially for the first box. The most anomalous feature is a fall from the forties

TABLE 8.7. *Errors, readings and times taken on Clay's problem boxes*

Means per subject

	Age group			
	Twenties	Thirties	Forties	Fifties
Number of subjects . . .	38	33	27	8
Accuracy				
First box presented:				
Errors (maximum 6) . .	0·5	0·6	1·4	1·8
Subjects making errors . .	6	6	8	4
Second box:				
Errors	0·5	0·6	0·9	2·0
Subjects making errors . .	7	5	4	3
Readings taken				
First box	19·3	25·2	26·4	31·5
Second box	19·1	19·6	24·1	29·5
Time taken (seconds)				
First box:				
Time spent taking readings ('search' time) . . .	43·9	56·9	72·4	99·4
Time spent otherwise ('interpretation' time) . . .	318·1	382·4	423·9	305·1
Total time . . .	362·0	439·3	496·3	404·5
Second box:				
Time spent taking readings .	35·9	35·8	56·1	117·3
Time spent otherwise . .	252·5	250·3	248·4	225·6
Total time . . .	288·4	286·1	304·5	342·9

to the fifties. Such a feature, coupled with a rise in the number of errors, has appeared in other problem-solving tasks and will be discussed more fully in relation to further experiments by Clay to be outlined later.

Taking the results together we see a change with age both of achievement and of the manner in which this achievement was attained. In the twenties there was little difference between performance on the first and second boxes except for a slight decrease of 'interpretation time'. Compared with the twenties, the thirties appeared to have maintained accuracy at the expense of time and a few more readings on the first box, but were able to benefit from practice to the extent that they gained equality with the twenties in all respects on the second box. The forties were initially poorer in all respects, but with practice they improved both as regards accuracy and speed, although they continued to take a larger number of readings. The fifties showed on average higher scores than younger subjects in all the measures taken except 'interpretation time', and while improving substantially with practice on this score, they remained essentially unchanged as regards others.

Observation of the subjects at work revealed that many wrote down readings instead of trying to carry them in their heads, and that this behaviour was linked with greater accuracy, as shown in Table 8.8. The proportion of subjects writing down readings was, as shown

TABLE 8.8. *Association between accuracy and writing down readings in Clay's problem-box experiment*

Numbers of subjects

	Numbers of buttons correctly identified						
	6	*5*	*4*	*3*	*2*	*1*	*0*
First box presented							
Subjects who wrote .	54	..	5	..	1	..	..
Subjects who did not write	28	1	4	2	3	3	5
Second box							
Subjects who wrote .	57	..	5	1	2	1	..
Subjects who did not write	30	..	2	..	5	2	1

in Table 8.9, somewhat higher in the twenties and thirties than in the forties and fifties and the question obviously arises of whether the lower accuracy among the older subjects was due to this fact. Almost certainly, however, it was not wholly so. For example, on the first box the thirties, forties and fifties attained very different degrees of accuracy but differed only slightly in the proportion of subjects writing down readings. Again, on the second box, the twenties, thirties and forties attained very similar accuracy but showed rather different proportions writing. Looking at the evidence another way, the forties, as a group, substantially improved their accuracy on the second box without adopting the writing technique. To an observer, the writing down of readings did in fact appear to be the result rather than the cause of a better grasp of the problem.

The relations between accuracy, age and making notes of this kind would seem to be worth further exploration, however, since

writing was likely to have reduced the load upon short-term retention
at all ages, so that if in fact such retention enters significantly into
the solving of problems of this type, writing should have made a

TABLE 8.9. *Association between age and writing down readings in
Clay's problem-box experiment*

Numbers of subjects

	Age group			
	Twenties	*Thirties*	*Forties*	*Fifties*
First box presented				
Subjects who wrote . .	25	19	12	4
Subjects who did not write .	13	14	15	4
Second box				
Subjects who wrote . .	27	22	14	3
Subjects who did not write .	11	11	13	5

solution easier. If so, the failure of older people to write would seem
inevitably to have handicapped them to some extent, and it would
seem reasonable to suppose that encouragement of writing, if given
in the instructions, would have benefited their performance.

Some additional evidence confirming the trends shown in Bernardelli's and Clay's experiments comes from a rather simpler problem

FIG. 8.3. Example of a set of patterns used in Schonfield and Shooter's experiment

experiment devised by Schonfield and used by him and Shooter. The
subjects were presented with an apparatus having a number of
hinged flaps about 3 inches square which could be raised to reveal
patterns of black dots in one or more of five possible positions.
There were four series of four problems involving 2, 3, 4, and 5
patterns respectively. An example is shown in Fig. 8.3. The task
was to discover, by raising the flaps one at a time, in which of the
positions (if any) a dot occurred only once. Thus in the example
shown the correct answer would be 'top right of pattern 2 (second
from left) and centre of pattern 3'. The subject was instructed that

before giving his answer he should press the morse key situated at the right-hand side of the apparatus. Table 8.10 shows times spent, errors made and the numbers of times flaps were raised.

TABLE 8.10. *Errors, times taken and numbers of observations in Schonfield and Shooter's experiment*

Means per subject per set of four problems

Age group	Number of patterns in problem			
	2	3	4	5
*Numbers of errors**				
15–29	6·1	5·7	5·4	2·6
30–39	3·8	5·3	3·4	1·8
40–49	5·1	7·3	4·1	2·6
50–71	7·4	8·8	5·2	4·4
Times in seconds				
15–29	33·0	57·5	87·3	87·9
30–39	39·5	87·3	126·2	117·8
40–49	38·5	106·9	136·1	131·8
50–71	50·4	121·3	121·0	121·6
Numbers of observations				
15–29	11·1	19·2	30·3	37·1
30–39	12·7	33·7	56·7	57·3
40–49	12·4	34·8	56·3	63·6
50–71	13·2	34·6	46·6	49·5

* The errors included both incorrect identifications and failures to identify.

If difficulty in problem-solving tasks is related to the need to integrate data, we should expect it to increase with the amount of data to be handled. Unfortunately, interpretation of Schonfield and Shooter's experiment on this point is not possible because the problems were always presented in the same order so that the effect of size cannot be sorted out from those of order and practice. The overall fall in the number of errors as one passes from the smallest to the largest problems is presumably due to practice and is perhaps substantial enough for us to assume that the main effect of practice was to increase accuracy, although this effect seems to have diminished somewhat in the older age groups.

In all four sizes of problem, accuracy rose from the twenties to the thirties and then fell to the forties and again to the oldest group. The times rose fairly consistently with age for the two- and three-pattern problems but for the four- and five-pattern showed the same anomalous fall in the oldest group that was observed by Clay. The same was true for numbers of observations. The transition from the twenties to the thirties is consistent with the view that the former were putting up a somewhat careless performance, saving time at the expense of accuracy, but some different and more complex explanation seems to be needed for the older subjects' results.

An incidental but interesting finding was the rise with age in the number of times the key was forgotten, shown in Table 8.11. Pressing

TABLE 8.11. *Numbers of times subjects forgot to press the key before giving judgements in Schonfield and Shooter's experiment*

Age range	15–20	21–29	30–39	40–49	50–71
Mean omissions per subject . .	0·6	1·7	2·7	3·5	5·6

the key was, so to speak, a detached and 'unessential' part of the task and the clear tendency for this to be dropped by the older subjects may be compared with the results of experiments by Craik, Drew (1940) and Davis (1948) on fatigue, using an artificial aircraft cockpit. They found that in the course of a 2-hour session, the performance of some subjects became disorganized and that operations which did not form an essential part of the task of 'flying' tended to be forgotten. Pilots would, for instance, towards the end of the session omit the periodical resetting of the petrol tap that was required. There would seem to have been a narrowing of the field of attention in an attempt, albeit unconscious, to minimize the requirements of a task and thus maintain reasonable performance in the face of falling capacity. In the cockpit experiment, the omissions saved time which could be diverted to the main task. What would seem to be saved in Schonfield and Shooter's experiment, is the possibility of interference with the short-term retention of the solution of the problem between the time the last flap has been closed and the verbal statement of the subject's judgement.

Clearer evidence that the amount of data to be handled does have a substantial effect in relation to age is contained in a series of experiments by Clay (1954, 1957) which also provides an explanation of the anomalous results in the preceding experiment by her and in that by Schonfield and Shooter. In the first of these experiments, subjects were required to place numbered ivorine counters in the squares of chequer-boards so as to add up to given totals. Four boards were used, as shown in Fig. 8.4. Subjects were divided into three age groups —18-24, 55-69 and 70-78—each subject doing only one board so as to obviate complications due to practice effects. In the

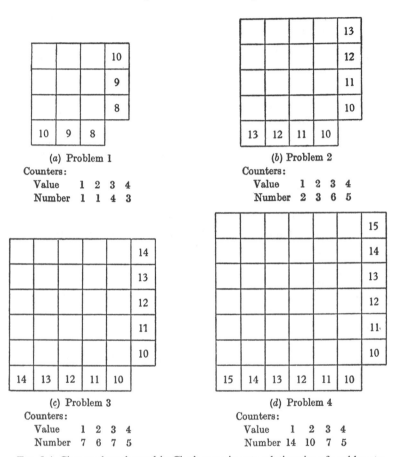

(a) Problem 1
Counters:
Value   1 2 3 4
Number 1 1 4 3

(b) Problem 2
Counters:
Value   1 2 3 4
Number 2 3 6 5

(c) Problem 3
Counters:
Value   1 2 3 4
Number 7 6 7 5

(d) Problem 4
Counters:
Value   1   2   3 4
Number 14 10 7 5

FIG. 8.4. Chequer-boards used in Clay's experiments relating size of problem to change of performance with age

second experiment a 5×5 board only was used with groups of subjects in each decade from the twenties to the seventies. The third experiment was conducted with groups in each decade from the twenties to the sixties. The subject was given the 3×3 board and, when he had completed this, a supplementary board, covering the marginal totals and extending the squares to 6×6, was presented together with additional numbered counters to complete the larger problem. It had originally been thought that to divide the task in this way would make it substantially easier for older people. This did, in fact, prove *not* to be the case; the results for the two stages were very similar in almost every respect to those for the 3 × 3 and 6 × 6 boards in the first experiment.

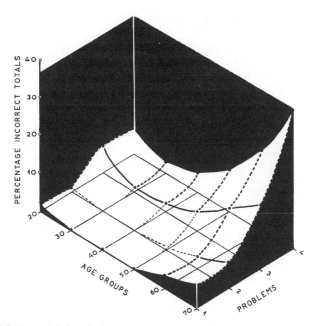

FIG. 8.5. Errors left in solutions of chequer-board problems as a function of age and problem size

The results of these three experiments were sufficiently similar for them to be considered together. Those for accuracy are shown in Fig. 8.5, from which it can be seen that there was a rise in the number of errors as one passed from the 3 × 3 to the 6 × 6 problem, and after a fall from the early twenties to the thirties, the rise with age became steeper as the size of the problem increased. The pattern of results for errors was from the thirties onwards very similar to that obtained by Kay (1954) and shown in Fig. 6.8 (p. 151).

The relationship between time taken, age and size of problem was less regular and the picture presented by Fig. 8.6 is very different from that of Kay's experiment. Times for the 3 × 3 task rose somewhat irregularly until the sixties and dropped in the seventies. In the 4×4 task, times for the sixties were substantially higher than for the twenties and there was again a drop to the seventies. For the 5×5 task, there was a sharp rise from the thirties to the fifties followed

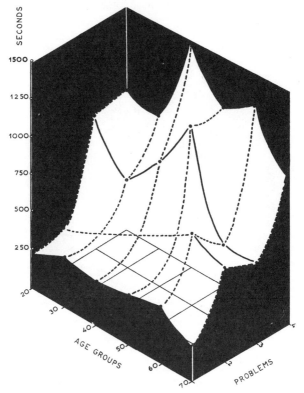

FIG. 8.6. Times taken over chequer-board problems as a function of age and problem size

by an even sharper fall to the sixties and seventies, while for the 6×6 task there is a similar rise from the thirties to the forties followed by a fall to the fifties and beyond. There seemed in each case to be a rise of time with age to a peak followed by a fall at later ages, the peak coming earlier as the size of the problem increased.

Looking at the time and error results together, it can be seen that as the times fell from their peak levels, a rise appeared in the number of errors. It seemed, in fact, that difficulty increasing with age showed first as an increase in the time taken with accuracy held constant, but that a point was reached when the expenditure of extra time would no longer lead to a successful solution, and that the older subjects were able to recognize this and did in consequence abandon the task relatively quickly, leaving a number of errors uncorrected. The point at which such a change occurred came earlier and earlier as the size of the problem increased. Thus with the 3×3 problem it did not come until the seventies, whereas with the 5×5 problem it appeared in the sixties and in the 6×6 problem among the fifties. The difference between Clay's results and those of Kay would seem to have been due to the conditions of the two experiments. Kay was measuring time and errors required to reach a uniform criterion performance. Clay, on the other hand, imposed no limits on accuracy or time, so that there was opportunity for the balance spontaneously struck between the two to be shown in the results.

What, we may ask, is the nature of the difficulty found by the older subjects at these tasks? Detailed studies by Clay of the results, and observation of the way the subjects tackled the task, showed that there was little or no difference with age in the 'strategies' adopted, and little difference in the type of error left in the solutions. Some of the errors could have been corrected by a simple exchange of two counters; others would have necessitated a more complex series of moves. Examples are given in Fig. 8.7. There was a slight tendency for the older subjects to make more of the simplest type of error than the younger, but there was no marked qualitative change in the type of error with age. It would seem, therefore, that the effect of age was to accentuate the difficulties present amongst the younger subjects and not to introduce any radically new type. The difficulties seemed to lie mainly in the making of corrections for errors when all, or almost all, the counters had been placed upon the board. Subjects would make one or two alterations in the arrangements of counters, and then seemingly become confused. This was shown in some cases by their preferring to remove all the counters from the board and to start again, rather than attempt to continue to make corrections. It seemed to be this confusion which acted as the 'cue' to the older subjects to stop, and the pattern of times and errors shown in Figs. 8.5 and 8.6 appears to have resulted from its acting at an earlier and earlier age as the size of the problem became greater.

Such confusion would seem likely to have arisen from the need to hold a considerable amount of data in mind in order to effect corrections, especially those of the more complex variety. Thus, for instance, in the second type of correction shown in Fig. 8.7, it is necessary as a minimum procedure, having identified the two totals which are wrong, to add a pair of counters together in the one column and hold

FIG. 8.7. Examples of changes necessary to correct errors left in solutions of Clay's chequer-board problems

(a) *Direct exchange of two counters*
Column 13 adds to two less than the required number, column 11 to two more. The columns can be corrected by exchanging the two counters indicated in heavy type

```
4   3   2   4    13
3   3   4   2    12
1   4   3   3    11
3   2   4   1    10
13  12  11  10
   -2      +2
```

(b) *Exchange of two pairs of counters*
The error cannot be corrected by the exchange of two counters only but requires that both those indicated in column 13 be exchanged with both those indicated in column 10.

```
4   2   3   3   2    14
4   2   3   3   1    13
1   4   4   1   2    12
2   1   1   3   4    11
3   3   1   1   2    10
14  13  12  11  10
   -1              +1
```

(c) *More than two totals wrong, requiring a series of changes to correct*
Three separate moves are required:
  (i) Exchanging the two indicated counters in column 14 corrects row 13 and reduces the error in row 10.
  (ii) Exchanging the two indicated counters in column 11 corrects row 10 and reduces the error in row 12.
  (iii) Exchanging the two indicated counters in column 10 corrects rows 12 and 11.

```
3   4   1   2   4    14
4   3   4   2   1    13+1
2   4   3   3   3    12+3
2   1   3   2   1    11-2
3   1   1   2   1    10-2
14  13  12  11  10
```

(d) *As an intermediate stage to correction a correct total has to be made temporarily wrong*
Two moves are required:
  (i) Exchanging the two indicated counters in rows 11 and 13 corrects these, but makes columns 10 and 11 wrong.
  (ii) Exchanging the two indicated counters in row 10 corrects columns 10 and 11.

```
4   3   3   4    13+1
2   4   3   3    12
4   1   3   2    11-1
3   4   2   1    10
13  12  11  10
```

(e) *An unusual case where correction of four totals can be made elegantly by the exchange of two counters*
Exchange of the two indicated counters corrects both rows 14 and 11 and columns 14 and 11

```
3   3   4   2   2   1    15
4   2   3   1   1   4    14+1
3   4   1   3   1   1    13
2   4   1   2   2   1    12
2   1   2   3   1   1    11-1
1   1   2   1   3   2    10
15  14  13  12  11  10
   +1              -1
```

their sum while adding the corresponding pair in the other column. Such procedures place a considerable strain upon short-term retention, as discussed in connexion with Bernardelli's electrical problem experiment. It was interesting to see, in confirmation of this, that many of Clay's subjects used aids to memory such as indicating incorrect totals by moving a counter slightly out of place, for the acknowledged purpose of helping them to remember which total needed correction.

It seemed possible, however, that some of this confusion arose from the presence of a large number of counters in close proximity

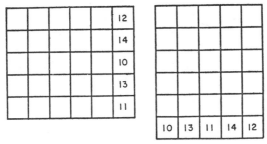

Condition (A)

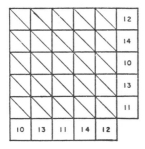

Condition (B)

FIG. 8.8. Chequer-boards used in Clay's experiment on spatial arrangement of data

leading to difficulty in keeping apart and treating separately counters similar to others which were not relevant to the correction in hand. Further examination of this point was made in a control experiment by Clay (1956a).

The task in this consisted of placing fifty numbered counters upon a chequer-board so as to add up to given marginal totals, but instead of totals for rows and columns having to be satisfied simultaneously, one set of twenty-five counters was used for the rows, and another set of twenty-five for the columns. The problem was presented in two forms which are shown in Fig. 8.8. Condition (B) is exactly the same as condition (A) with the exception that instead of two blocks of twenty-five squares being kept entirely separate, the subjects had to place the counters in the bottom left-hand halves of the squares to make up the column totals and the top right-hand halves to make up the row totals. All subjects completed condition (A) before starting condition (B) and it was pointed out to them that the essential problem for condition (B) was the same as that for condition (A). The results are set out in Table 8.12. Those for condition (A) show

TABLE 8.12. *Errors left in solutions and times taken over Clay's chequer-boards with the two different spatial arrangements shown in Fig. 8.8*

	Age group					
	Twenties	*Thirties*	*Forties*	*Fifties*	*Sixties*	*Seventies*
Number of subjects .	15	10	11	13	9	8
Errors						
Condition (A):						
Mean errors per subject	0·13	..	0·26	0·77	..	..
Number of subjects making errors . .	2	..	1	3	..	..
Condition (B):						
Mean errors per subject	..	..	1·0	0·70	0·44	0·67
Number of subjects making errors . .	..	..	4	5	3	3
Mean times per subject in seconds						
Condition (A) . .	294	366	405	385	382	407
Condition (B) . .	286	336	329	636	413	522

no consistent changes with age except for an insignificant rise of time taken between the twenties and the forties. The problem seemed clearly to be within the capacities of the oldest subjects tested. This indicates that the limitation upon the performance of older subjects in Clay's former chequer-board problems was not difficulty in adding, which had been found by Birren and Botwinick (1951) and by Birren *et al.* (1954) to increase with age. With condition (B) the results were somewhat irregular, but there was a significant rise with age in both errors and time taken. The irregularities were due to the balance between these two scores shifting from one age group to another. Comparing performances under the two conditions, we can see that the twenties improved slightly in condition (B) in both time and accuracy. The thirties also improved as regards time, but had no room for improvement of accuracy, as they made no errors in condition (A). The forties were quicker but considerably less accurate in condition (B). The fifties took very substantially longer time for about equal accuracy. The sixties and seventies were on average both less accurate and slower. We see as before the 'break' in the time scores as one goes up the age scale, with times rising a little from the twenties to the thirties and forties, then very sharply to the fifties and falling back again to the sixties.

Commenting upon these results, Clay remarks:

The subjects in the over-40 groups became confused and had difficulty in keeping the two blocks of squares separate on Problem B. Their comments made it clear that they understood the instructions before they began, but they seemed to forget them as they went on. Some added the counters in the upper halves of the squares to equal a column total instead of a row total. Others added up both sets of counters to equal the same total. Several were observed to take a counter from a correct row for an error in a column, or vice versa, because it was the nearest counter of the required value, and to replace it with another counter without any regard to the effect the exchange would have on the previously correct total. Several said they found the display of Problem B much more confusing than that of Problem A, and it seems clear that this resulted from having counters referring to both rows and columns in the same square. Some subjects had difficulty in locating a second incorrect row or column when faced with one incorrect total, and when trying to find it sometimes forgot where they had found the original error. One remarked: 'I can't find it, but I'm only looking down not across.' Another remark: 'If only I could remember where there is one too many', indicates that the subject found it difficult to hold certain facts in mind while looking for other errors.

Several older subjects made use of verbal cues as an aid to memory. For instance, one subject completed all the rows on Problem B and looked at each column total before placing a counter in it, saying 'Now 10' and then 'Now 13', and so on.

We have already suggested, in comment upon the experiments outlined so far, some reasons for the difficulty they seem to have presented for older subjects. The important question remains of why time taken should flatten out or fall at higher ages in every problem where subjects covering a full age range have been tested. Why should there be, as one goes up the age scale, a seemingly radical change of method marked by a shift in the balance between the scores for time and errors? Clay points out that this procedure by the older subjects avoided what would otherwise have been a nearly impossible situation. For example, we can see from Fig. 8.6 that had the times for the 5×5 and 6×6 problems continued to rise after the 'break' at the same rate as they appeared to have been doing before it, the older subjects would have been spending very long times indeed over the task.

One possible factor which might at first sight seem reasonable may be ruled out, namely *lack of motivation* on the part of the older subjects. This point has already been discussed in Chapter III, where it was noted that the short time spent by the older subjects on these problems appears to have been the result rather than the cause of their inability to do the task.

The evidence would seem to point to a 'mechanism' where there are at least two major interacting factors at work. In order to solve this sort of problem the subject must be able, as we noted at the beginning of the chapter, to relate together a certain minimum amount of data. This he must do not only in order to deal with the problem as a whole, but in order to deal successfully with each unit of it; for instance, to identify each terminal in the electrical problem or to correct an error on the chequer-boards. The gathering and the holding in mind simultaneously of these data involves the building of a conceptual framework which in its turn is dependent upon processes of short-term retention. We have seen already that the efficiency of such a system would be considerably impaired by the longer time taken by older subjects to gather data and identify objects—in other words, by perceptual processes. These must precede the storage of data in short-term memory and partly determine the time during which any material already held has to be retained while further data are being gathered. It would seem also, as we shall see in the next chapter, that short-term memory processes become increasingly liable to disruption by intervening activity as we go up the age scale. This imposes an additional complication in those cases where data have to be held in mind while further data are gathered. As a case in point we may note that in the problem illustrated in Fig. 8.2 considerably greater difficulty was found over the three 'horses' indicated by the circles on the right-hand side of the diagram than by the three indicated on the left. These latter could be identified unambiguously by readings of '0' or of 'no connexion', whereas identification of the others required the piecing together of readings of 3, 6, and 9.

The disruption produced by intervening activity may perhaps be compared with that of neural 'noise' discussed in Chapter VII as affecting perception. The analogy becomes closer when we realize that short-term retention is almost certainly carried by self-regenerating neural circuits which would be liable to interference from other neural activity going on at the same time. It may well be that such short-term retention can be more firmly held if extra time is taken for the establishment of the self-regenerating activity. If so, some compensation for lowered capacity of short-term memory could be achieved by spending longer time, just as effective visual acuity can be increased by longer viewing time. Such extra time would, however, obviously bring about an increased chance of the very interference it is intended to avoid. The net result would seem to depend upon the relative rates at which the gain of clarity and the intrusion of inter- ference occur with time and many possibilities need to be explored before any definite pronouncement can be made on this matter. For our present purpose it is sufficient to note, firstly, that if short-term retention is to take place successfully at all, there must be some point of balance at which information can be registered more rapidly than interference can disrupt it: if this were not so, the subject would be incapable of any higher co-ordinated activity at all. Secondly, if as one passes beyond this point the extra time has less effect upon the establishment of short-term memory than it does upon the possibility of interference, a stage will be reached at which longer time will not improve short-term retention any further, and it will be to the subject's advantage to 'cut his losses' by doing the best he can with shorter times, putting up with any resulting inaccuracy.

A numerical example of this kind of interaction is shown in Fig. 8.9. Values of time (t) to establish short-term retention at four levels of problem difficulty are plotted against values of a linear variable (A) assumed in the present case to be a factor decreasing with age. The curves in Fig. 8.9 show time as increasing with diffi- culty at a rapidly accelerating rate as A declines, until the falling curve at the right-hand side is reached. This curve shows the level for each value of A at which any further increase of t will lead to *less* and not more retention. It thus represents an optimum level of performance which, although it may fall short of the level demanded by the task, will make the best of a situation where perfect performance is impossible. It will be obvious that once this falling curve has been reached performance will become more and more inaccurate, and that errors will begin earlier and be greater the higher the level of difficulty. The curves in Fig. 8.9 are similar in type to those of Fig. 8.6 except that, beyond their peaks, the times for the different levels of difficulty fall along a common curve instead of along curves roughly similar in shape but at a level rising with difficulty. This is probably due to the fact that the times shown in Fig. 8.6 include not only those taken to obtain and store data but the times required for actions

CONCLUSION ON PROBLEM SOLVING

The work we have surveyed in this chapter shows that for the type of problem in which several pieces of data have to be related together there is, at least in the cases studied, a decline of performance with age, and that the decline becomes more severe as the complexity of the problem is increased. Close examination of the data reveals, however, no evidence of a change with age in the actual capacity to make the intellectual 'leaps' or insights required. Rather it would appear that limitations for the older subjects lie in the gathering and the holding in mind of the data on which such insights depend. If this is so, it means that we have evidence, not of an actual decline of insight with age, but rather of certain necessary pre-conditions for its occurrence. Such a view would explain the common observation that many of the oldest people display wisdom and judgement at a very high level, especially regarding matters upon which they possess considerable knowledge and experience. Such experience would enable better coding of incoming data and make it both substantially easier and quicker to handle, and requiring of less short-term storage capacity. The practical point follows that attention either to efficient coding or to methods and procedures whereby the load on short-term memory can be minimized—even if only by enabling notes to be used for tasks that would otherwise have to be carried out 'mentally'—would be likely to improve performance considerably as people become older at tasks demanding insight into a mass of data.

IX

LEARNING AND MEMORY

STUDIES using a wide variety of materials have nearly all shown that performance at learning tasks declines from early adulthood onwards. Evidence has been summarized by Ruch (1933) and more recently by McGeoch and Irion (1952). A valuable survey which includes evidence from clinical studies is given by Jones and Kaplan (1956). Thorndike, whose work is classical in this field (Thorndike *et al.* 1928) puts the peak age in the early twenties with a slow decline thereafter, but there are suggestions (Belbin 1953) that for some industrial tasks the peak has come by the teens. If various studies are taken together the general picture is of a slow decline until the seventies with possibly a sharper fall thereafter (Kubo 1938). The *rate* of decline may, in some tasks at least, be less among more able subjects (Gilbert 1941). Thorndike matched his subjects in the different age groups for intelligence test scores and the fact that he still obtained a decline in learning performance means that the changes of learning with age are relatively severe.

Some tasks which have been included loosely under the heading of learning, such as substituting one letter for another or a digit for some other symbol according to a code, are not primarily learning tasks at all, and should be considered in other contexts. Declines with age at tasks which genuinely involve learning vary with the material to be learnt. Thus Thorndike, comparing three groups of subjects aged 20–24, 25–34 and 35 or over, concluded that declines with age were less marked when previous experience could provide some positive help than when there was no way of mitigating the requirement to learn—where the task involved 'sheer modifiability' of the organism. Again, he found among the groups of subjects he obtained that where the learning was 'for use', such as with university studies, the older might be superior to the younger even though showing declines on more artificial tasks. The matching of Thorndike's subjects for intelligence scores means that the absolute learning deficits might be greater in a more representative population, but this would be unlikely to affect the differences between the rates of decline in different tasks.

The lack of age change when learning is 'for use' raises the question of how far lack of willingness to try their best could account for poorer learning by older people. The problem of motivation among older subjects has been considered in previous chapters (pp. 48 and 220), and evidence given that it probably does not account for lowering of performance with age. More positive evidence that it cannot be the sole cause of learning deficit among older people is given in results obtained by Shooter *et al.* (1956). For example, they found that the time taken to retrain London tramdrivers as bus-drivers when trams were withdrawn tended to take longer for older drivers, although their continuance in a driving job depended upon their success. These data will be given in Chapter X.

It is clear that the decline of performance with age at most learning tasks must be accepted as a well-established fact. What we need to know is the nature of the difficulty encountered by older people, its cause and, if possible, the means of preventing or removing it. Some indication can be obtained from the differential rates of decline for different types of material, categories of subject and conditions under which the task is done, but for the most part it would seem necessary to study learning in more detail than is usually attempted, trying to go beyond the overall learning achievement to the process whereby this achievement is attained.

Loss of plasticity is often spoken of as the cause of the decline. 'Plasticity', however, is a vague term which needs further definition if it is to be of use in this connexion. It presumably implies inability to modify pre-existing habits to meet new conditions, but would seem, as commonly used, to be merely descriptive and not explanatory. If, however, we look behind the term, we find it used to cover two types of theory, both special cases of the main types of theory advanced to account for age changes in general. The maturation–degeneration theory suggests that loss of ability to learn is due to a loss of ability to 'register' new information. The alternative theory which stresses the effects of experience points out that when we confront a new task we inevitably do so in terms of knowledge and habits acquired in the past, and that these may or may not be appropriate, and will help or hinder performance accordingly. It further implies that the wide range of experience that older people possess and the greater extent of its channelling increase the chance of their bringing inappropriate experience to bear.

Before attempting to assess the validity of these theories we must recognize that for learning to take place, and for the subject to be able to furnish evidence that it has, a number of stages must be gone through. These will vary somewhat from one situation to another, but the following would seem to be essential:

1. The material to be learnt must be *perceived* and *comprehended* and any *responding actions selected* or *built*. This will inevitably be done in terms of material derived from past experience to some extent codified and 'schematized'. The subject will perceive and respond by selecting, qualifying and reordering this schematized material, and what is learnt appears normally to be the result of this process rather than directly dependent on sensory data (Zangwill 1937, 1939; Kay 1955*b*). On the effector side it would seem that we can learn a fresh selection, fine control and temporal ordering of action. On the receptor side and in the translation process it would appear that we learn in terms of categories or 'codes' which we derive by recognizing how the various pieces of data are related together, and which enable us to reconstruct on a future occasion an approximation to what we have perceived (Bartlett 1932; Oldfield 1954). It is true that we appear sometimes very shortly after witnessing an event to be able to recall more detail than we make use of subsequently, and can thus be said to be recalling on the basis more of the *stimulus* than of our perception. When, however, this short period is past, all that remains seems to be what we have made of the material in perceiving and dealing with it.

2. The material is held by some *short-term retention* mechanism, which can store very rapidly but impermanently. We may reasonably assume that the mechanism consists of self-regenerating neuronal circuits in the brain which provide a dynamic 'memory' lasting a few seconds or minutes but which soon run down or are broken up by fresh neuronal activity. As was discussed in Chapter II, this short-term retention partly overlaps in time with, and is often essential for the completion of, comprehension at stage 1.

3. Some kind of *durable trace* must be established which is capable of remaining relatively unimpaired by subsequent activities of the organism and of standing up to gross depressions of neural activity from anaesthetics or other causes such as very low body temperature (Andjus *et al.* 1956). It seems necessary to postulate some alteration in the micro-structure of the brain or a stable biochemical change as the carrier of these traces. The observations of Eccles and his co-workers (Eccles 1953) on the growth of synaptic junctions under

the influence of repeated stimulation provide a possible lead: it would be interesting to know how far this kind of plasticity of the nervous system is preserved into old age.

4. The structural or biochemical changes must *endure* until the time of recall, although they may undergo some changes either by way of simplification or as the result of intervening activity by the organism.

Stages 3 and 4 may be absent in the case of relatively short-term retention, but would seem essential to long-term learning.

5. There must be *recognition of a further situation* demanding the re-use of this material, as modified by any changes during stage 4.

6. The material must be *recovered from among other material* in memory, either by active recall or in some less overt way.

Stages 5 and 6 may, at first sight, appear to be the same; but should be distinguished from one another. We can often recognize what material is required without being able to recall it, as when we cannot remember a name although it is 'on the tip of the tongue'. This would indicate a failure at stage 6. On the other hand, we show a failure at stage 5 when we recall material without being able to see its relevance to a new situation.

7. Finally the *recalled material has to be used* in the new situation in such a way as to produce an overt, communicable response, which may result from many pieces of recalled material together with material arising from the present situation. Normally, in a learning experiment this final result is all we observe, but it may be affected by any previous stage.

From what has been said in earlier chapters it is clear that many apparent failures to learn by older people are not the result of any true learning disability but are due to difficulties of perceiving or comprehending the material presented at stage 1. This is especially likely when the material is complex, or when the pace at which it is presented is not under the subject's own control as, for instance, when listening to a training lecture, or when the material to be learnt is shown to the subject for a short time and then removed. In these circumstances any slowness of comprehension, even momentary, may cause part of the material to be missed. Such an effect of pacing is well shown in the experiment by Brown (1957) (see p. 109) in which subjects were required to plot positions on a grid within a rigid time-limit. Several subjects, especially in the older age groups, would sometimes attempt to use the edges of the grid as reference lines instead of the co-ordinates drawn on the grid. This procedure led to a 'large' error as they were attempting to plot in the wrong large grid square. When carrying out the task without time-limit subjects making this mistake would try several times without success to find the correct point on the grid, would eventually realize what they were doing wrong and seldom, if ever, make the same mistake again. Subjects whose first experience of this task was with the time-limit never had the opportunity to gain this insight and thus made

TABLE 9.1. *Prevention by 'pacing' of learning to avoid a certain type of error*

The figures are means per subject for 'large' errors in Brown's grid-matching experiment (p. 109) expressed as percentages of the total attempts—successes and errors—shown in Table 5.2 (p. 113)

	Age group	
	20–49	50–79
1. Effect of practice at paced task upon performance at unpaced		
Group B: unpaced task without previous practice .	3·66	8·14
Group A: unpaced task after paced . . .	3·69	7·92
Practice effect: i.e. difference A−B . . .	+0·03	−0·22
2. Effect of practice at unpaced task upon performance at paced		
Group A: paced task without previous practice .	6·34	17·75
Group B: paced task after unpaced . . .	4·34	6·69
Practice effect: i.e. difference B−A . . .	−2·00	−11·06

1. shows that practice at the paced task had practically no effect on the incidence of 'large' errors, whereas
2. shows that a substantial reduction followed practice at the unpaced task.

as many large errors after transferring to doing the task unpaced as did those doing the unpaced task without previous practice. Subjects who transferred to the paced condition after a period of work under the unpaced showed the effect of practice in that they made many fewer errors at the paced task than did those for whom this came first. The figures are given in Table 9.1.

Long-term retention

Actual retention at stage 4 is usually assumed to be little affected by age when uncomplicated by senile changes of clinical degree. This is suggested by the common observation that older people

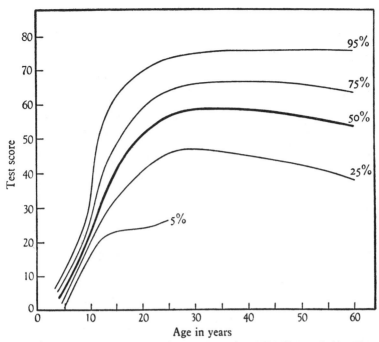

FIG. 9.1(a). Changes with age in scores on the Mill Hill Vocabulary Test. Percentile points

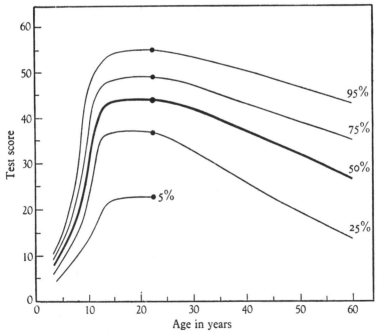

FIG. 9.1(b). Changes with age in scores on the Matrices Test. Percentile points

apparently remember well events which occurred many years before even though they are forgetful of more recent happenings. Better evidence is contained in the results of several vocabulary tests, for instance those of Foulds and Raven's (1948) given in Fig. 9.1(a), which show that knowledge of the meanings of words, presumably acquired over the years, remains high in old age even though Matrix Test scores fall markedly.

TABLE 9.2. *Mean performance figures for three skilled operations at two printing works. The number of men in the group is given in brackets after each figure*

	Age group				
	Twenties	Thirties	Forties	Fifties	Sixties
Machine compositors					
Works A . . .	106·5 (2)	99·4 (7)	138·2 (4)	127·5 (2)	..
Works B . . .	125·5 (5)	127·0 (4)	122·3 (6)	114·8 (5)	94·9 (1)
Hand compositors					
Works A . . .	104·0 (2)	125·9 (15)	133·6 (12)	130·2 (5)	117·0 (2)
Works B . . .	114·3 (3)	142·9 (11)	133·2 (20)	120·5 (17)	124·6 (12)
Readers					
Works A . . .	81·0 (2)	121·5 (5)	119·1 (3)	133·1 (3)	127·4 (3)
Works B . . •	..	..	130·9 (9)*	152·3 (6)	140·3 (8)

The performance figures are for the third year after the introduction of an incentive scheme. Figures for the first and second years were closely similar.
* All readers under 50 years of age have been grouped together.

Further evidence is contained in performance figures for high-grade occupational skills such as those given by Clay (1956b). In Table 9.2 are shown productivity figures for three skilled operations at two printing firms shortly after the introduction of an incentive payment scheme. The figures show that productivity among compositors tended to rise from the twenties to the thirties or forties, and among readers to the fifties. Thereafter it declined somewhat, but not as severely as the results of many experiments on performance might lead one to expect. Productivity of machine compositors fell more than that of hand compositors, probably because the relationship between what is seen and done is less 'direct' in the former operation and causes a difficulty of the kind discussed in Chapter VI.

The figures suggest that in most cases the skills concerned take many years to attain full maturity, but that once mastered they show little deterioration with age, or at any rate that compensation can be made fairly well for any deficiencies. The fall of productivity in the older age groups may admittedly have been somewhat greater than the figures indicate because some of the older men contracted out of the incentive scheme and thus furnished no productivity data. These men, many of whom had remained after normal retiring age, tended to be less productive than the rest, but were still regarded as worth employing from an economic point of view. As we have seen in Chapter III, we can only regard such figures as evidence that skill is maintained into middle and old age if labour turnover is low. In these printing works it was in fact negligible, so that maintenance of performance could not have been the result of progressive selection as it seems to be in some semi-skilled factory operations. For example, Belbin's studies discussed in Chapter V (p. 115) suggested that although markedly lower productivity was seldom found among older people actually employed in the factories he visited, they tended to move away from certain operations so that those who remained were, in effect, a selected group.

This suggestion was taken up in a study by King (1956) who examined the records of both productivity and labour turnover for a number of sewing-machine operations. As shown in Fig. 9.2, productivity again increased up to the thirties and thereafter declined somewhat on average but not very much or very consistently. The labour turnover was, however, high, as shown in Fig. 9.3, and there was a clear correlation between ratings for efficiency and for learning which indicated that those who remained were more able than those who left. This obviously implies that those in the higher age ranges were, on average, more able than those in the lower. We cannot be sure how far skill would have been retained by a less selected group, but it seems clear that it was maintained well enough by those who had stayed on. This may perhaps illustrate the point shown in Gilbert's (1941) results, and also in those of Foulds and Raven in Fig. 9.1, that declines with age are less among the more able performers.

The experimental evidence about long-term retention is at first sight conflicting, although it would seem to be not irreconcilable. The commonly held view is supported by the results of Shakow et al. (1941) who compared scores for 'old' and 'new' recall using a modification of the Wells Memory Test (Wells and Martin 1923). The 'old' items included personal and current information, things commonly learnt at school, counting backwards, naming common objects, &c. 'New' items included repetition of figures forward and backwards, memory of sentences and of ideas in a story, recognition

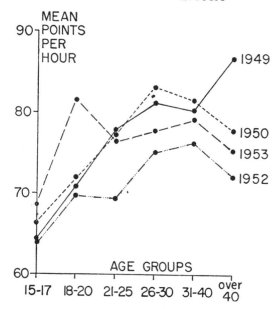

FIG. 9.2. Productivity levels among sewing-machine operators during four 8-week
periods

The operatives, all women, numbered 82 in 1949, 85 in 1950, 68 in 1952 and 59 in 1953. These
numbers were spread fairly evenly among the age ranges indicated

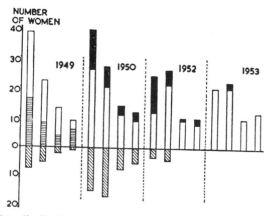

FIG. 9.3. Age distributions of employees, starters and leavers. Sewing-machine
operations

Key. Above base line, women employed at date shown. The black portions indicate newcomers
since the previous period. The horizontally shaded portions in 1949 indicate women still employed
in March, 1953. Below base line, those women at present employed who had left before the next
period began. Age groups: 15–20; 21–30; 31–40; over 40.

of pictures shown previously, &c. The results are given in Fig. 9.4 which shows a clearly less steep decline for old items than for new.

In contrast to this finding are the results obtained by Speakman (1954) in the experiment testing the incidental learning of stamp

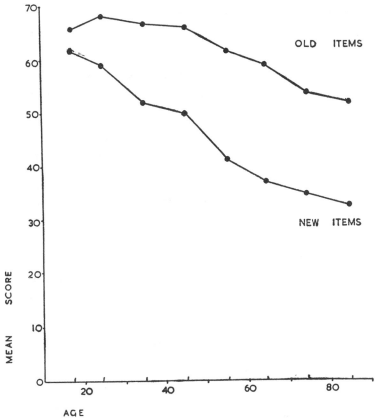

Fig. 9.4. Comparison of scores for 'old' and 'new' recall items

values which was outlined in the previous chapter, and the results of which are set out in Table 8.4 (p. 200). One might have expected that the older subjects would have been able to recall the old values relatively well, but have been less able than the younger to recall the new. Surprisingly, the reverse occurred: the younger were better able to recall the old values and young and old were little different in their recall of the new. The relatively good recall by the older subjects of the new series was not due to their better memory of the unchanged 3*d.* stamp: their recall of this was no better than that of the younger subjects.

It is just possible that in spite of the association of nearly forty years between the colours and the old values the older subjects had never learnt them, but this seems hardly likely as every one of the values except the 3*d.* had been in common use for a substantial time during the period. Alternatively, the difficulty for older people may have lain in recall at stage 5 or 6, but if this had been so we should have expected the recall of the new values to be affected also. If these possibilities can be discounted, it seems fairly certain that the older subjects had forgotten more than the younger.

One difference which may explain the conflict between the results of this experiment and the other evidence is that almost certainly the subjects had little or no occasion to use or maintain their knowledge of the colours during the twenty months elapsing between the change of colours and the experiment. On the other hand, all the other evidence comes from situations where the information recalled has been in more or less continuous use. Vocabulary, personal data and industrial skill may have been acquired many years ago but they had almost certainly been used at intervals since by the people on whom the studies were made. When this happens we do not need to postulate *very* long-term memory in order that the material should be preserved—it is enough that the memory process should span the interval since the material was last used. For example, most of us can recall a number of childhood memories, but we do not need to postulate a single memory process spanning the whole gap between childhood and the present time to account for our ability. Almost, if not quite all our present childhood memories must have been re-called many times since the original occurrences, and what we almost certainly remember is not the original but our memory 'rewritten' at the time of last recall.

Speakman raises the question with regard to his own results of whether the forgetting of old material is actually the result of acquiring the new. If so, there should have been a negative correlation between numbers of old and of new stamp values recalled. Rank correlations for each age decade separately and for each of the two age groups 20–49 and 50–86 were, however, all *positive*—significantly so in the 20–49 group. Recalls of old and new values, in so far as they were not independent, appeared to be related to some common factor such as a general retentive ability.

More work is needed on the problem of how far skills learnt when young are retained over a long period without intervening practice. If it could be shown that they were well preserved, or easily recoverable, it would mean that training given at school for work or hobbies could be taken up in middle life or at retirement with obvious advantages to older people, giving them a flexibility which would enable them to take up new work or pursuits more easily than they could otherwise.

Human studies are inevitably weak at providing evidence about long-term retention because it is usually difficult to be sure there has been no rehearsal during the intervening time. In addition, we commonly have recourse to testing a subject's present performance or knowledge and attempting to relate this to experience in the past over which we have had no control. Ideally, we need longitudinal studies in which both initial experience, activity during the period of retention and conditions of recall can all be controlled. This cannot be done with human subjects, but could perhaps be achieved with animals: with them we can at least control *overt* practice at the task, and it is traditionally assumed that limited powers of conceptualization would preclude any important amount of running over the material in their minds, although we may perhaps doubt whether such a view of animals, at least of mammals, is entirely justified.

Longitudinal studies of this kind by Verzár McDougall (1955) using rats as subjects provide evidence of retention over a substantial portion of the life span, without intervening overt rehearsal, by at least some individuals. Rats were trained to run through a maze for food and retrained at intervals of 2–9½ months after the end of their original training. The results indicated that both learning and relearning were quickest among young adult rats. Some of the old adult rats were able to relearn rapidly. Others, however, were unable to relearn the maze and continued to make errors with no sign of improvement although they ran eagerly for the food. Clearly there was loss of memory in these individuals, although we cannot be certain whether this was due to a loss of *retention* or to a failure of *recall*.

To sum up, the available evidence, especially as regards human beings, suggests that *very* long-term memory may be much poorer than is commonly supposed and that the long-term memories from the past that older people preserve remain because they have some part to play in the person's life and are recalled at intervals. If this is not done they have a considerable likelihood, increasing with age, of being forgotten. Thorndike's idea that learning by older people is better done if it is 'for use' seems to be echoed in their readier forgetting of what is useless. Whether mere use is sufficient for maintenance or whether some notion of 'usefulness' needs to be added we do not at present know. Nor can we be sure in any particular case whether loss of memory is due to loss of retention or to failure of recall. We can, however, say with some confidence that skills and other learnt material can be maintained with relative ease to an age well beyond that at which they can be easily learnt. Just how much maintenance is required is a matter of both practical and theoretical interest upon which further research would seem worth while.

Registration for long-term retention

To return to the discussion of 'plasticity', the maturation-degeneration type of ageing theory assumes that difficulty in learning by older people is due to a breakdown at stage 3: the process of 'registration' becomes more difficult, requiring longer time or stronger signals or more practice for its establishment. If it is true that long-term retention implies some anatomical change in the brain, this type of theory is perhaps plausible in view of the slowing with age of tissue changes, such as those involved in healing. The connexion is, however, extremely tenuous and speculative, and could only be proved by demonstrating the physiological basis of the memory trace—a feat which seems to be a long way from realization.

Clearly older people learn some things about as well as younger: learning of university subjects by some of Thorndike's groups and of new stamp colours in Speakman's experiment are cases in point. The difficulty in these cases is that it was not possible to keep control of the amount of practice so that older people may well have put more time and trouble into their learning. This objection can hardly apply, however, to an experiment by Belbin (1956) who presented men in their teens and twenties and over-sixty with Road Safety posters, and measured their retention of them by (a) asking for recall in words, and (b) asking for comments on photographs of road scenes illustrating points made in the posters. Those over 60, although markedly poorer than younger subjects at (a), were about the same as them at (*b*). Both younger and older subjects in a control group, given the photographs for comment without having seen the posters, made less relevant comments than subjects who had seen the posters. It thus appears that the posters did affect comment upon the photographs, and also that the older subjects who had seen them, had learned something about them, although they were unable to recall the details in words. Recall as demanded in (*a*) would undoubtedly require the retention of much more detailed information than that needed for (*b*) and we may well suppose that the essential difference between the older and younger subjects was in the *amount* they retained. Whether the older subjects retained only certain portions of the material or 'half-retained' it all, we cannot say.

Detailed analysis of the process of learning

The truth or falsity of a breakdown with age in the process of registration cannot be decided by simply looking at over-all learning achievement but requires the examination in detail of the process of arriving at mastery of a learning task. An experiment designed to do this has been made by Kay (1951). The task was one of rote-learning, but the lists of words or syllables or digits which are customarily used for this purpose in psychological experiments were avoided because it seemed possible that subjects would regard them as pointless and not worth serious effort. Kay's task was designed in the hope that it would be interesting and did in fact prove to be so.

The subject sat facing a box containing a row of ten small electric-light bulbs. Below and in front of each bulb was a morse-key. The lights and keys were numbered 1–10 from left to right by means of figures about an inch high placed between them.

The bulbs and keys were connected to an apparatus arranged in such a manner that, when one bulb was lit, the pressing of one of the morse-keys would put it out and light another bulb. This could in turn be put out and a third bulb lit by pressing another of the keys, and so on for a series of any length up to ten. The task set the subject was thus one of learning a series of keys which would produce a series of changes in the lighting of the bulbs. A detailed description of the apparatus has been given by Welford (1952*b*).

Each subject was shown the apparatus, its working was explained and demonstrated, and typewritten instructions were left beside him in case he wanted to go back over any point. He was then required to discover and learn a sequence among the keys 1–5, repeating the series over and over until he had pressed the keys in correct sequence without making any errors for two consecutive 'trials'. Having achieved this, he learnt another sequence on keys 6–10, until the same criterion of performance was reached.

As soon as he had learnt the second series he was asked to repeat the first series. If he did not do so without error on the first 'trial', he went on to further trials until he achieved a correct performance. Having done so, he repeated the second series in a similar manner.

TABLE 9.3. *Standard deviations of the learning scores in Figure 9.5.*

Age range	Trials	Errors	Times (in seconds)
20–29	2·4	15	20
30–39	4·3	18	37
40–49	5·1	22	36
50–59	6·9	44	86
60–69	11·3	70	153

Finally the first lights of both series were put on together and the subject was asked to make moves in the two series alternately beginning with the first move of series I, then the first move of series II, the second of series I, and so on. This alternation was continued for two complete trials only.

Scores for the *learning* stage of the experiment are set out in Fig. 9.5 and show that, on average, there was a clear fall with age. This appeared first as a slowing in the thirties, then as a fall of accuracy in the forties, and finally as a fall of both accuracy and speed in the fifties and sixties.

A further point about the changes of performance between the different decades is not brought out by Fig. 9.5. It is that the *variability of performance* increased very greatly with age. In Table 9.3 are shown the standard deviations of the three scores. It will be seen that all rose consistently. These standard deviations were roughly proportional to the corresponding means, so that the relative variability of the different decades was more or less equal. In absolute measures, however, the variation between subjects in the higher age ranges was very much greater than in the lower, so that whereas some subjects were considerably poorer than the group means would suggest, others were putting up performances not very different from those of younger subjects.

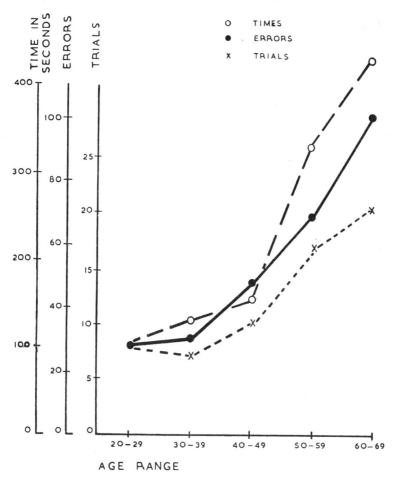

FIG. 9.5. Times, errors and trials per subject for learning both series in Kay's experiment (excluding criterion trials)

Scores for *relearning* are set out in Fig. 9.6 from which it will be seen that average numbers of trials required, errors made and times taken all increased markedly with age. Correspondingly the numbers of subjects, set out in Table 9.4, who recalled both series correctly at the first trial fell sharply, until in the fifties and sixties no subject recalled both series without error.

The increase of errors with age appeared earlier in the relearning than it did in the learning-task, being pronounced among the subjects in their thirties, who in learning had been as accurate as the twenties. The two sets of scores do, however, generally support each other: as the age of the subjects increased not only did performance at

TABLE 9.4. *Numbers of subjects recalling correctly at first relearning trial in Kay's experiment*

Age range	Series I	Series II	Both series
20–29	10	8	8
30–39	4	8	3
40–49	4	5	3
50–59	1	3	0
60–69	1	1	0

TABLE 9.5. *Times, errors and numbers of correct trials for two trials in which subjects were required to alternate items of series I and II in Kay's experiment*

Means per subject

	Age group				
	Twenties	Thirties	Forties	Fifties	Sixties
Time (secs.) . . .	48·9	48·4	59·4	76·3	117·9
Errors	2·8	5·5	7·5	7·7	15·2
Correct trials (out of 2) .	0·9	0·7	0·5	0·2	0·0

learning fall but there was also less retention of what had been learnt.

The results for the subsequent task of *alternating the two series* are given in Table 9.5 and show the same trends.

Some of the changes of performance that went with age are probably to be explained by different methods of tackling the experiment. Those in their twenties seemed to approach the learning task without any very clear idea of what they were going to do, and allowed the task itself to dictate their method. The subjects in the thirties and forties were more circumspect, carefully examining the lights and the keys before beginning their first trial. They asked questions about the method of learning they should adopt, often of a deductive nature: 'Then I don't need to look at . . .', &c. As a result, they usually started with some definite idea in mind of how to proceed. It was probably because of this that their performance when learning was relatively so much better than it was when re-

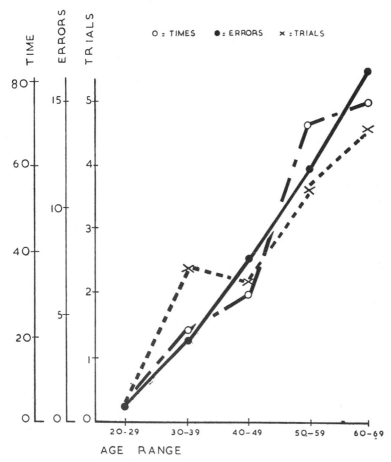

FIG. 9.6. Times, errors and trials per subject for relearning both series in Kay's experiment (excluding criterion trials)

learning. The learning-task was—very much more than the re-learning—a matter of *problem-solving*, in which the superior application and technique of the subjects in their thirties could show to advantage.

The approach of the subjects in their fifties and sixties was, like their achievement, much more varied. Some showed the same characteristics as subjects in their thirties and forties, and when examining the apparatus were clearly trying to evolve a technique. Others, however, seemed to have difficulty in understanding the task. Often their questions revealed that they had erroneous preconceptions about the nature and purpose of the apparatus, and that their lack of comprehension was due to their having difficulty in modifying these preconceptions in the light of the instructions.

A more detailed understanding of what was happening during learning, as opposed to the way in which the subjects approached the task, can be gained from a study of the errors. Kay found that errors made during the early trials were tending to persist. It seemed that during these trials the subjects built up a pattern of responses, and that they tended to impose this pattern on the task in later trials in spite of evidence that it was wrong. Learning during the later trials thus tended not to be a filling in of 'blanks', but a *modification* of this initial pattern. It is worth noting, in support of this point, that often when an error was about to be eliminated the subject would move his hand towards the wrong key, but at the last moment avoid pressing it, making some remark such as 'No, *not* that one'.

The reason for the persistence of these errors appeared to be that the pattern of responses built up during the early trials was more difficult to modify than to form in the first place. This would seem to be akin to the problem commonly recognized by teachers of games and of skills such as typewriting, who maintain that it is important to build the correct habits right at the beginning because faults quickly become ingrained, and are then difficult to eliminate. Experimental support for this view in the case of young subjects comes from work by von Wright (1957) who found that the pattern of errors made on a single serial maze changed greatly between the first and second trials but relatively little thereafter—the pattern of errors which persisted was that built up during the first trial. He obtained further confirmation in the fact that subjects prevented from making errors in the first trial made fewer errors subsequently than did those who had not been so aided. Subjects in the forties and fifties showed somewhat closer correspondence between the errors on the *first* and subsequent trials than did younger subjects, probably indicating that the effect on the first trial of presuppositions brought to the experiment tends to rise with age. The older subjects took more trials and longer time to learn the maze and made somewhat more errors although not significantly more. There were no significant *over-all* differences with age in the repetition of errors, although repeated errors were substantially more frequent among the older subjects in the last stages of learning. The evidence is not sufficient to say whether the difficulty for older people lay mainly in modifying their initial pattern of performance or in the overdetermination of performance by presuppositions brought to the task, and indeed in this type of experiment it seems impossible to separate the two conclusively.

Both Kay's and von Wright's results indicate that the older subjects, as in Belbin's experiment, learnt *something* about as quickly and thoroughly as the younger, even if only to make a particular selection from among their guessing habits, but suggest that they were unable to learn *so much* material at the first trial as could the younger. If this is true it would mean that the difference between older and younger subjects in effecting registration at stage 3 lay not so much in speed or in signal-strength required as in the *amount* of material they could deal with at any one time.

The results from Kay's relearning and reordering tasks make it clear that the initial learning was remarkably stable. The errors made in both these were the same as those made during the learning task. The initial pattern of responses built up during the very first learning trial appeared to have persisted right through the three parts of the experiment. What dropped out between learning and relearning and again before the alternation task were the modifications to this initial pattern achieved during the learning and relearning trials.

The persistence of the initial scheme and the ephemeral nature of the modifications made to it suggest that the two were being carried by different mechanisms in the memory chain. In particular, it seems worth while to consider whether the modifications may have been carried by the short-term memory of stage 2 and whether this shows declines with age. We shall take up this point again later, and produce evidence for the view that it does so, not only in clinical senile conditions but in normal older people as well.

Effects of past experience

We shall now turn to the other type of 'plasticity' theory—that which regards learning deficit in old age as due to the effects of increased experience. The general point that past experience has an effect on *performance* which changes with age is not in doubt: such an effect is well shown in Brown's figure-tracing experiment (p. 73) in which older subjects treated reversed figures for what they were whereas younger subjects tended to treat them as 'nonsense' shapes. The present problem is how may past experience influence *learning* in relation to age.

It is obvious that past experience can make the task of learning *easier*. If we can use knowledge already in our possession or motor skills already acquired to deal with parts or aspects of a new task there is less to learn. Most students of ageing will have met cases where this benefited older people to a marked degree, reversing for individuals a trend clear enough in an older group as a whole. One example has already been mentioned (p. 186).

Past experience might impair learning performance in that it could lead to a subject misidentifying a situation which demanded that something fresh be learned as one in which an already known way of responding would be adequate. To put it another way, an established mode of response tends automatically to assert itself in a situation similar to the one it was originally designed to meet. This could have three results. Firstly, the subject might fail to recognize the need to learn until the action he took proved ineffective, and would waste his first 'trial' with the new situation. Secondly, the errors he made on the first trial might impair his subsequent performance. Thirdly, established habits of perception and action may tend to impair the accuracy of recognition at stage 5 and of recall at stage 6, intruding themselves in the place of the correct responses which, although they have been retained, are thus rendered unavailable. In order to overcome this a subject would have to learn not only to do what was correct, but also *not* to do what was incorrect, and thus would have to learn more than if he started fresh.

Much of the evidence called in favour of this theory is, to say the least, doubtful. For instance, we have already seen in Chapter VI that the poorer performance of older people at mirror aiming and similar tasks which is often attributed to the difficulty of dealing with unfamiliar relationships between display and control, seems better considered as a case of the difficulty encountered by older people in making complex spatial transpositions.

The classical experiment quoted in support of the present theory is that of Ruch (1934) who compared the performance of subjects of different ages learning by rote (*a*) meaningful associates of the type HOUSE; VISIT, (*b*) nonsense equations such as $A \times M = B$, and (*c*) false equations such as $3 \times 4 = 2$. He found a greater decline with age on (*b*) and (*c*) than on (*a*). The results are given in Table 9.6. Ruch maintained that these results showed that the greatest decline was on (*c*), i.e. the task which ran counter to established experience,

TABLE 9.6. *Learning of different types of material. Data from Ruch*
(*1934*)

Numbers of correct responses out of 150, mean per subject

Type of material	Meaningful associates	Nonsense equations	False equations
Age range			
12–17	134·7	78·5	106·1
34–59	123·7	62·8	76·1
60–82	111·6	37·9	49·4
Ratio 60–82/34–59 . . .	0·90	0·60	0·65

and thus confirmed his theory. The figures do, however, show the *percentage* decline for (*c*) to be very similar to that for (*b*). The evidence for Ruch's view is, in fact, far from conclusive and other possibilities need to be considered. For instance, nonsense and false equations require more learning than meaningful material in the sense that with the latter one part does to some extent imply the other. Ruch's results might, therefore, again be due to older people finding learning progressively harder as the amount to be learned is increased. Systematic work on the relationship of amount to be learnt and learning performance with age would seem to be worth while.

A further consideration against the view that past experience is in itself a prime cause of learning deficit in older people comes from the fact that learning tasks often force action. When recall is demanded, the subject is virtually compelled to do something about the situation with which he is confronted, whether or not he remembers what he is supposed to have learnt about it previously. If he has any gaps in his knowledge, he will almost inevitably be forced back upon his previous experience. The filling of gaps in this way will appear in his performance as the 'transfer of previously acquired habits', but such transfer may be a sign of failure not only at stage 5, but at any stage previous. The experience he uses in this kind of situation may derive from his general background of experience, or, as in Kay's experiment, from an erroneous pattern of responses built up during the early stages of practice. Whichever is the case, this way of acting would appear to be an understandable and very reasonable attempt to make the best of an otherwise impossible situation.

Learning as a skill

A very different type of theory relating age changes in learning to factors of experience regards learning as a skill that can itself be learnt and maintained by continued exercise, and assumes that difficulties of learning by older people are due to their having allowed this skill to fall into disuse. The general point that we can 'learn how to learn' and that learning performance itself improves with practice is well substantiated (see McGeoch and Irion 1952). This theory does not contain any definite implications about what stage is involved, but one might expect that practice at learning would lead to a better ordering of events in stages 1, 5, 6, and 7, and to such factors as improved control of the subject's attention to the task. The actual loss of learning ability would be attributable to the failure of its retention at stage 4, operating, so to speak, at second hand.

Some evidence in support of this view as an explanation of age changes in learning is given by the work of Sorensen (1930), who found that the fall of learning achievement among members of university extra-mural classes was more closely related to age in a class resuming studies after many years' gap than in two classes of comparable age range who had kept up studies more nearly continuously. The difficulty about Sorensen's evidence is that it seems doubtful whether the mental status of the groups was really the same: people who maintain attendance at extra-mural classes are probably different from their contemporaries. In other words, there is no evidence of which way the causal connexion lies between maintained attendance and higher learning ability. It may be that the first causes the second, but it may also be that those who continue their attendance tend to be those whose learning ability has remained high.

The evidence already considered on the maintenance of skill leads us to regard the theory as perhaps a reasonable explanation of learning deficit in at least some older individuals. Just how important it may be is difficult to assess with human subjects but could well form the topic of experiments with animals in which learning tasks could be given at various stages of life, with and without other learning tasks during the intervening periods.

Short-term retention

We have already noted short-term retention at stage 2 as a possible cause of learning difficulty among older people in Kay's experiment. Further indications that short- rather than long-term memory tends to break down in late middle and old age is contained in the results of an experiment by Jones, Conrad and Horn (1928) who tested the recall of three motion pictures shown to a representative group of 765 people from New England villages. They found that the recall scores rose to a peak in the early twenties and by the late fifties had dropped to the same level as that attained by children of thirteen. For our present purpose the important point to note is that the age decline when recall was delayed was no greater than when it was required immediately after the pictures had been shown.

'Short' and 'long' as terms in relation to memory differ widely according to the context in which they are used: what is called short-term in one experiment may be long-term in another. Jones, Conrad and Horn's experiment did not really test retention over the length of interval—a few seconds or a minute or so—normally considered as the span of short-term memory. However, relationships between memory processes spanning different periods of time are not at all clear and it is impossible to lay down definite limits for 'short' and 'long' at present.

Results of experiments on retention over periods of seconds in relation to age are at first sight conflicting. Gilbert (1941) compared a group of people aged 60–69 with a group aged 20–29 on a number of memory tasks with results shown in Table 9.7. The two groups had previously been matched for score on a vocabulary test. Once again we find that short-term and longer-term retention for the same task show very similar percentage changes with age. The striking differences are in the amount of change with different types of material. In particular, 'Memory Span for Digits' which might be regarded as a test of a rather pure form of very short-term retention shows only a small decline with age. Wechsler (1944) has also pointed out that immediate memory span for digits declines less with age than some other intellectual abilities.

As against Gilbert's and Wechsler's findings for digit-span are the results of what might seem even simpler short-term retention experiments by Kay (1953) and by Kirchner. In Kay's experiment the subject sat facing a row of twelve light-bulbs, with a morse key directly under each. For the first part of the task one of these lights was put on by the experimenter. By pressing the key immediately under

TABLE 9.7. *Age differences in learning as a function of type of material. Data from Gilbert (1941)*

Mean scores of age groups

Task	20–29	60–69	Difference	Difference as percentage of younger
Memory span for digits: highest number correctly repeated.				
Visual presentation . . .	8·21	7·51	0·70	8·5
Auditory presentation . . .	6·87	6·06	0·81	11·8
Reversed . . .	5·53	4·36	1·17	21·2
*Repeating sentences: 1 mark for whole sentence with no error, ½ mark with 1 error . .	16·76	13·29	3·47	21·3
Knox cubes: number of designs repeated correctly.	8·71	6·44	2·27	26·2
Memory of paragraph learnt from Stanford-Binet 10-yr. level: number of 'memories' produced correctly.				
Immediately.	10·85	6·32	4·53	41·8
After longer interval . . .	14·01	9·16	4·85	39·7
*Memory of designs: Scored as in Babcock test . . .	13·54	7·32	6·22	45·9
*Paired associates: number correct out of 9 in two trials.				
Immediately.	6·27	2·59	3·68	58·7
After longer interval . . .	7·51	3·41	4·10	54·6
*Retention of Turkish-English vocabulary given at beginning of tests and tested at end. Number of Turkish words correctly underlined	7·49	2·97	4·52	60·4

* These items were taken from the Babcock test of mental efficiency.

it the subject put this light out and another on. Pressing the key under this second light made it go out and a third appear, and so on through the whole twelve in random order. This simple task caused no difficulty to any subjects. The task was then changed so that the lights came on automatically in a random order at 1·5 seconds intervals, and the subject had to press the key under each light *which had just gone off*: in other words, he had to work 'one back' in the series. The order was then changed again and the subject required to work two back, then three back, then four back. The experiment was one of several designed to test fatigue in civilian air-crew and was given to two groups of radio officers, stewards and stewardesses, one group being tested before and one after flight.[1] Each group was divided into two age ranges—above and below 30. The 'one back' task was found by almost all subjects to be easy: they simply moved their hand to the key where the light was on, waited until it went out, pressed the key and then moved to the new position of the light. Two-, three and four-back were more difficult. On the two-back task subjects would sometimes mark the position of the intermediate light with a finger of the hand they were not using, thus making the task somewhat similar to one-back, but beyond this a subject in order to make a perfect score was compelled to carry the intermediate light positions in some form of running short-term memory. This they found extremely difficult and many attempted to avoid doing so by placing a finger on the key under the light which was on, counting the required number of changes, pressing the key, then moving to where the light was again and repeating the same procedure. This clearly involved abandoning any attempt to deal with more than a third of the lights in the three-back condition or a quarter in the four-back, but seemed often to be the alternative to complete inactivity.

Kay's results are given in Table 9.8. Comparing the subjects of different ages tested before flight there was clearly a fall with age in the number of correct responses. We may note that the age difference was much reduced among the subjects tested after flight. It seemed as if fatigue had depressed the performances of younger subjects but left those of the older relatively unchanged. This rather surprising result is paralleled by that of the experiment by Botwinick and Shock (1952) mentioned in Chapter III, who found that performance at an adding task, although initially lower among older subjects, showed both absolutely and relatively less fatigue decrement than among young subjects.

Kirchner repeated Kay's experiment as far as 'two-back' with two age ranges similar to those tested by Gilbert, but with the simplest (no-back) task paced like the others and with the light changing at the slightly longer interval of 2 seconds. His results, given in Table 9.9, showed closely similar performances in both age groups at the no-back task, indicating that speed of motor perfor-

[1] The same subjects were not tested twice owing to the influence of the first test performance upon the second. See Welford, Brown and Gabb (1950).

mance was not a limitation. The one- and two-back conditions, however, showed definite changes with age. Even at one-back the older subjects made considerably more errors than the younger. At two-back some of the older subjects were unable to make any showing of

TABLE 9.8. *Results of an experiment on serial short-term retention by Kay on aircrew. Percentage responses correct*

	Number of items back in the series subject was required to work			
	1	2	3	4
Subjects tested before flight				
Under 30	99	71	59	42
Over 30	94	61	37	33
Difference	5	10	22	9
Older as proportion of younger .	0·98	0·86	0·63	0·79
Subjects tested after flight				
Under 30	92	66	47	35
Over 30	89	63	40	33
Difference	3	3	7	2
Older as proportion of younger .	0·89	0·96	0·85	0·94

TABLE 9.9. *Results of an experiment on serial short-term retention by Kirchner. Percentage responses correct*

	Number of items back in the series subjects were required to work			
	0	1	2	3
Younger subjects aged 18–25				
Students	100	99	93	73
Naval ratings . . .	100	99	81	51
Older subjects aged 64–78 . .	99	80	33	Not attempted
Older as proportion of younger .	0·99	0·81	0·38	

performance at all, owing to difficulty in understanding the task, and those who did fully understand made only about 40 per cent. as many correct responses as the younger.

The significant difference between Kirchner's experiment and digit span tasks such as those of Gilbert would seem to lie in the fact that in the latter all information is taken in before any responding action is begun, while in the former there is a continual alternation between intake of information and use of it in responding action.

It would seem that some process involved in responding exerts a serious interfering effect upon the information stored in short-term memory.

The hypothesis that intervening activity has a greater interfering effect upon short-term retention among older than among younger subjects has been indicated by the observations of Cameron (1943), who compared senile patients having retention defect with a group of young adults. Subjects were required to retain three digit numbers over periods of a few minutes, the periods between presentation and reproduction either being occupied by spelling out a list of words or being left unoccupied. The senile subjects were able to retain the digits accurately over an unoccupied period of up to a few minutes, but, unlike the younger subjects, showed much poorer recall after the filled intervening periods.

Intervening activity alone does not, however, seem to be a sufficient definition of the conditions leading to interference. Speakman, in an experiment described more fully later, spoke to subjects a four-figure number (0954) which they at once repeated. Immediately after this they turned over, one by one, a pack of numbered cards, counting to find how many they had to turn to reach a card with a given number on it. They were then asked to recall the four-figure number and also to say how many cards they had turned. All subjects of all ages from 11 to 63 performed this task without error. It is clear that it must have been easy but it is not clear why it should have been so—one would have expected the intervening activity of turning the cards to have interfered with retention of the number. It is possible that the repetition of the number before the intervening task played an important part in fixing it in the subject's memory. As support for this view, we may mention that subjects in Kay's (1953) experiment sometimes verbalized the numbers of the intermediate lights in the two-, three- and four-back conditions. Also in Kay's and Kirchner's experiments, the allowing of more time between successive lights, and thus more chance of rehearsal, improved performance for all age groups. It is also fairly certain that not every intervening activity will cause interference: research on so-called 'retroactive inhibition' indicates clearly that some aspects of 'similarity' are important in determining how much interference an intervening activity will cause.

If it is true that short-term retention is, at least under certain conditions, increasingly liable to interference by other activity as age advances, it seems possible to tie together many diverse facts about learning and other changes of performance with age.

Interference of this kind would seem likely to play an important part in any learning task where the amount to be learned is larger than the immediate memory span, if only because the responses made in attempting to rehearse or recall some of the material would interfere with the retention of the rest. The hypothesis that this interference increases with age would thus predict a relative increase of difficulty among older people as the amount of material to be learnt becomes greater, and in this way also provides an explanation for the results of Ruch's experiment. It also suggests one possible explanation both for the difficulty of modifying erroneous responses found by Kay in his original experiment, and for the impermanence of these modifications even when they had been achieved. Modifications at any one point in the series would inevitably have to be 'carried' during the responses involved in the rest of the series, and would thus be liable to interference from them. When an attempt was being made to correct an error the chances of interference would be increased because, seemingly, more has to be 'carried' in short-term memory to make a change in an already established sequence than to learn a sequence in the first place. In order to be able to run off a sequence which contains no errors a subject has only to remember which is the next move at each position in the series. To correct an error, however, he must hold in memory the position moved from together with both the wrong and the correct positions before the correct move can be substituted for the erroneous one.

Several other inferences also follow from this hypothesis. For instance, we should expect that older people would find learning easier if the material were split up and learnt a little at a time—the so-called 'part-method'—or if practice periods were spaced with brief periods of rest at frequent intervals. These inferences await experimental test, but upon two others there is some evidence already. The first is that the amount of deficit shown by older people should depend to some extent upon the method of measurement adopted: in particular an immediate memory-span test, where the score is the maximum that can be retained with complete accuracy, should give less decrement with age than a test of what is retained from an amount of material too great to be retained without error. Confirmation of this is contained in Gilbert's results already quoted (Table 9.7): except for the reversed span test which introduces complications of reordering beyond sheer rote retention, the digit span tests stand clearly apart from the others in having a smaller decline with age.

The second inference upon which some evidence exists is that we should expect 'incidental' or unintentional learning by older people in the course of other activity to be poor. The poorer recall by the older subjects in the experiment by Jones, Conrad and Horn on the memory for motion pictures might be taken as confirmation of this point, since the subjects did not know they would be questioned until after the performance. A slight doubt could, however, be raised about whether the learning shown in this case was truly incidental, because some retention of the subject matter during viewing would be necessary in order to keep track of the events in the films. Doubt also attaches to the results of Willoughby (1929) already mentioned in Chapter VI, which at first sight confirm this point. His subjects worked for $2\frac{1}{2}$ minutes substituting symbols for digits according to a code placed in front of them. The code was then removed and they were asked to recall as much of it as they could. The amount recalled declined by about 50 per cent. from the teens to the seventies. However, the amount of substitution done in the time-limit allowed, and thus the degree of practice with the symbols, also diminished with age.

An experiment free from these objections is one by Speakman to part of which reference has already been made. He presented subjects with a pack of numbered cards and asked them to turn them over one by one until they reached the card with a certain number on it, and to count the number of cards turned. While they were doing this he said 'eight, five, seven, three' slowly and audibly. At the end of the trial, the subject was asked how many cards he had turned, whether he had heard anything and if so what. The subject was then given a card bearing eight four-digit groups including 8573 and a close variant of it, 8753, and asked whether he recognized the number which had been spoken.

The same procedure was then repeated with the subject searching for a different number and with a different group of spoken digits (6241). The recognition card again bore a close variant (6421). The difference from the previous trial was, of course, that the subject now expected to be required to remember something spoken while turning the cards.

These two trials were given after a 'warming-up' task in which the subject simply turned cards until he found an indicated number.

They were followed by two control tasks. The first of these has already been described on p. 251. The second control was a simple forward digit span.

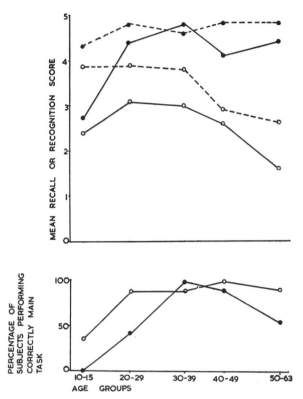

FIG. 9.7. Scores for incidental learning and for retention of main task in experiment by Speakman

Open circles: first trial.
Filled circles: second trial.
Continuous lines: recall scores.
Dashed lines: recognition scores.

The retention and recall scores were somewhat crudely calculated by assigning one point for each digit correct and a further point if all were in the correct order. More refined methods of scoring would clearly have produced very similar results.

The results of the two main trials are given in Fig. 9.7. On the first, mean recall and recognition scores fell from a peak in the twenties, but practically no adult subject forgot how many cards he had turned.

It thus appeared that while there was progressively less incidental learning as age increased, the spoken number did not interfere with the main task. On the second trial, recall and recognition of the number were much better, but in the twenties and again in the 50–63 group several subjects forgot how many cards they had turned. On the second trial the spoken number did appear to interfere with the main task, so that except among the thirties and, perhaps also among the forties, there was a substantial tendency for one or the other to be forgotten. In contrast, as has already been noted, on the first control task, where the four-figure number was presented before the cards were turned, no subject in any age group failed to remember both the number and how many cards he had turned. The results for the digit-span test showed a small, but only small, decline with age from the twenties and were thus in line with those of previous studies.

It seems clear from this experiment that the interference effect of *simultaneous* activity upon short-term retention is much greater than when the potentially interfering activity is separated in time. We might argue from this that the failure of retention is due to a failure to perceive, but while this may well be true in some cases it does not appear to be so in all. The subjects genuinely seemed to have difficulty in holding the number while counting. As one man put it 'I didn't stop counting, but remembering the number just seemed to drive it out', and another 'I tried to hold it all, but ended by losing the lot', and a third 'I tried to remember the number but it got lost during the experiment. I had been counting the cards, but when I stopped I just seemed to forget them.'

The precise nature of the impairment to short-term memory with age is still not quite clear but two possible leads may be suggested. Firstly, Speakman's results on incidental learning suggest that it may be due to confusion between items arriving in close temporal proximity, in much the same way as Clay found that older people tended to confuse items in close spatial proximity (see p. 212).

A second possibility links impairment of short-term retention to the lowered 'signal-to-noise ratio' in old age discussed in relation to perception in Chapter VII. The known changes in the brain—smaller number of brain cells, lowered general activity and tendency to disorganization of the EEG all suggest that dynamic traces carried by self-regenerating neuronal circuits would be less viable in old age, lasting for a shorter time and being less able to maintain their pattern while other activity was going on in the brain.

X

ADAPTABILITY

THE fact that performance at learning tasks declines with age is often taken to support the view that people become less adaptable as they grow older. In a general way this would seem to be undoubtedly true. It would appear, however, that the nature and causes of change in adaptability with age are not entirely straightforward and that further study would be likely to reveal ways in which such changes could be at least minimized if not entirely avoided. 'Adaptability' in the present sense is usually taken to cover both response to training for new work or in new methods for existing jobs, and also attitudes to social and other types of change. The two are really separate problems, and in the present chapter we shall survey evidence about each in turn, further separating, under the heading of 'training', field and experimental studies.

A. TRAINING

1. *Field data*

A survey conducted between 1949 and 1951 by Shooter and Schonfield of over seventy firms and management and research organizations revealed that very few people in industry over the age of 40 were being trained in a way which permitted the precise recording of results. Even for younger persons the records of training were seldom sufficient for research purposes. Evidence about industrial training in relation to age is thus fragmentary and it is impossible to say from present knowledge whether the data they gathered were truly representative.

Records fell into four main classes:

(*a*) Marks in examinations taken during or at the end of courses.

(*b*) Ratings by training staff.

(*c*) Length of training required to reach a given criterion of performance.

(*d*) Measured progress at work when training is accomplished by working at the actual task.

Examples of the first two of these came from a course at an engineering training school. The course was for technicians employed on the installation or maintenance of certain types of electrical equipment and for engineers supervising such work who had not had considerable experience of it. The syllabus included circuit diagram reading, correct methods of fault diagnosis and clearance, and the development of skill in making mechanical adjustments. The course lasted eight weeks and comprised lectures, demonstrations and

TABLE 10.1. *Examination of scores of trainees for course on electro-mechanical equipment*

	Age groups				
	20–24	25–29	30–34	35–39	40 and over
Theory examinations					
Number of trainees.	95	56	32	15	6
Mean marks out of 100 in					
first examination	75	72	70	60	48
second examination	78	78	75	60	55
Fault clearance					
Number of trainees	78	47	26	12	4
Mean marks out of 10 in					
examination	7·3	7·3	6·8	6·3	3·9

Marks for fault clearance were not available for all trainees.

TABLE 10.2. *Number of trainees rated as 'Highly Qualified' for mechanical adjustments to five types of apparatus*

Age group	Number of machines for which a rating of 'Highly Qualified' was given			Total number of trainees
	0	1 or 2	3, 4 or 5	
20–24	28 (29%)	44 (46%)	23 (24%)	95
25–29	17 (30%)	30 (54%)	9 (16%)	56
30–34	14 (44%)	13 (41%)	5 (15%)	32
35–47	17 (81%)	3 (14%)	1 (5%)	21

practical work, more than half the time being spent on mechanical adjustments. Written tests on theory were given midway through the course and at the end. There were also practical tests of fault clearance and mechanical adjustment. In the former, circuit faults were introduced into the apparatus and the student had to trace them. For the latter, a piece of equipment was dismantled and had to be reassembled after the component parts had been mixed up.

The results, given in Tables 10.1 and 10.2, showed a substantial fall of performance with age and it is clear that this cannot have been due to such factors as the trainees being unable to express themselves in written examinations because it occurred in fault clearance and mechanical adjustment as well as in the theory tests.

Data of type (c) were contained in the results of an oral test at which London taxicab drivers must qualify before they are licensed. The questions were taken from a list of journeys given to the applicant

TABLE 10.3. *Length and variability of time required by trainee taxicab drivers to reach given levels of learning the geography of London*

Age group	Number of trainees	Level of learning in terms of number of questions answered correctly		
		4	7	12
(a) Mean times per trainee in weeks				
British Legion students				
Twenties	12	30·5	37·7	41·3
Thirties	9	30·0	37·8	41·1
40 and over*	13	41·6	50·8	55·9
Private students				
Twenties	21	34·4	39·1	44·4
Thirties	12	37·5	41·3	47·9
Forties	10	50·6	59·7	62·6
(b) Standard deviation in weeks				
British Legion students				
Twenties		4·6	6·9	6·6
Thirties		4·5	5·7	6·3
40 and over*		18·1	21·0	19·6
Private students				
Twenties		10·8	10·9	11·2
Thirties		12·3	11·6	12·5
Forties		19·3	22·6	21·3

* All those in the '40 and over' group were in the forties except two who were in the fifties.

for study: he was asked to describe the shortest route between two points by naming all roads followed and crossed. He had also to know the whereabouts of squares, hotels, hospitals and so on. The candidate was interrogated until he had given six wrong answers, when the test stopped and the number of correct routes was scored. Twelve correct answers were required for qualification. The tests were held monthly at first and fortnightly once a man had reached four correct answers. Table 10.3(a) gives the lengths of training required by two groups of students studying full time. The private students had no formal instruction, but the British Legion students, who had an eight-month grant, were given one 6-hour lesson a week and also learnt the routes by cycling along them with maps. The students over

40 in both the British Legion and the private groups were slower than those in their twenties and thirties, and although the two groups differed, they did so to a much smaller extent than did the age ranges. As is frequently found in experimental studies of ageing, the variability of performance was greater among the older subjects than among the younger. This is shown in Table 10.3(*b*).

TABLE 10.4. *Output record of trainees on cigarette inspection.* Mean number of trays inspected per trainee

Age group	Number of trainees	Weeks			
		1	4	7	10
Under 21 .	3	26·4	58·4	75·7	66·3
21–25 . .	5	29·1	50·0	64·3	67·9
26–30 . .	8	23·8	51·4	67·4	76·2
31–35 . .	6	22·5	54·8	56·7	74·2
36–40 . .	12	22·4	46·4	54·6	64·8
41–45 . .	13	24·0	47·9	60·8	67·3
46 and over .	3	30·6	50·6	68·5	80·0

An example of type (*d*) data showing actual work performance is given in Table 10.4. These women were placed on cigarette inspection because they had become redundant elsewhere in the factory. There is no trend either upward or downward with age in these figures. They are, of course, for speed only and before equal performance at different ages could be confidently assumed it would be necessary to show that the older women were not maintaining speed at the expense of accuracy. It can be assumed, however, that any marked tendency to inaccuracy would have been detected and remedied, so that the figures in Table 10.4 may be taken to indicate approximately equal performance. They thus stand in marked contrast to the others surveyed so far. Why this is so, it is impossible to say on the present evidence, but some data were obtained from other training courses upon two factors which may well have influenced the level of performance and which we have seen in previous chapters to be fundamental to ageing studies, namely comparability of subjects and type of task.

Comparability of subjects in different age ranges

Not all the redundant women in the cigarette factory were retrained for inspection. We may suspect therefore that some acknowledged or unacknowledged selection took place and the members of the group whose results are given in Table 10.4 were not fully representative of their age ranges.

Such preselection of trainees can take place in several ways and may, indeed, have affected the validity of age comparisons in all the data surveyed so far. Any tendency on the part of an employer to dismiss less efficient men and women is likely to raise the standard of older people retained and lower that of older people seeking training elsewhere. The same result follows from the fact that once a person is settled in a job he is unlikely to move unless circumstances force him to do so. On the other hand, where a firm has a policy of recruiting only young labour and some barrier exists to the engagement of people in middle and old age, those who overcome this barrier are likely to be the abler individuals among the older people available. In the same way, many older people knowing or believing that age barriers exist will assume it is not worth applying and those who do will thus be unusually bold or perhaps desperate. Study of such preselection of trainees is difficult since much of it is probably due to unrecognized attitudes of mind on the part of those engaging workpeople and of those applying. Some check on the effects of preselection can, however, be made by studying cases where (a) all those on one job are transferred to one other, or refresher courses are given to all those on a particular job, or when (b) trainees are selected irrespective of age by means of some defined criterion such as a performance test.

(a) Perhaps one of the finest sets of field data on the training of older people comes from the retraining of tram-drivers as bus-drivers. During the changeover from trams to buses in South London all tram-drivers were given the opportunity to train as bus-drivers. The course lasted three weeks (with an extra week if needed), made up of about 40 hours at the wheel and 8 hours in the classroom, including demonstrations on mechanical models. Few men refused the offer of retraining. Many of those who failed were allowed to take the full course a second time.

Data were obtained for about half the total number of men who accepted and are set out in Table 10.5. The proportion passing in three weeks showed a continuous fall after the early thirties, indicating an increase with age of difficulty at learning the new task. The difficulties of the unsuccessful older trainees included poor control, poor road sense, poor retention of the London positioning rules and a lack of comprehension of the gear-box. The commonest difficulty lay in 'nearside judgement', many older trainees tending to leave the vehicle some 4 to 5 feet away from the kerb at stops and to pass other vehicles too widely. A few others showed a dangerous tendency in the opposite direction, passing too closely or scraping the kerb. Most of those who failed at three weeks did,

TABLE 10.5. *Results of retraining tram-drivers as bus-drivers*

Age group:	26–30	31–35	36–40	41–45	46–50	51–55	56–60	61–67
Number of persons .	104	106	146	92	63	62	61	60
% passing in 3 weeks .	96	97	90	83	65	71	44	32
% passing in 4 weeks .	3	2	9	12	23	8	25	10
% passing in 7 weeks .	1	1	..	2	5	11	24	21
Total % passing . .	100	100	99	97	93	90	93	63

TABLE 10.6. *Relationship between success of tram-drivers retraining as bus-drivers and previous experience of driving other road vehicles*

Age range:	Twenties and thirties	Forties	Fifties	Sixties
Trainees passing in 3–4 weeks Experience with				
Trolley-bus . . .	2	..	13	10
Car or lorry . . .	43	11	15	8
Both kinds . . .	4	1	1	..
No experience with other road vehicles . . .	17	9	22	3
Trainees failing or discontinuing Car or lorry (none with trolley-bus)	..	..	1	3
No experience with other road vehicles	2	7	11	16

Note: The numbers in this table differ from those in Table 10.5 because data regarding previous driving experience were collected from only some of the trainees.

however, pass in four or seven weeks, so that in the proportion who passed eventually there was little fall until the sixties. Even at this age, two-thirds of the trainees passed. Experience at driving other road vehicles clearly helped, as shown in Table 10.6: very few failed who had this previous experience. It was, however, not essential as is shown by the substantial numbers even as late as the fifties who passed without it.

(b) An example of a course where trainees were selected according to a defined criterion is that for postmen promoted to the rank of Postman Higher Grade. These attended a two-week course on registered mail, including lectures, demonstrations and practical work on rules, postal geography, classes of postal packets, mail dispatching, parcel post and other relevant aspects of Post Office procedure. Trainees were selected by a letter sorting and intelligence test. A test was given in the middle and another at the end of the second week; in each a dispatch of 250 letters had to be dealt with, the time taken

TABLE 10.7. *Results of tests during course on dispatch of registered letters*

Means per subject

Age group:	16–25	26–30	31–35	36–40	41–45	46–55
Number of trainees . .	12	14	20	12	13	11
Test 1						
Time taken (minutes). .	151	155	159	154	151	162
Entry errors . . .	0·7	0·9	1·4	1·2	1·9	1·6
Non-entry errors . .	1·8	2·3	1·8	2·1	2·2	1·9
Test 2						
Time taken (minutes) .	101	105	111	105	104	122
Entry errors . . .	0·5	0·6	0·8	0·9	1·0	1·1
Non-entry errors . .	0·7	0·9	0·8	0·7	0·6	1·3

and the errors made being recorded. Errors were separated into two kinds, 'entry' and 'non-entry'; the former consisting of clerical errors in recording particulars of the letters in the register, and the latter of non-clerical errors such as failure to seal the bag properly or attaching the wrong label.

The results set out in Table 10.7 show that the age trends, although somewhat irregular, still indicate a fall of performance with age. It is understandable that the trends should be reduced by the pre-selection procedure and the fact that they occur at all would seem to be evidence confirming that the taking of training is indeed a relatively severe task for older people, and shows changes with age greater than those which are reflected in the selection test scores. In this respect the results agree with the experimental studies of Thorndike *et al.* (1928).

The type of task

Common observation indicates that the difference between older and younger people at learning some jobs is greater than at learning others, just as the relation of learning performance to age has been seen to vary with type of material. What features of the task are important in this respect are uncertain, but three possibilities deserve consideration:

(a) Training staff often say that older people take less readily to *theoretical* than to practical training. Such evidence as is available lends little support, however, to the view that theoretical training is of itself difficult for older trainees. The difficulty would seem rather to lie in the method of instruction employed than in the actual theoretical content. The theory marks in Table 10.1 show, if any-

TABLE 10.8. *Ratings of learner drivers for different aspects of driving: means each out of a maximum of 5*

Age group:	Under 21	21–30	31–40	Over 40
Number of trainees . .	8	15	9	16
Mechanical theory. . .	3·4	3·5	3·4	2·5
Mechanical practical . .	3·4	3·4	3·0	2·4
Steering	3·6	3·5	3·0	2·5
Road sense	3·6	3·5	3·1	2·1
Confidence	3·5	3·4	2·8	2·5

thing, a smaller decline with age than do those for the more practical task of fault clearance, although since the equivalence of the scales of marks for theory and fault clearance cannot be assumed, little weight can be attached to this comparison.

Further evidence was obtained from courses in car driving at a police driving school and at a commercial school of motoring. Test results at the police school and ratings by the commercial school's training staff showed little consistent difference of age trend between results for mechanical theory on the one hand and the practical aspects of driving on the other—indeed, what little difference there was appeared to be in favour of the former. Results of ratings for the last three lessons before taking the driving test or discontinuing by private motorists taking courses at the commercial school's branch in Cambridge are shown in Table 10.8.

Any difficulty associated with theoretical training is more probably due to its being given by means of lectures which are difficult for older people because they impose a pace for taking in information by the listener. A second difficulty likely to arise in theoretical training is due to descriptions being verbal and abstract. In this connexion we may note that older trainees asked to have examples of apparatus in front of them during lectures on the working of the electro-mechanical equipment mentioned earlier, finding it very difficult to understand without being able to see the actual articles which were being described.

(*b*) Training for a new job in middle age will imply a change from previous work in the course of which *deeply ingrained habits* will have been acquired, and it is very likely that these will sometimes have to be unlearnt in order to master the new task. Some indication of this may be given in the results of a training course for blind telephonists. The course lasted for three terms of four to six weeks and a test was given at the end of each term. Scores for the last of these are given in Table 10.9. The age trends in the other two tests were in almost all cases closely similar. The striking feature of Table 10.9 is that the figures for typewriting changed hardly at all with age, whereas all the other tests showed substantial declines. It seems possible that age of onset of blindness was an important factor in producing these results. It had been, on the average, considerably later for the older subjects, so that many would have acquired habits of reading and writing which would have had to be modified to work in Braille, while some of them might have acquired skill at touch typing before becoming blind.

The rates of decline for the various Braille tasks did, however, differ considerably among themselves, so that previous experience cannot be the sole operative factor. In particular, the writing tasks, in which new responses had to be given to familiar signals, seemed less affected than the reading tasks, in which familiar meanings had to be attached to new signals. This is the reverse of what would be expected on the theory of Wylie (1919) following Poffenberger (1915) that 'transfer effect is positive when an old response can be transferred to a new stimulus, but negative when a new response is required to an old stimulus'. A possible reason is that we have here an example of a tendency, which would be a reasonable inference from the work surveyed in previous chapters, for declines with age in processes of comprehension to limit performance sooner than declines in expressive processes.

(*c*) One feature likely to be important is *complexity* of various kinds especially when combined with demand for speed. For example, the one rating in Table 10.8 which seems to have a somewhat greater average decline than the rest is 'road sense' which implies the ability to make judgements based on a variety of incoming data which must be used within narrow time-limits if they are to be

TABLE 10.9. *Performance of blind trainees on several tests. All figures are per subject*

	Teens	Twenties	Thirties	Forties	Ratio, teens to forties
Number of trainees . . .	19	20	13	16	
1. Typing from dictation on ordinary typewriter for 10 minutes					
Strokes made . . .	1,209	1,164	1,165	1,176	0·97
Errors	8·3	6·7	11·2	9·6	0·86
2. Writing 20 telephone numbers from dictation on braille machine					
Time (secs.)	*82*	*86*	*95*	102	0·80
Errors	*0·8*	1·1	1·3	2·2	0·36
3. Writing prose from dictation on braille machine for 5 minutes					
Words written . . .	*148*	*136*	128	111	0·75
Errors	4·5	4·7	4·5	8·2	0·55
4. Reading aloud 20 telephone numbers from braille					
Time (secs.)	*77*	*90*	*91*	131	0·59
Errors	*0·7*	*0·9*	*0·9*	2·3	0·30
5. Reading aloud prose from braille for 5 minutes					
Words read	*425*	*338*	*405*	203	0·54
Errors	1·8	2·2	*1·1*	2·9	0·62
6. Switchboard operation: dealing with 21 calls and a telegram					
Time (mins.) . . .	*30·3*	*30·6*	*35·2*	44·5	0·68
Errors in manipulating plugs, &c.	3·2	2·8	3·5	3·6	0·89
Errors in recording . .	2·5	2·2	3·0	3·4	0·74

Results significantly different from those of the forties are printed in italics.

effective. In an earlier study, Belbin (1953) had found evidence that difficulty of industrial training occurred mainly on jobs which involved the acquisition of rhythm or of rapid sensori-motor coordination, such as sewing-machine operations. The difficulty in these cases appeared to be not so much that older trainees could not acquire the skill at all as that they could not attain sufficient speed.

It would seem that it may be necessary to consider relatively small differences of complexity on nominally similar tasks. Table 10.10

gives the results of ratings for tests following a seven-week course on electro-mechanical equipment similar to, but more complex than, that of Table 10.1. The student was given demonstrations and practical work on stripping and reassembling the equipment and then, for the final test, was allowed 15 hours spread over three days to make a complete assembly and adjustment. Each functional unit

TABLE 10.10. *Ratings on reassembly of electro-mechanical equipment.*
B and C ratings as percentage of total

Age groups:	20–25	26–30	31–35	36–40	41–45
46-unit machine . . .	5·4	5·0	5·7	5·4	9·3
58-unit machine . . .	8·6	9·0	7·9	12·2	18·3

The amount by which the number of B and C ratings on the larger machine was greater than on the smaller rose significantly with age in the thirties and forties.

of the apparatus was checked by the examiner and the adjustments rated according to a three-point scale: (A) adjustment to within restricted tolerance; (B) to within normal tolerance; and (C) outside normal tolerance. It can be seen from Table 10.10 that (B) and (C) ratings for the smaller 46-unit machine were similar in all age ranges except the oldest. In the larger 58-unit machine they were again similar until the early thirties but rose in the late thirties and again in the forties.

The suggestion that in the more complex task errors rose with age to a greater extent and that the rise began at an earlier age is in line with the results of experiments on performance already discussed in Chapters VI and VIII. The similarity of this and of other training results to experimental findings does, indeed, raise the question of how far the limits lie in the ability to acquire training and how far in more general aspects of performance. The fact that Belbin (1953) found difficulties of training and difficulties of maintaining performance with age to be reported from different types of operations, indicates that a distinction between training and performance difficulties should be drawn. On the other hand, Kay (1954) has pointed out that some of the difficulties of the older people at experimental tasks may well be due to their having failed to acquire the necessary 'training' from the instructions given by the experimenter and thus not understanding fully what is required of them. In the experiment outlined in Chapter VI (p. 147), he checked carefully the subjects' understanding of the instructions before they began the main task. The results, given in Table 10.11, show a striking increase with age in the proportion who did not understand what they had to do without further instruction. It is of some comfort to note that the proportion of subjects in the somewhat dangerous condition of erroneously believing they knew what was required, did not increase with age. There would seem to be a need for research in which the factors

TABLE 10.11. *Ability of subjects to carry out written instructions for an experiment. Numbers out of 10 except in the 55–64 group in which they are out of 14*

	Age group					
	15–24	*25–34*	*35–44*	*45–54*	*55–64*	*65–72*
Could carry out the instructions correctly .	6	5	3	3	4 (28%)	2
Thought they could carry them out but had interpreted them wrongly .	4	5	5	4	6 (44%)	4
Did not understand what they had to do .	0	0	2	3	4 (28%)	4

of training and performance are separately controlled to an extent greater than has been achieved hitherto.

Some practical implications

In spite of their many and obvious limitations, these results would seem to lead to three practical conclusions:

(*a*) The wide scatter of scores specifically noted in one case and present in at least some others implies that *some* older people can be trained to a good standard of performance at tasks for which the average results might lead one to expect failure. Even if selection has to be exercised, a rigid age bar would seem unjustified for at least many training courses, and although the training of older people may sometimes take longer than that of younger, the lower labour turnover in the higher age ranges might often more than offset its cost.

(*b*) It is clear that although preselection may often distort the picture of how easy or difficult it is for older people to train, it cannot be the whole cause of variation between the results of one course and another in relation to age. The nature of the task would seem to be an important variable. It follows that attention to the details of the job for which the training was required might substantially simplify its demands for older people and thus reduce the severity for them of the training required. Suggestions along these lines have already been made (Welford 1953*b*).

(*c*) The receiving of training is itself a task making demands which vary greatly according to the methods used. We have noted in previous chapters that a rise of demand may result in a disproportionate fall in the performance of older people. It follows that poor training methods may disproportionately affect their chances of success. Belbin *et al.* (1957) have already stressed the difficulties inherent in common methods of training.

2. *Experimental studies of training methods*

The field studies of training do not in themselves give a clear lead as to what modifications to existing training methods would benefit older people. For this we must turn to the results of experiments on learning and performance generally. Broadly speaking, these imply four recommendations:

(*a*) The subject should be given control of the pace of instruction and the amount required to be learnt at any one time should be limited.

(*b*) The relationship between instruction and task should, other things being equal, be as direct as possible. Thus, manipulatory skills should be neither taught nor tested by using words—as, for instance, in the T.W.I. system. A verbal medium implies translation from words to action or vice versa which may be disproportionately difficult for older people.

(*c*) Care should be taken to ensure that the material presented is at all stages of training understandable to the subject so that he *never* has to perform a task he does not comprehend.

(*d*) Errors should be prevented during the early stages of training so that they do not become fixated and have to be 'unlearnt' later.

These are, of course, only a few among the many factors likely to affect older people in training. For example, subtle considerations of the relationships between trainer and trainee need to be taken into account at all ages and may become of increasing importance as people get older. A possible indication in this direction is contained in the replies collected by King (1955a) answering a questionnaire sent to instructors of rural craftsmen. The instructors teach individuals or small groups of blacksmiths, agricultural engineers, carpenters and others in their place of work. King found that the older instructors tended to rate the performance of older trainees higher than did younger instructors. It is, of course, impossible to tell from such data alone how far higher ratings reflect an objectively higher standard of performance. It is understandable that older trainees should have a greater respect for and rapport with an older instructor and such rapport might, upon analysis, prove to be resolvable into factors such as older instructors tending to teach more slowly or having a common background of early experience and outlook with older trainees leading to a common language and set of presuppositions.

We shall here outline some exploratory experiments which have attempted to study the effects of the four factors which have been listed.

(a) Pace of instruction

Effects of allowing the subject to set his own pace of learning are shown by the results of the electrical problem experiment described in Chapter VIII (p. 203). The two age ranges (above and below 30) were each divided into two groups. To one group the experimenter demonstrated the method of tackling the problem, and to the other written instructions were given.

Differences of time and meter-readings between the training methods were small and insignificant. There was, however, a relationship which varied between the younger and older subjects between training method and the accuracy with which the first box was solved. From Table 10.12 it will be seen that the older subjects made rather more errors than the younger when training had been by demonstration and a little less than the younger when it had been by written instructions.

Both demonstration and written instructions used a verbal medium thus running counter to the second of our recommendations, and it is possible that the written instructions made somewhat more severe demands in this respect than the demonstrations. Written instructions do, however, have the important advantage that if for any reason a subject is slow to comprehend the task he can look over them several times, and if he forgets any detail he can go back and recover it. When training is by demonstration, any detail not grasped or forgotten will be lost unless the subject asks to have the point gone over again. Because it tends to be embarrassing to have to do this frequently, an older subject trained by demonstration is likely to have a number of gaps in his grasp of the methods of solving the problem when he begins the test. This is not to say, however, that the difficulties inherent in demonstration are always overcome by

TABLE 10.12. *Relationships between training-method, accuracy and age in solving an electrical problem*

Numbers of subjects attaining different levels of accuracy

	Number of errors on first box					
	0	*1*	*2*	*3*	*4*	*5*
Training by demonstration						
Younger	10	3	1	..	..	..
Older	5	1	4	..	..	3
Training by written instructions						
Younger	5	2	..	1	1	6
Older	5	1	1	1	1	1

written instructions—manifestly the difficulty of understanding these will often be a more severe limit upon performance than any drawbacks inherent in demonstration. Where, however, the educational level of subjects is adequate (as was the case in the present experiment) written instructions would seem at least worth consideration.

(b) *Relationship between training method and task for which training is given*

Experiments by Belbin (1958) have shown that older subjects may learn substantially better by 'doing'—'activity' learning as she has termed it—than by conscious memorization of instructions.

In the first of these, the subjects were required to 'post' fifty numbered cards into five slots (ten cards in each slot) in the lid of a box, each slot bearing a distinctive colour. There was a systematic relationship between colour and number; thus, all the cards in the 20's had to be posted into one slot and all those in the 30's into another. The subjects had to learn the relationship between colour and number so that they could post cards as quickly as possible without making errors. Two methods of training for this were used.

In the first—the 'memorization' method—subjects were given a chart showing the relationships between colours and numbers and were left to study this, with the box into which the cards would have to be posted in front of them. The subject studied the chart until he was satisfied that he had learned the relationships. The chart was then removed. His learning was tested by asking him to state the relationships and if he did so correctly, he began the task of posting.

TABLE 10.13. *Performance at card-sorting following two different training methods in Belbin's first experiment*

	Twenties	Thirties	Forties	Fifties and sixties
Number of subjects . .	10	12	8	14
Median times (in secs.) to 'post' 50 cards as main task after training by:				
Memorization. . .	96	152	150	153
'Activity learning' . .	96	112·5	122	131
Percentage subjects attaining completely correct performance after:				
Memorization. . .	60	33	38	21
'Activity learning' . .	70	67	50	50
Median learning times (in secs.) for:				
Memorization. . .	33·5	60·5	77·5	42·5
'Activity learning' . .	54·0	115·0	122·5	144·5

The second method of training—the 'activity' method—required the subjects to find out for themselves the relationship between colour and number. They were given a large pack of coloured cards, each of which bore a number. They were told to post these cards into the appropriately coloured slots, noting the numbers as they did so, and gradually building up the idea of which numbers were associated with which colour. When they were satisfied that they had achieved this, they were transferred to the main task. Each subject performed the task twice—once with the first and once with the second set of instructions. Half performed first with the first set and then transferred to the second, and half performed the tasks in the opposite order. Different sets of relationships between numbers and colours were used in the two tasks.

The results are set out in Table 10.13 for a point in the performance at which the median times for the youngest group were the same for the two methods. It can be seen that with the memorization method median time to post the fifty cards rose sharply from the twenties to the thirties and beyond, while the proportion of subjects attaining completely correct performance fell. With the activity method, the median time rose gradually from the twenties to the fifties, but was, at all ages beyond the twenties, lower than that for the memorization method. This quicker performance was not achieved at the expense of accuracy, which did indeed, in all age ranges especially the oldest, tend to be higher with the activity method.

Belbin suggests four possible reasons for these results. Firstly, it is clear from Table 10.13 that the older people were taking substantially longer than the younger to learn, especially by the activity method. The possibility arises therefore that the older people were not allowing themselves enough time to learn by memorization. Belbin points out, however, that this cannot be the complete explanation, as three subjects in the sixties, who were unable to do the task at all when trained by the memorization method, performed reasonably well following training by the activity method. Secondly, learning by memorization involved 'translation' between the chart and the box, which may have been relatively difficult for older people: in the activity method, no such translation was needed, as the numbers to be associated with the colours were always seen going into the appropriate slots. Thirdly, memorizing from the chart inevitably required the learning of colour-number relationships as such, whereas with the activity method it was possible to ignore the colours and to learn number-spatial relationships, which might have been somewhat easier for older people. Fourthly, with the activity method, the learning task was similar to the main task and thus gave practice at it: if older subjects, after learning by memorizing, had performed the main task for a longer time, they might have come substantially closer to the younger subjects and the times achieved by the two methods might have been considerably nearer together.

Belbin's second experiment was designed to compare activity learning and memorization at different ages, with these four possibilities either eliminated or controlled. The task was to post cards numbered from 20 to 79 into six different slots in the lid of a box. All the 20's were to go into one slot, all the 30's into another, and so on. The subject was required to learn the association between slots and numbers.

One group (1) of subjects learnt by first memorizing small numbered slips attached to the slots. The main task was then done without the slips. The other group (2) learnt the task by actually posting a pack of special numbered cards on which the pattern of the six slots appeared and numbers were printed in the appropriate positions as

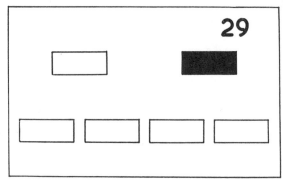

FIG. 10.1. Example of card used for training by the 'activity' method in Belbin's second card-sorting experiment

TABLE 10.14. *Times taken to reach 'criterion' performance of 10 secs. per 6 cards in Belbin's second card-sorting experiment*

Totals per group of 8 subjects in mins. and secs.

		Memorization		'Activity learning'	
Age group:		18–22	30–49	18–22	30–49
Cycle at which criterion was reached .		12th	27th	7th	6th
Total time to reach criterion . .		24′ 14″	60′ 39″	32′ 17″	43′ 3″
Total made up of:					
Learning time		5′ 34″	11′ 15″	22′ 10″	33′ 47″
Time performing main task . .		18′ 40″	49′ 24″	10′ 7″	9′ 16″

shown in Fig. 10.1. Both groups were told to go on until satisfied they had learnt the positions and were then transferred to the main task. Time taken over the learning and also the time required for each six cards of the main task was measured by a stop-watch.

In Table 10.14 are shown the times required by each age range in each learning method to reach an arbitrary criterion performance of 10 seconds to post six cards. The older were slower than the younger with each method of training, but the difference was both absolutely and proportionately very much greater with the memorization method than with the activity method. With the younger subjects, the criterion performance was reached more quickly following memorizing than after activity learning, but with the older subjects the activity learning was clearly superior.

In Table 10.15 the figures are analysed in a different way to show performances attained after constant time, adding together time taken learning and time taken performing the main task. Once again we see the same pattern of results, the younger subjects doing better following memorization and the older showing better performance

TABLE 10.15. *Mean individual cycle times (in secs.) reached after 2,027 seconds in Belbin's second card-sorting experiment*

	Memorization		'Activity learning'	
Age group:	*18–22*	*30–49*	*18–22*	*30–49*
Cycle time	9·5	13·4	10·3	11·0

after learning by the activity method. Again, as in the first experiment, the superiority of the activity method as regards time was not at the expense of accuracy: the errors did in fact tend to be fewer after learning by the activity method than following memorization.

(c) *and* (d) *Ensuring initial comprehension of the material and preventing errors in the early stages of learning*

Experiments incorporating these two factors together were carried out by Belbin (1958) with a view to improving the training of women engaged on invisible mending in factories making woollen cloth. The normal method of training requires the trainee to watch an experienced mender and then to do the work herself under supervision. The method is slow, taking several months, and many trainees, even young girls, leave because they find the work too exacting. For older trainees it is commonly regarded as nearly impossible. The task is one which makes severe demands on visual acuity both during the initial training period and during subsequent practice of the skill once it has been acquired. Trainees have often complained that stitches 'disappear as you look at them'. Preliminary studies indicated, however, that the limitation imposed by acuity operated more during the initial training period than it did thereafter. It would seem that once the pattern of the weaves has been learnt, it is not necessary to observe them in such precise detail, and the task becomes less visually exacting than it was initially. An alternative training method devised by Belbin aimed at overcoming this initial difficulty by using cloth specially woven with threads very much larger than normal. Trainees learned the weaves with this and only transferred to the

TABLE 10.16. *Median times (in minutes) taken by subjects aged 30–50 to mend 6 in. of weave after 8 hours' training by two training methods*

	Type of weave		
	1 × 1 plain	*2 × 2 hopsack*	*2 × 2 twill*
Training method:			
Traditional 'sit by me' method .	6·6	5·9	Unable to do task*
Belbin's alternative method .	4·5	3·1	5·5†

* Three subjects out of 5 were unable to do the task.
† One subject out of 6 was unable to do the task.

TABLE 10.17. *Comparison of trainee menders aged 30–50 with those starting training on leaving school*

	Type of weave		
	1 × 1 plain	*2 × 2 hopsack*	*2 × 2 twill*
Training by Belbin's method:			
Median times taken by 30–50 group to mend 6 in. of weave after 8 hours of training	4·5 mins.	3·1 mins.	5·5 mins.
Training required by school leavers to attain same speeds as older group .	5½ weeks	10 weeks	3–4 weeks
Time required by school leavers to attain same speeds when trained by 'Training Within Industry' method .	7 weeks	Not at all	4 weeks

normal cloth when the patterns had been thoroughly mastered. Throughout the training, care was taken to ensure, as far as possible, thorough understanding of each weave and of what had to be done to mend it, and efforts were made to avoid errors which would have to be 'unlearnt' later.

The results for a group of eleven trainees in their thirties and forties are given in Table 10.16, and show the new method to have yielded clearly superior results. The older subjects put up perform-ances which were remarkably good when compared with those of trainees who had just left school. The figures in Table 10.17 are striking: we see the older subjects attaining in a matter of hours speeds which it took the school leavers weeks to reach. These results must be qualified by the fact that the mends involved were relatively simple and that the older subjects might not have been able to maintain performance at this level over long periods. They do, however, refute the belief that this work cannot be learnt by middle-aged people—they did in fact do so very quickly. Belbin suggests that the reason for these results is that mending is predominantly a perceptual skill and that her method of training was designed to take account of this fact. Older people find difficulty essentially because their limited visual acuity makes it impossible, or very difficult, to master the perceptual task when it is unfamiliar. Removal of the limitation imposed by acuity during the early stages enables them to learn the perceptual skill successfully and this in turn permits them to benefit from the more strictly manual skill which Belbin suggests they have acquired gradually over the years in the performance of household mending, especially darning.

The study of special training methods for older people is as yet in its infancy. Enough has already been done, however, and the implications of work on learning seem sufficiently definite, to make it clear that attention to the manner of presenting material and to the circumstances and pace of training can profoundly affect the likelihood of success for trainees in middle age and beyond. Such new training methods would not only seem capable of shortening training time for older people, but, perhaps even more important, are also likely to help in avoiding the danger of discouragement during instruction. This is frequently mentioned by training staff as a reason why many older trainees discontinue after a short time. It probably tends, as the training officer of a Royal Ordnance Factory pointed out, to operate on a vicious circle principle: difficulties and failures owing to unsuitable methods early in training may introduce anxiety and lead to failure which will so shake older people's confidence that they are then unable to do jobs which they would otherwise have been able to tackle well.

Any change of work in middle and old age must inevitably present problems, not only because the new task has to be learnt, but also because social and emotional adjustments will often be required. Training courses designed to take account of the particular needs of older people may not be able to remove these difficulties entirely, but it is reasonable to suppose that by reducing the actual problems of learning they would enable older people to face, with more equanimity than they can at present, necessary changes of work due to accidents or ill health, or resulting from new processes or changing emphasis in production.

B. RESISTANCE TO CHANGE

Older people are commonly believed to be opposed to social changes and to show increasing conservatism in social and political attitudes. These beliefs have been queried by Pollak (1943) and also by Lorge and Helfant (1953). More recently a detailed study has been made by Speakman using material from Public Opinion Polls in a number of countries over the period 1935 to 1946, collected by Cantril and Strunk (1951). Speakman extracted from the published results details of 104 polls in which age data were available together with questions about some proposed political, social or domestic change. The criterion of what questions involved change for this purpose was the agreement of three judges to whom they were shown, together with a number of other questions which did not involve such changes. The percentages voting in favour of and against the proposed changes were computed for three age groups—20–29, 30–49 and 50 and over—and it was found that there was a small but significant tendency towards greater opposition as one went up the age scale. The absolute difference with age was, however, small. It was similar to those associated with sex and population density and less than differences associated with social class and political belief, as is shown in Table 10.18.

Closer inspection of the data indicated, however, that the very small over-all change of resistance did not give a true picture of the trends with age. The degree of opposition shown by older people as compared to younger differed greatly according to whether the proposed change was popular or unpopular. Percentages voting against proposals of different levels of popularity are shown in Fig. 10.2, from which it appears that older people tended to vote less favourably towards popular changes and less unfavourably towards unpopular changes than did younger people. The small over-all tendency of the older people to greater opposition was very largely because more popular than unpopular changes were canvassed in the opinion polls concerned.

Further analysis by Speakman indicated that these results could not be due to some peculiarity whereby older people were tending to espouse unpopular causes, nor could they be attributed to a pre-ponderance of questions touching upon some special interest attached to middle and old age, as for instance proposals to increase old-age benefits. The data from public opinion polls do not normally report the

TABLE 10.18. *Differences of resistance to change associated with age compared with differences associated with other factors*

	Sex	Social class	Political party	Population density
Group showing, on average, greater resistance to change . . .	Women	Upper	Conservative	Country
Less resistance . .	Men	Lower	Radical	Large towns
(a) Mean difference (regardless of sign) between percentage voting against proposed changes* .	5·6	14·5	25·6	15·0
(b) Mean difference (regardless of sign) between those over and under 50 years of age in these groups .	7·5	7·1	6·4	12·1
(c) Ratios of (a) to (b) giving effects of age relative to other factors . .	1·34	0·49	0·25	0·81

* These percentages were calculated after removing all replies of 'uncertain' or 'don't know'.

strength with which opinion is held but deal with percentages of those voting 'yes' or 'no' or 'uncertain', and it is always hazardous to argue from unanimity of opinion in a group to strength of opinion in the individuals composing that group. If, however, it is legitimate to do this in the present case, the conclusion seems inescapable that the older people were displaying, on average, more moderate, less extreme opinions than younger people. Similar evidence has also been obtained in a different connexion and with a quite different technique (Welford 1946).

It can be seen from Fig. 10.2 that issues upon which opinion was fairly equally divided tended also to generate substantially greater numbers of 'uncertain' or 'don't know' answers than did those where opinion was more definitely favourable or unfavourable. It seemed, therefore, arguable that the moderate opinions of older people might be linked with ignorance or uncertainty. The data from public-opinion polls have indicated that there are significant reductions with age in the percentages of those showing accurate knowledge of

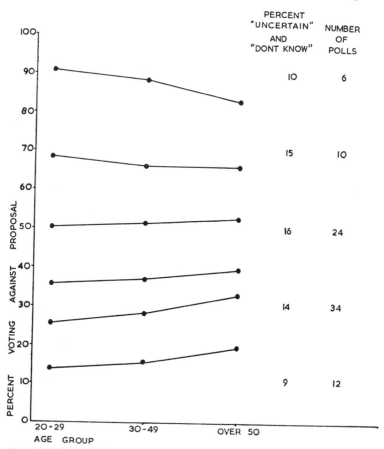

Fɪɢ. 10.2. Relation between resistance to change by older people and the popularity of the change proposed

The proportion voting in favour of popular changes tends to diminish with age; so also does the proportion voting against unpopular changes.

The percentages plotted were calculated after removing all replies of 'uncertain' or 'don't know'.

a current topic, of those reading newspapers and books and listening to radio, &c., and of those partaking in various types of social activities. These trends might perhaps in turn be the result of education having been less well developed fifty or so years ago than during the last twenty years. Uncertainty does not appear, however, to be the sole cause of the age differences in Fig. 10.2. If we compare the third and the last lines of Table 10.19 we see that when the percentage replying 'uncertain' or 'don't know' is held constant, age differences

TABLE 10.19. *Relationship between resistance to change and age with 'uncertainty' controlled*

	Age comparisons	
	Over 50 with 20–29	Over 50 with 30–49
Cases where more people in the older group than in the younger voted 'uncertain' or 'don't know' Number of polls on which the comparison was based	10	11
Difference of percentage voting 'uncertain' or 'don't know' (older minus younger) . .	8·16	7·58
Difference of percentage of the remainder voting against change (older minus younger) . .	8·16	4·78
Cases where equal proportions in both the older and the younger group voted 'uncertain' or 'don't know' Number of polls on which the comparison was based	10	11
Difference of percentage voting 'uncertain' or 'don't know'	0	0
Difference of percentage of the remainder voting against change (older minus younger) . .	4·16	0·14

in the proportions resisting change are reduced but a substantial difference remains between the 'over 50' and the 20–29 groups.

The cause of the moderation shown by the older people must for the moment remain in doubt. It is probably in part due to the factors which have been discussed and in part to a genuine clinging to old opinions or, in other words, to *inertia* of opinion. Whatever the cause, the simple over-all generalization that older people are more resistant than younger to change as such, is not borne out. The avoidance of extreme opinions means that although older people may not be so enthusiastic over some proposals for change which are generally popular, they may be less opposed to unpopular changes.

Taking these somewhat tentative and fragmentary results together with the data available on training, we can see evidence that there is indeed some restriction of adaptability as people grow older and that in this respect popular opinion is borne out. Equally, however, it seems clear that this restriction is of limited extent and can hardly be regarded as precluding the successful achievement of change by older people, especially if suitable care is taken to make the process as easy as possible. Such care might be expected to benefit people of all ages, but to be of disproportionate advantage in the middle and older years.

greater individual differences than do younger. The disproportionate effect of increased difficulty is by no means universal, and instances have been given in which the opposite has been observed. It is clear, therefore, that we must go beyond the readily observable facts to more fundamental principles of the operation of human sensory, central and motor mechanisms. This the work reported here has attempted to do by looking in detail at the nature and causes of changing performance among older people.

The studies have revealed clearly that the changes with age lie essentially in the central control and guidance of actions. In some cases they may represent the indirect effects of impairment to the peripheral organs of sense and motor action. For example, if we cannot see clearly we can compensate to some extent by looking for a longer time at what we have to observe, or if our hand becomes unsteady we can largely offset the resulting difficulty of making accurately graded movements by altering the manner in which we support and steady it. There is no doubt, however, that some, and probably the most important, age trends in performance are due directly to effects associated with age in the central mechanisms themselves. These may be thought of as due to changes in the central nervous system which are analogous to those more obvious changes in tissues we can see. They are organic in nature and are to be thought of as dispassionately as we think of the signs of maturing years in face and hands. Their effect upon behaviour is due to the fact that they occur in the tissue by which behaviour is mediated.

These effects would seem to be of two main types. The first is the lowering of the 'capacity' of the organism's 'information channel', due either to a reduction in the strength of the signals from one part of the mechanism to the next, or to an increase in the amount of random nervous activity (i.e. 'noise'), or to both. The reduction of 'signal to noise' ratio implied by these changes results in a need for stronger signals or for the integration of data over a longer time before it can become a sufficient basis for action. This applies not only to signals coming from the sense organs to the brain, but to the many stages of signalling within the brain itself. Because many mechanisms of this kind are involved, the form of slowing varies from one task to another according to which mechanism in the chain is setting the limit to the subject's performance—in other words, according to the demands of the task he is doing.

The second major effect of central change with age lies in a little-understood process seemingly common to short-term memory and conceptualization. We have described it as the holding in mind of a quantity of data so that it can be used simultaneously. It is conceived that data are somehow held in a form of short-term storage while other data are being gathered. Obviously, unless data can be so held, the amount of information that can be simultaneously applied to any problem is very small indeed. It would appear that in old people the amount that can be stored tends to diminish, and that what is stored is more liable than it is in younger people to interference and disruption from other activity going on at the same time. Such a decline in short-term retention would be capable of accounting for a very wide range of observed age changes in learning and problem-solving, although it must be recognized that the evidence at present available does not rule out other explanations.

Diminished channel capacity, lowering of 'signal to noise' ratio and lessened short-term storage would all on average tend to produce limitations of performance measurable by simple over-all achievement scores. It is important to recognize, however, that these limitations are not likely to exert their effects upon all parts or aspects or stages of a task equally. They will only become serious at certain points at which 'peak' demands occur leading to 'overloading'. Thus the pacing of performance by an external agency is likely to lead to occasional overloading of the subject's capacity to handle information, and complex problem-solving tasks may at certain points on the way to a solution make excessive demands for short-term retention, so that the capacity for this will limit the complexity of problem that can be tackled successfully. Intermittent overloads of these kinds may well be the cause of some of the momentary 'lapses' of attention to which both young and old are to some extent prone, and which are often said to increase with age.

A possible explanation of the limitation of both channel capacity and short-term retention is contained in the fact that the number of active brain cells tends to diminish from young adulthood onwards. Such a diminution would almost certainly lead to a lessening of signal strength in the brain: the fact that random activity would be averaged over a smaller number of cells would tend to increase the relative 'noise' level, and the reduced number of cells would mean less capacity for the establishment of the reverberant circuits which probably underlie short-term retention. The same kind of explanation might well account for other observed changes with age, for example, the finding by Botwinick and Shock (1952) that a mental task showed less fatigue effect among older people than it did among younger: if we can conceive of fatigue as in any sense an aftermath of over-activity of the brain, it is clear that reduction of signal strength would, in certain circumstances at least, reduce liability to fatigue effects.

This kind of explanation would not, however, explain the fact noted in many experiments that older people have a remarkable ability to compensate for any changes which may tend to impair their performance and show an automatic and unconscious ordering of their activity to make the best use of what capacities they have. This process of what we may call *unconscious optimization* is probably a feature of much if not most normal human performance. The fact that it is striking in later middle and old age indicates that whatever difficulties may be experienced at these times of life, the ability to organize behaviour 'strategically' has not been lost. It must be emphasized that such over-all planning should not be taken as in any sense supporting the view that there is 'a little man up aloft in control', but simply that behaviour is organized in a hierarchical manner, as described in Chapter II, with different controlling processes operating on different time scales.

It is clear that each one of the areas of research surveyed here requires a great deal of further work. The results already obtained constitute little more than an extensive exploration and a beginning of the definition of essential problems. What has been achieved would seem to be the demonstration that certain age changes which might prima facie be due to either organic causes or to experience are likely to have been caused predominantly by the former. The time would now seem opportune for a more thorough-going study of the effects of experience, especially long experience, upon performance in later middle and old age. We do not know, for example, the relationship between demands early in life and the subsequent changes of performance level with age, although we know that moderate demands in childhood and adolescence appear to bring out an individual's potentialities better than demands which are either too high or too low, and we also know that age changes are less among individuals who show high achievement as young adults.

Research aimed at studying the results of long experience would seem inevitably to involve longitudinal studies following individuals over a considerable period of years and imply the need for the highly stable investigating groups that these longitudinal studies require. They would also seem to need considerable flexibility of thought in designing ways of studying performance. It would be necessary to solve the problem of how to study those performances in which older people excel and of how to discover in just what ways this excellence is attained. There is little doubt that the more thorough 'coding' in perception and in action that experience makes possible is potentially a means of offsetting the limitations we referred to earlier, and may often far more than compensate for them. Such 'coding' and the experience that lies behind it, is, however, highly individual, and it would seem necessary, therefore, to face the task of assessing uniquely individual abilities and their changes with age. It is difficult to do this in an acceptably scientific manner, but the task would seem not to be impossible. We might, for example, consider the progress over a number of years of those things which a man can do best, and compare these 'best' performances with other aspects of his ability. Again, a potentially useful line of approach is to measure really well-established skills such as those attained by industrial operatives at their work, because these are probably the most highly practised activities that we have available for study, apart from simple actions such as eating and walking.

Viewing the work in this book from a strictly practical standpoint, we see that it provides no dramatic suggestions for the elimination or reversal of age changes. What it does indicate, however, is that in many tasks subjects, young and old alike, are working well within their capacities and changes of capacity, even in old age, are un-important. Perhaps more significant is the indication that where age changes do impinge upon performance some relatively trivial factor may often be limiting what can be done, so that comparatively small changes in the task could bring it within the capacities of older people. It follows that a promising line for future research in industry lies in attempting to change the layout of work or of machine tools in order to make them more suitable for operation by older people. It would seem likely that relatively minor modifications could pro-foundly affect the chances of success by older people at certain jobs: the modifications would benefit both young and old, but especially the latter. Attempts to 'fit the job to the man' in such ways would seem a far better approach to the problem of employment for older people than attempting to move men to other jobs. Older people who at the present time change their jobs seem seldom to take up work at a level appropriate to their past attainments, and in consequence a move in middle or old age usually leads to the wasting of skills which have been established and brought to a high level over a period of many years. Where changes of work must be made, we may expect that the acquisition of new skill would be easier if arrangements could be made for it to be acquired gradually over a substantial period of time—if, in other words, a man could always look 'one jump ahead' and prepare for his new work in advance. The same might well be true of preparation for retirement.

An industrial medical officer once said to the writer that data were needed which would enable a doctor to prescribe work for older people in much the same way as he now prescribes drugs or treatment. We are not yet in a position to make suggestions either for work or for leisure which attain this degree of definiteness. It is, however, fair to say that a foundation has been laid upon which such an 'ergopoeia', analogous to the pharmacopoeia, can eventually be based, and the way has been shown round some of the extremely difficult problems besetting the studies of ageing in industry which must precede such specification.

In conclusion, it must be remarked with all humility that anyone who has a sympathetic interest in his fellow men and seeks to understand them cannot but recognize that everything which has been done so far towards the scientific study of ageing leaves aside some of the most characteristic and important qualities of older people, qualities which are elusive in nature and must be broadly classed as attitudinal. Many so-called attitudes and interests have been the subject of investigations which have shown changes in the patterns of what men and women consider desirable or important as they grow older, but over and above these are many qualities of attitude which have up to the present escaped systematic study. Some of these seem rather clearly based on organic or other fundamental factors; for example, the gnawing suspiciousness that seems to derive from deafness or loss of memory, the disagreeability and laziness which often result from failing energy, or, on the other hand, the gentle enjoyment of people that comes from the inability to pursue the energetic pastimes of former years, or the helpfulness to others that many old people show when increased leisure in retirement gives them opportunity for its practical expression.

Other attitudinal qualities do not seem to have any such clear and obvious organic foundations. For example, the bitterness resulting from failure to achieve ambitions, or the fearless simplicity that derives from having reconciled oneself to the fact that some of what one set out to do has been done and the rest can be forgotten. Perhaps we may say of these that old age is a *revealing* time when the best and the worst in us stand out in sharp relief.

Whatever the cause of these attitudes, they are of profound practical and social importance and the understanding of them must surely form a part of the programme of future research in the field of ageing. How to proceed to study them in a significant way we do not yet know and for the present all we can do is to remember what the pioneers of psychology realized, but has since often been forgotten, namely that preconceived theory is a tool and a servant that must never be allowed to usurp a position of control. We shall do less than justice to our subject if we try to force these aspects of the behaviour of older people into the strait jacket of present psychological theories. For the present we must observe as accurately and objectively as we can, searching forward step by step, content never to be quite sure where we shall eventually arrive.

REFERENCES

ANDJUS, R. K., KNOPFELMACHER, F., RUSSELL, R. W., and SMITH, AUDREY U. (1956). Some effects of severe hypothermia on learning and retention. *Quart. J. exp. Psychol.* viii. 15–23.

APPEL, F. W., and APPEL, E. M. (1942). Intracranial variation in the weight of the human brain. *Human Biology*, xiv. 48–68.

ATTNEAVE, F. (1954). Some informational aspects of visual perception. *Psychol. Rev.* lxi. 183–93.

BARKIN, S. (1933). *The Older Worker in Industry.* New York Legislative State Document No. 60. Albany, Lyon.

BARTLETT, F. C. (1932). *Remembering.* Cambridge University Press.

—— (1950). Programme for experiments on thinking. *Quart. J. exp. Psychol.* ii. 145–52.

—— (1951). Anticipation in human performance. In *Essays in Psychology dedicated to David Katz.* Upsala: Almquist and Wiksells.

BELBIN, E. (1956). The effects of propaganda on recall, recognition and behaviour. II. The conditions which determine the response to propaganda. *Brit. J. Psychol.* xlvii. 259–70.

—— (1958). Methods of training the older worker. *Ergonomics*, i. (in press).

—— BELBIN, R. M., and HILL, F. (1957). A comparison between the results of three different methods of operator training. *Ergonomics*, i. 39–50.

BELBIN, R. M. (1953). Difficulties of older people in industry. *Occupational Psychol.* xxvii. 177–90.

—— (1955). Older people and heavy work. *Brit. J. industr. Med.* xii. 309–19.

BELLIS, C. J. (1933). Reaction time and chronological age. *Proc. Soc. exper. Biol. Med.* xxx. 801–3.

BIRREN, J. E. (1955). Age changes in speed of simple responses and perception and their significance for complex behaviour. In *Old Age in the Modern World.* Edinburgh; Livingstone, pp. 235–47.

—— ALLEN, W. R., and LANDAU, H. G. (1954). The relation of problem length in simple addition to time required, probability of success, and age. *J. Gerontol.* ix. 150–61.

—— and BOTWINICK, J. (1951). Rate of addition as a function of difficulty and age. *Psychometrika*, ii. 219–32.

—— —— (1955a). Age differences in finger, jaw and foot reaction time to auditory stimuli. *J. Gerontol.* x. 429–32.

—— —— (1955b). Speed of response as a function of perceptual difficulty and age. *J. Gerontol.* x. 433–6.

—— CASPERSON, R. C., and BOTWINICK, J. (1950). Age changes in pupil size. *J. Gerontol.* v. 216–21.

BOTWINICK, J., and SHOCK, N. W. (1952). Age differences in performance decrement with continuous work. *J. Gerontol.* vii. 41–46.

BROADBENT, D. E. (1954). The role of auditory localization in attention and memory span. *J. exp. Psychol.* xlvii. 191–6.

BROWN, J. (1955). An experimental study of immediate memory. Unpublished thesis. Cambridge University Library.

BROWN, RUTH A. (1957). Age and paced work. *Occupational Psychol.* xxxi. 11–20.

BROZEK, J., and KEYS, A. (1945). Changes in flicker-fusion frequency with age *J. consult. Psychol.* ix. 87–90.

BRYAN, W. L., and HARTER, N. (1899). Studies on the telegraphic language. The acquisition of a hierarchy of habits. *Psychol. Rev.* vi. 345–75.

CAMERON, D. E. (1936). Studies in depression. *J. ment. Sci.* lxxxii. 148–61.

—— (1943). Impairment of the retention phase of remembering. *Psychiatric Quart.* xvii. 395–404.

CANTRIL, H., and STRUNK, M. (1951). *Public Opinion 1935–46.* Princeton University Press.

CARPENTER, A. (1946). The effect of room temperature on performance of the resistance box test. *Medical Research Council Applied Psychology Research Unit Report No. 50.*

CATHCART, E. P., Hughes, D. E. R. and Chalmers, J. G. (1935). The physique of man in industry. *Industrial Health Research Board Report No. 71.* London: H.M.S.O.

CLAY, HILARY M. (1954). Changes of performance with age on similar tasks of varying complexity. *Brit. J. Psychol.* xlv. 7–13.

—— (1956a). An age difficulty in separating spatially contiguous data. *J. Gerontol.* xi. 318–22.

—— (1956b). A study of performance in relation to age at two printing works. *J. Gerontol.* xi. 417–24.

—— (1957). The relationship between time, accuracy and age on similar tasks of varying complexity. *Gerontologia,* i. 41–49.

CONRAD, R. and HILLE, BARBARA (1955). Comparison of paced and unpaced performance at a packing task. *Occupational Psychol.* xxix. 15–28.

COVELL, W. P. (1952). The ear. In *Cowdry's Problems of Ageing* (ed. A. I. Lansing). Baltimore: Williams & Wilkins. pp. 260–76.

CRAIK, K. J. W. (1943). *The Nature of Explanation.* Cambridge University Press.

—— (1948). Theory of the human operator in control systems. II. Man as an element in a control system. *Brit. J. Psychol.* xxxviii. 142–8.

CROSSMAN, E. R. F. W. (1953). Entropy and choice time: the effect of frequency unbalance on choice response. *Quart. J. exp. Psychol.* v. 41–51.

—— (1955). The measurement of discriminability. *Quart. J. exp. Psychol.* vii. 176—95.

—— (1956). The information capacity of the human operator in symbolic and non-symbolic control processes. In Ministry of Supply Publication WR/D 2/56 *Information Theory and the Human Operator.*

—— (1957). Personal communication.

—— and SZAFRAN, J. (1956). Changes with age in the speed of information intake and discrimination. *Experientia Supplementum,* iv. 128–35.

CULLUMBINE, H., *et al* (1950). Influence of age, sex, physique and muscular development on physical fitness. *J. appl. Physiol.* ii. 488–511.

DAVIS, D. R. (1948). *Pilot Error.* Air Ministry Publication A.P. 3139A. London: H.M.S.O.

—— (1949). The disorder of skill responsible for accidents. *Quart J. exp. Psychol.* i. 136–42.

DAVIS, R. (1956). The limits of the 'psychological refractory period'. *Quart. J. exp. Psychol.* viii. 24–38.

DENTON, G. (1953). Times spent handling and transporting shoes. British Boot, Shoe and Allied Trades Research Association Report No. TM 1123.

DREW, G. C. (1940). An experimental study of mental fatigue. Air Ministry, Flying Personnel Research Committee Paper No. 277, 11 F.

DROLLER, H. (1955). Falls and accidents in a random sample of elderly people living at home. In *Old Age in the Modern World.* Edinburgh: Livingstone. pp. 374–84.

ECCLES, J. C. (1953). *The Neurophysiological Basis of Mind*. Oxford University Press.

EYSENCK, H. J. (1952). Schizothymia-cyclothymia as a dimension of personality. II. Experimental. *J. Personality*, xx. 345–84.

FERREE, C. E., and RAND, G. (1930). Study of factors which cause individual differences in size of form field. *Am. J. Psychol.* xlii. 63–71.

FISHER, M. B., and BIRREN, J. E. (1947). Age and strength. *J. appl. Psychol.* xxxi. 490–7.

FITTS, P. M. (1947). A study of location discrimination ability. In *U.S.A.A.F. Research Report No. 19: Psychological Research on Equipment Design* (ed. P. M. Fitts).

—— (1954). The information capacity of the human motor system in controlling the amplitude of movement. *J. exp. Psychol.* xlvii. 381–91.

—— and DEINIGER, R. L. (1954). S-R compatibility: correspondence among paired elements within stimulus and response codes. *J. exp. Psychol.* xlviii. 483–92.

—— and SEEGER, C. M. (1953). S-R compatibility: spatial characteristics of stimulus and response codes. *J. exp. Psychol.* xlvi. 199–210.

FOULDS, G. A., and RAVEN, J. C. (1948). Normal changes in the mental ability of adults as age advances. *J. ment. Sci.* xciv. 133–42.

FRIEDENWALD, J. S. (1952). The eye. In *Cowdry's Problems of Ageing* (ed. A. I. Lansing). Baltimore: Williams & Wilkins. pp. 239–59.

GALTON, F. (1885). On the Anthropometric Laboratory at the late International Health Exhibition. *J. Anthropol. Inst.* xiv. 205–18.

—— (1889). On instruments for (1) testing perception of differences of tint and for (2) determining reaction time. *J. Anthropol. Inst.* xix. 27–29.

GARVEY, W. D., and KNOWLES, W. B. (1954). Response time patterns associated with various display-control relationships. *J. exp. Psychol.* xlvii. 315–22.

—— and MITNICK, L. L. (1955). Effects of additional spatial references on display-control efficiency. *J. exp. Psychol.* l. 276–82.

GILBERT, J. C. (1941). Memory loss in senescence. *J. abn. and soc. Psychol.* xxxvi. 73–86.

GREGORY, R. L. (1955). A note on summation time of the eye indicated by signal/noise discrimination. *Quart. J. exp. Psychol.* vii. 147–8.

—— (1956). An experimental treatment of vision as an information source and noisy channel. In *Information Theory: 3rd London Symposium 1955* (ed. C. Cherry). London: Methuen.

—— and CANE, VIOLET (1955). A statistical information theory of visual thresholds. *Nature*, clxxvi. 1272.

HARTLINE, H. K. (1934). Intensity and duration in the excitation of single photo-receptor units. *J. cell. comp. Physiol.* v. 229–47.

HECHT, S., and MINTZ, E. U. (1939). The visibility of single lines at various illuminations and the retinal basis of visual resolution. *J. gen. Physiol.* xx. 831–50.

HEIM, A. W., and WALLACE, J. G. (1949). The effects of repeatedly retesting the same group on the same intelligence test: Part I. Normal adults. *Quart. J. exp. Psychol.* i. 151–9.

—— (1950). Part II: High Grade Mental Defectives. *Quart J. exp. Psychol.* ii. 19–32.

HICK, W. E. (1952a). On the rate of gain of information. *Quart. J. exp. Psychol.* iv. 11–26.

—— (1952b). Why the human operator? *Trans. Soc. instrum. Technol.* iv. 67–77.

HOCHBERG, J. and McALISTER, E. (1953). A quantitative approach to figural 'goodness'. *J. exp. Psychol.* xlvi. 361–4.

HUGH-JONES, P. (1952). A simple standard exercise test and its use for measuring exertion dispnoea. *Brit. Med. J.* i. 65–71.

HYMAN, R. (1953). Stimulus information as a determinant of reaction time. *J. exp. Psychol.* xlv. 188–96.

INDUSTRIAL WELFARE SOCIETY (1950). *The employment of elderly workers.* Report of a survey on the practice and experience of 400 member firms.

JONES, H. E. (1928). A first study of parent–child resemblance in intelligence. *27th Yrbk. of Nat. Soc. for Study of Educ.*

—— CONRAD, H., and HORN, A. (1928). Psychological studies of motion pictures. II. Observation and recall as a function of age. *Univ. Calif. Publ. Psychol.* iii. 225–43.

—— and KAPLAN, O. J. (1956). Psychological aspects of mental disorders in later life. In *Mental Disorders in Later Life* (2nd ed.), (ed. O. J. Kaplan). Stanford University Press. pp. 98–156.

JUNG, C. G. (1918). *Studies in Word Association.* London: Heinemann.

KALLMANN, F. J. (1957). Twin data on the genetics of ageing. In *Ciba Foundation Colloquia on Ageing*, Vol. 3 (ed. G. E. W. Wolstenholme and Cecilia M. O'Connor). London: Churchill. pp. 131–43.

KAY, H. (1951). Learning of a serial task by different age groups. *Quart. J. exp. Psychol.* iii. 166–83.

—— (1953). Experimental studies of adult learning. Unpublished thesis. Cambridge University Library.

—— (1954). The effects of position in a display upon problem solving. *Quart. J. exp. Psychol.* vi. 155–69.

—— (1955a). Some experiments on adult learning. In *Old Age in the Modern World.* Edinburgh: Livingstone. pp. 259–67.

—— (1955b) Learning and retaining verbal material. *Brit. J. Psychol.* xlvi. 81–100.

KING, H. F. (1953). Age and Work in Agriculture. Unpublished thesis. Cambridge University Library.

—— (1955a). The response of older rural craftsmen to individual training. *J. Gerontol.* x. 207–11.

—— (1955b). An age-analysis of some agricultural accidents. *Occupational Psychol.* xxix. 245–53.

—— (1956). An attempt to use production data in the study of age and performance. *J. Gerontol.* xi. 410–16.

—— and SPEAKMAN, D. (1953). Age and industrial accident rates. *Brit. J. industr. Med.* x. 51–58.

KOGA, T., and MORANT, G. M. (1923). On the degree of association between reaction times in the case of different senses. *Biometrika*, xiv. 346–72.

KORCHIN, S. J., and BASOWITZ, H. (1956). The judgement of ambiguous stimuli as an index of cognitive functioning in ageing. *J. Personality*, xxv. 81–95.

KUBO, T. (1938). Mental and physical changes in old age. *J. genet. Psychol.* liii. 101–18.

LASHLEY, K. S. (1929). *Brain Mechanisms and Intelligence.* University of Chicago Press.

LE GROS CLARK, F. (1954). The working fitness of older men. Report issued by the Nuffield Foundation.

—— (1955). Ageing men in the labour force. Report issued by the Nuffield Foundation.

LEONARD, J. A. (1952). Some experiments on the temporal relation between information and action. Unpublished thesis. Cambridge University Library.

—— (1953). Advance information in sensori-motor skills. *Quart. J. exp. Psychol.* v. 141–9.

LEONARD, J. A. (1954). The effect of partial advance information. Medical Research Council Applied Psychology Research Unit Report No. 217.

LORGE, I., and HELFANT, K. (1953). The independence of chronological age and sociopolitical attitudes. *J. abn. soc. Psychol.* xlviii. 598.

MACKWORTH, N. H., and MACKWORTH, J. F. (1956). Remembering advance cues during searching. Medical Research Council Applied Psychology Research Unit Report No. 258.

McGEOCH, J. A., and IRION, A. L. (1952). *The Psychology of Human Learning.* New York: Longmans.

MACPHERSON, S. J., DEES, VALERIE, and GRINDLEY, G. C. (1949). The effect of knowledge of results on learning and performance—III. The influence of the time interval between trials. *Quart. J. exp. Psychol.* i. 167–74.

MILES, W. R. (1931). Measures of certain human abilities throughout the life span. *Proc. Nat. Acad. Sci.* xvii. 627–33.

—— (1933). Age and human ability. *Psychol. Rev.* xl. 99–123.

—— (1934). Age and the kinephantom. *J. gen. Psychol.* x. 204–7.

MILLER, G. A. (1956). The magical number seven, plus or minus two: some limits on our capacity for processing information. *Psychol. Rev.* lxiii. 81–97.

MISIAK, H. (1947). Age and sex differences in critical flicker frequency. *J. exp. Psychol.* xxxvii. 318–32.

MONTPELLIER, G. DE (1935). *Les Altérations morphologiques des mouvements rapides.* Louvain: Institut Supérieur de Philosophie.

MURRELL, K. F. H., GRIEW, S., and TUCKER, W. A. (1957). Age structure in the engineering industry: a preliminary study. *Occupational Psychol.* xxxi, 150–68.

NORRIS, A. H., SHOCK, N. W., and WAGMAN, I. H. (1953). Age changes in the maximum conduction velocity of motor fibres in human ulnar nerves. *J. appl. Physiol.* v. 589–93.

O'LEARY, J. L. (1952). Ageing in the nervous system. In *Cowdry's Problems of Ageing* (ed. A. I. Lansing). Baltimore: Williams and Wilkins. pp. 223–38.

OBRIST, W. D. (1954). The electroencephalogram of normal aged adults. *EEG clin. Neurophysiol.* vi. 235–44.

OLDFIELD, R. C. (1954). Memory mechanisms and the theory of schemata. *Brit. J. Psychol.* xlv. 14–23.

OSHIMA, M., *et al.* (1954). Changes in physical functions by age. *Annual Report of the Japanese Institute for Science of Labour,* No. 47. pp. 12–15.

OWENS, W. A. (1953). Age and mental abilities: a longitudinal study. *Genet. Psychol. Monogr.* xlviii. 3–54.

PACAUD, S. (1955*a*). Experimental research on the ageing of psychological functions. In *Old Age in the Modern World.* Edinburgh: Livingstone. pp. 279–89.

—— (1955*b*). Le vieillissement des aptitudes. In *Précis de Gerontologie* (ed. L. Binet and F. Bourlière). Paris: Masson. pp. 40–67.

POFFENBERGER, A. T. (1915). The influence of improvement in one simple mental process upon other related processes. *J. educ. Psychol.* vi. 459–74.

POLLACK, I. (1953). Assimilation of sequentially encoded information. *Am. J. Psychol.* lxvi. 421–35.

POLLAK, O. (1943). Conservatism in later maturity and old age. *Am. sociol. Rev.* viii. 175–9.

RICHARDSON, I. M. (1953). Age and work: a study of 489 men in heavy industry. *Brit. J. industr. Med.* x. 269–84.

RUCH, F. L. (1933). Adult learning. *Psychol. Bull.* xxx. 387–414.

—— (1934). The differentiative effects of age upon human learning. *J. gen. Psychol.* xi. 261–86.

RUGER, H. A., and STOESSIGER, B. (1927). Growth curves of certain characteristics in man. *Ann. Eugen.* ii. 76–111.

SHAKOW, D., DOLKART, M. B., and GOLDMAN, R. (1941). The memory function in psychoses of the aged. *Dis. Nerv. System*, ii. 43–48.

SHELDON, J. H. (1948). *The Social Medicine of Old Age*. Oxford University Press for the Nuffield Foundation.

SHOCK, N. W. (1947). Older people and their potentialities for gainful employment. *J. Gerontol.* ii. 93–102.

SHOOTER, ANTIONIA M. N., SCHONFIELD, A. E. D., KING, H. F., and WELFORD, A. T. (1956). Some field data on the training of older people. *Occupational Psychol.* xxx. 204–15.

SIMONSON, E. (1947). Physiological fitness and work capacity of older men. *Geriatrics*, ii. 110–19.

SINGLETON, W. T. (1954). The change of movement timing with age. *Brit. J. Psychol.* xlv. 166–72.

—— (1955). Age and performance timing on simple skills. In *Old Age in the Modern World*. Edinburgh: Livingstone. pp. 221–31.

SMITH, K. R. (1938). Age and performance on a repetitive manual task. *J. appl. Psychol.* xxii. 295–306.

SNODDY, G. S. (1926). Learning and stability. *J. appl. Psychol.* x. 1–36.

SORENSON, H. (1930). Adult ages as a factor in learning. *J. educ. Psychol.* xxi. 451–9.

SPEAKMAN, D. (1954). The effect of age on the incidental relearning of stamp values. *J. Gerontol.* ix. 162–7.

SWARD, K. (1945). Age and mental ability in superior men. *Am. J. Psychol.* lviii. 443–79.

SZAFRAN, J. (1951). Changes with age and with exclusion of vision in performance at an aiming task. *Quart. J. exp. Psychol.* iii. 111–18.

—— (1953). Some experiments on motor performance in relation to ageing. Unpublished thesis. Cambridge University Library.

—— (1955). Experiments on the greater use of vision by older adults. In *Old Age in the Modern World*. Edinburgh: Livingstone. pp. 231–5.

—— and WELFORD, A. T. (1949). On the problem of generalized occupational transfer effects in relation to studies of ageing. *Quart J. exp. Psychol.* i. 160–6.

—— —— (1950). On the relation between transfer and difficulty of initial task. *Quart. J. exp. Psychol.* ii. 88–94.

TANNER, W. P., and SWETS, J. A. (1954). A decision-making theory of visual detection. *Psychol. Rev.* lxi. 401–9.

THOMAS, G., and OSBORNE, B. (1950). *Older people and their employment*. Social Survey Report No. 150. London: Central Office of Information.

THORNDIKE, E. L. *et al.* (1928). *Adult Learning*. New York: Macmillan.

VERVILLE, E., and CAMERON, N. (1946). Age and sex differences in the perception of incomplete pictures by adults. *J. genet. Psychol.* lxviii. 149–57.

VERZAR-McDOUGALL, J. (1955). Learning and memory tests in young and old rats. In *Old Age in the Modern World*. Edinbrugh: Livingstone. pp. 247–59.

VINCE, MARGARET A. (1948*a*). The intermittency of control movements and the psychological refractory period. *Brit. J. Psychol.* xxxviii. 149–57.

—— (1948*b*). Corrective movements in a pursuit task. *Quart. J. exp. Psychol.* i. 85–103.

—— (1949). Rapid response sequences and the psychological refractory period. *Brit. J. Psychol.* xl. 23–40.

WACKWITZ, J. D. (1946). *Het Verband Tusschen Arbeidsprestatie en Leeftijd*. Delft: Waltman.

WALLACE, JEAN G. (1956). Some studies of perception in relation to age. *Brit. J. Psychol.* xlvii. 283–97.

WECHSLER, D. (1935). *Range of Human Capacities.* Baltimore: Williams and Wilkins.

—— (1944). *The Measurement of Adult Intelligence* (3rd ed.). Baltimore: Williams and Wilkins.

WEHRKAMP, R. A., and SMITH, K. U. (1952). Dimensional analysis of motion: II. Travel distance effects. *J. appl. Psychol.* xxxvi. 201–6.

WELFORD, A. T. (1946). An attempt at an experimental approach to the psychology of religion. *Brit. J. Psychol.* xxxvi. 55–73.

—— (1952a). The 'psychological refractory period' and the timing of high-speed performance—a review and a theory. *Brit. J. Psychol.* xliii. 2–19.

—— 1952b). An apparatus for use in studying serial performance. *Am. J. Psychol.* lxv. 91–97.

—— (1953a). The psychologist's problem in measuring fatigue. In *Symposium on Fatigue* (ed. W. F. Floyd and A. T. Welford). London: H. K. Lewis. pp. 183–91.

—— (1953b). Extending the employment of older people. *Brit. Med. J.* ii. 1193–7.

—— (1957). Methodological problems in the study of changes in human performance with age. In *Ciba Foundation Colloquia on Ageing,* Vol. 3 (ed. G. E. W. Wolstenholme and Cecilia M. O'Connor). London: Churchill. pp. 149–69.

—— BROWN, RUTH A., and GABB, J. E. (1950). Two experiments on fatigue as affecting skilled performance in civilian aircrew. *Brit. J. Psychol.* xl. 195–211.

WELFORD, N. T. (1952). An electronic digital recording machine—the SETAR. *J. sci. Instrum.* xxix. 1–4.

—— (1955). Let's reduce statistical drudgery. III. *Am. Psychologist,* x. 574.

WELLS, F. L., and MARTIN, H. A. A. (1923). A method of memory examinations suitable for psychotic cases. *Am. J. Psychiat.* iii. 243–57.

WESTON, H. C. (1949). On age and illumination in relation to visual performance. *Trans. Illum. Eng. Soc.* xiv. 281–97.

WHITFIELD, J. W. (1954). Individual differences in accident susceptibility among coal miners. *Brit. J. industr. Med.* xi. 126–39.

WILLOUGHBY, R. R. (1929). Incidental learning. *J. educ. Psychol.* xx. 671–82.

WRIGHT, J. M. VON (1957). An experimental study of human serial learning. *Soc. Sci. Fennica Commentationes Humanorum Litterarum,* xxiii. No. 1.

WYLIE, H. H. (1919). An experimental study of transfer of response in the white rat. *Behav. Monogr.* iii. No. 16.

ZANGWILL, O. L. (1937). An investigation of the relationship between the processes of reproducing and recognizing simple figures, with special reference to Koffka's trace theory. *Brit. J. Psychol.* xxvii. 250–76.

—— (1939). Some relations between reproducing and recognizing prose material. *Brit. J. Psychol.* xxix. 370–82.

INDEX